D1180596

THE COMPLETE BOOK OF
SEA FISHING

● *Ted Entwistle with part of the catch that won the 1985
TVS Championship for him in Iceland*

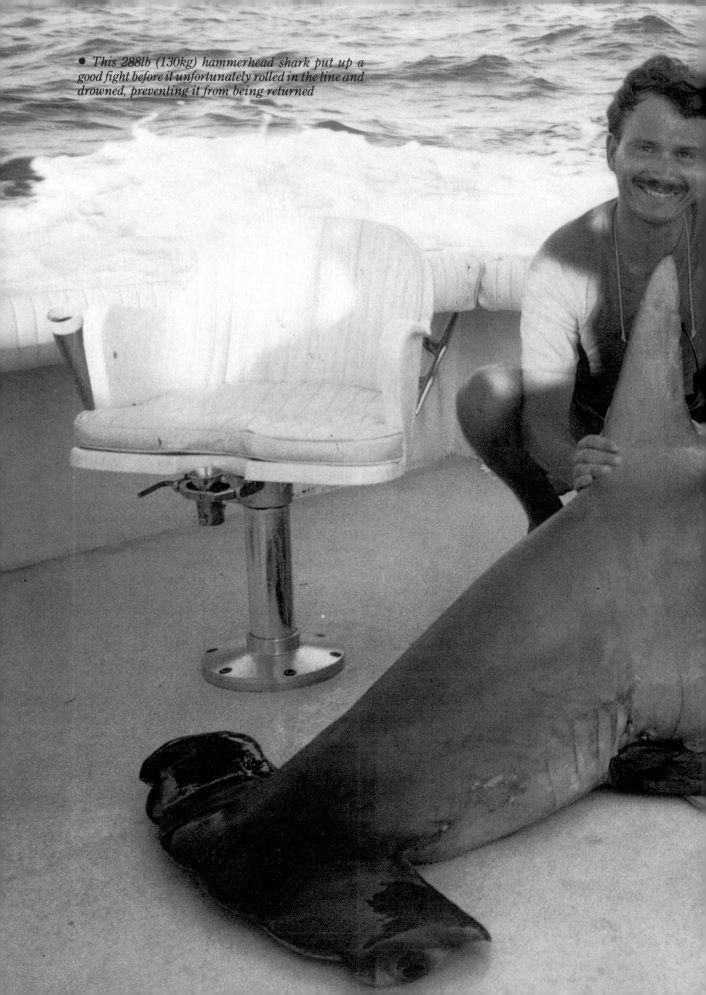

● This 288lb (130kg) hammerhead shark put up a good fight before it unfortunately rolled in the line and drowned, preventing it from being returned

THE COMPLETE BOOK OF
SEA FISHING

Tackle & Techniques

Alan Yates & Ted Entwistle

David & Charles

Illustrations by Philip Murphy

British Library Cataloguing-in-Publication Data
Yates, Alan
  The complete book of sea fishing: Tackle and techniques.
  I. Title II. Entwistle, Ted
  799.1

  ISBN 0-7153-9434-7

Copyright © Alan Yates & Ted Entwistle 1992

The right of Alan Yates and Ted Entwistle to be identified as
authors of this work has been asserted by them in accordance
with the Copyright, Designs and Patents Act 1988.

All rights reserved. No part of this publication may be
reproduced, stored in a retrieval system, or transmitted, in
any form or by any means, electronic, mechanical,
photocopying, recording or otherwise, without the prior
permission of David & Charles plc.

Typeset by Ace Filmsetting Ltd, Frome, Somerset
and printed in Italy by Milanostampa SpA
for David & Charles plc
Brunel House   Newton Abbot   Devon

Contents

PART I: SHORE FISHING

Alan Yates

Introduction

IT IS BECOMING INCREASINGLY EVIDENT that inshore fish stocks worldwide are gradually deteriorating. Pollution, over-fishing and the dreaded monofilament gill net have all played their part in making it increasingly difficult for the shore-based sea angler to enjoy continuous success with the techniques and methods of the past. In fact angling success is no longer guaranteed or even a matter of luck, not because the fish have grown more wary, but because there are just fewer of them to be shared amongst an increasing number of human predators.

In recent years the advances made in tackle and techniques have

resulted from anglers constantly trying to improve their chances of catching fish in this increasingly difficult angling environment. Tackle has become more refined and is custom-made, whilst techniques have changed accordingly; in particular, great strides forward have been made in distance casting and tackle presentation.

Whether you fish freelance, for specimens, or in competitions, the opportunity to improve your results can now be greatly influenced by personal commitment, skill and effort, so that Lady Luck takes a lesser – though still important! – back seat.

1 Tackle

NO ANGLING BOOK WOULD BE COMPLETE without an initial list of the basic tackle required, yet the choice of modern tackle is so vast that it would be impossible to list all that is good and bad about the stock items; in any case, choice is so often a matter of personal preference, and usually gained with experience. Modern rods and reels are in the main very efficient and well made. Quality generally comes with price – yet it will never be a rod or reel alone that makes the successful sea angler. The merits of the different makes and models will be noted throughout this book, but I would emphasise that the most expensive tackle is not a requirement of successful angling, whereas keeping tackle well maintained certainly is.

Rods

The choice of a rod is based on its function as a tool with which to cast a lead into the sea, its aptitude to signal that a fish is eating the bait, and also on how well it assists the angler in retrieving the fish. Usually one of these three qualities is evident in a rod, but not all three in equally good measure, so the angler must choose which is his priority or settle for a compromise of the three qualities. Shore rods in general range between 11ft 6in and 14ft (3.4m and 4.3m) in length, with different models available for use with multiplier reels and fixed spool reels, as well as those designed for casting with the reel positioned at the butt or up the butt of the rod. Usually rods come in two equal pieces, although the long tip/short butt system is favoured by the custom-built blank makers. The latter means that the spigot joint is not included in the activity zone of the blank during the cast, and this is considered to improve the action and the distances it achieves. The size and spacing of the rod rings differentiate the two types of rod.

The rod used with a fixed spool reel requires fewer rings as the reel is positioned below the rod. Larger rings are usually used as the line comes off the reel spool in large loops. Up to six intermediate rings are required, with the biggest ring closest to

the reel. Beware of using too few rings on fixed spool rods, because if the butt ring is too far away from the reel, the loop of line from the spool will belly out and catch on the ring, causing the line to snap.

With the multiplier, the reel is positioned on top of the rod so more rings are required to funnel the line along the length of the rod. Ring positioning on multiplier rods should be such that when the rod is compressed, the line does not touch the blank but follows its bend.

When choosing a rod, most anglers would place its casting capability as the priority feature. The distance the baited hook can be cast from the shore is of paramount importance and is one of the biggest single factors to influence the shore angler's success. However, rods capable of casting long distances are very often stiff, especially those designed to cope with the more forceful casting styles such as the pendulum cast. Thus they do not show bites from feeding fish very well, and are also more rigid and less of a pleasure to use when landing a fish. Modern rod-building materials are, though, ultra-light, and so even the stiffest rod is not heavy to use. The rod-builders' compromise is to mix modern materials such as carbon fibre, boron, Kevlar and fibreglass in the quest to create the best combination. Also, rods are built with power points – that is, they are strengthened at particular points along the blank's length: the blank wall thickness is increased, or a combination of materials is used in layers, in an attempt to impart

● *A 35lb (15.8kg) conger eel comes to the gaff*

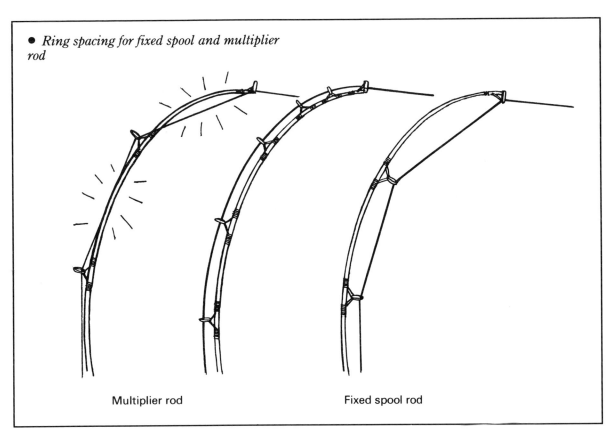

● *Ring spacing for fixed spool and multiplier rod*

Multiplier rod   Fixed spool rod

strength and power to the cast whilst retaining a soft or more active tip. There are many variations on this theme, which means that there is a very diverse range of rods catering for all tastes and requirements, and the angler is bound to find one that suits him. In the past, the off-the-peg models catering for the mass market were of low quality, but the English blank specialists – for example ZZiplex, Century, Conoflex – so cornered the market that several of the Japanese mass production companies (such as Daiwa Sports) now produce excellent quality rods which compare well with those from the blank manufacturers.

The angler can therefore choose either to buy a rod ready made up, or to purchase a rod blank and make up the rod, or have it made up to his own requirements. The latter option does give a greater degree of choice regarding the type of blank; this is especially significant when casting, and bite detection may be a particular consideration. Other options include a choice of rings, reel-fitting position and type, length of tip, and even the colour of the whipping. Furthermore, all offer a considerable saving in cash on the most expensive off-the-peg equivalents. There are excellent ready-made rods at the cheaper end of the market for the beginner,

notably those produced by Daiwa Sports, Shakespeare, Silstar and ABU Garcia Ltd.

The ultimate choice of rods by many of the top anglers includes the purchase of several different tips to fit the same butt, thereby giving a combination of rods to cope with different casting or fishing situations on pier or beach. Custom-building allows the personalisation of rods which is aesthetically pleasing, and the current trend towards fancy and colourful whipping and a high gloss finish does have practical value in providing additional protection and grip to the blank for casting or retrieving in wet weather situations.

Basic rod-building

Rings can be taped on the blank prior to whipping them. Tape one leg of the ring: this way, positions can be finalised without mistakes. The standard method of whipping a ring to the blank with thread has been used for years and is simple enough. However, beware of some makes of whipping silk which lose their colour when doped or varnished, and never come out looking as flash as they did in the tackle shop. Beware also of mixing some varnishes and, for example, nitrate cellulose-based dopes.

9

● *Multiplier reel up-the-butt position*

Gudebrod offers an excellent range of silk whipping – these are colour-fast, and do come out looking similar to when they went on the blank. There are several preferred finishes to rod whipping including dope, varnish and epoxy resin, but nothing approaches the finish of the professional rod-builders. For home rod-building, ten coats of varnish put on over a period of time takes some beating, and application with the finger has proved more effective than with a brush. Smooth and even whipping is obtained by whipping the silk from the ring leg towards the centre of the ring. The legs themselves can be chamfered down with a file, which enables the whipping to settle over the edge of the ring foot without creating a ridge.

There is a large choice in types of rod rings; the lightweight ranges from Fuji, Seymo and Daiwa are ideal, though remember that the type of ring should suit the blank. Stiff rings will alter the action of a flexible or soft blank. Most anglers prefer a hardened or stainless-steel-type tip ring at the end of their rod, as these are far stronger and less prone to line wear than most of the lightweight makes. The tip ring also comes in for extra wear when the rod is placed against promenade walls, for example, or on shingle.

Reel fittings range from the basic coaster which is a screw-up pipe clamp, to the more permanent

● *A multiplier overrun or birdsnest*

fixed reel seat. Coasters are ideal for situations where the reel's position is likely to be changed; and the fixed reel seat is more efficient if big fish are to be encountered. Of the fixed reel seats, the carbon plastic screw-up type is the most efficient. The clip-type seat can wear, with the result that the reel may be allowed to slip and even fall from the clamp in extreme cases. Reel seat positions are a matter of personal preference, although a rough guide is shown for up-the-butt casters. The down-the-butt caster puts the seat as low as he requires and then uses a short rod extension, known as a reducer, which fits into the butt to increase the distance the reel is away from the body for reeling in or when keeping the reel away from sand or mud.

When casting or reeling in, a better grip is obtained on the rod by using purpose-made rod grips, and there is a variety of grips available for the self-build rod enthusiast. These range from rubber cycle-type grips, to foam or even leather wraps as used on tennis rackets and so on. These are either stretched or glued in position.

A coat of silicon car wax over a completed rod gives it added protection from salt corrosion and the occasional collision with beach or promenade. Storing rods inside lightweight plastic tubes protects them during transit, with rod tips given added protection by placing them inside foam pipe lagging.

Reels

I use multipliers for all my beach and pier fishing and admit to being totally biased in their favour. For the beginner, however, nothing is more efficient or easy to use than the fixed spool reel. This design originated in coarse and game angling; the line comes off the front of a spool when it is cast,

and is called 'fixed spool' or 'fixed drum' as the spool does not turn. When the line is retrieved, the handle turns a bale arm which revolves around the spool to load the line. The multiplier, on the other hand, does have a revolving spool, and the retrieval rate of the spool is multiplied via the handle by a gearing system.

Both reels are highly efficient in sea fishing terms, and in capable hands both offer excellent casting distance ability. A drawback with the multiplier and its revolving spool is that it tends to tangle or overrun when it is cast. The beginner can experience some dreadful tangles with multipliers, especially if he tries to cast from the shore with those models designed for boat fishing, or those at the cheaper end of the market without bearings or with heavy metal spools.

The fixed spool, on the other hand, is easy to master and a distance cast of up to 100 yards (91.4m) is quite feasible, even at the first few attempts. However, the fixed spool is a more cumbersome reel to use, and the gearing mechanism involved makes direct winding difficult. Thus loads cannot be reeled in directly and the angler has to pump to retrieve heavy fish or objects. Furthermore, it is a myth that fixed spools give a faster line-retrieve: since the arrival of the Shimano Speedmasters and the Daiwa Sealine power mesh geared reels, the multipliers are now equal. The fixed spool reel is also inferior to the multiplier in out-and-out distance casting, especially in gale-force winds. On the tournament field in perfect conditions the fixed spool performs reasonably well, but it never lives up to its potential in practical angling conditions. The multiplier is capable of achieving distances approaching 300 yards (275m).

Most experienced sea anglers prefer the multiplier, whilst many novices are attracted by the easy-to-use fixed spool. However, in practice it is difficult to change from the fixed spool to the multiplier.

Multiplier line tangle can be horrendous – the line is thrown off a revolving spool faster than the lead can pull it through the rod rings, and the result is one loop catching up the next to form an overrun or birdsnest; at worst the line actually snaps and the sinker is lost. It is important that the line is laid on the spool evenly to help prevent all this from happening, and in fact the blame for all overruns can be laid firmly at the feet of the caster, with an overloaded reel or jerky cast being responsible –

● *ABU, Daiwa and Shimano multipliers (none is immune to birdnesting in the wrong hands)* very rarely is the reel at fault. There are a few basic rules to follow which will be dealt with later in the casting section (see p27); but in the main, tangles only happen because the angler causes them.

The type of reel chosen is related to where you fish. Fish from a sandy, snag-free beach or a place where long casting is necessary, and you will need to use a low-diameter line and a reel suitable for such a light line load. Fish over heavy kelp or boulders and strong line is required, and so also a bigger reel to cope with the larger diameter line which means a bigger line load.

If your choice is a fixed spool reel, then one model with two separate spools loaded with different breaking strain lines will cope. However, if you prefer a multiplier then two different models are required, one for each situation.

Multipliers

Many different sizes of multiplier are available, each catering for a different line load or fishing situation. For shore fishing in general two main sizes of multiplier are preferred. The examples given here are based on the ABU 0000 multiplier size system, as this is the one generally understood. For rock or heavy line fishing the ABU 7000 size and upwards are ideal; whilst for clear beaches when distance is required, the 6500 size and below are best. The 7000 size would be suitable for 20 to 30lb (9 to 13.6kg) bs line; and the 6500 size reel for 12 to 15lb (5.4 to 6.8kg) line. The latter is the combination of reel size and line diameter which gives the greatest casting distance capability. It is important that the spool of the reel should unload the line evenly when cast; thus different diameter/

● *Match the hook size to the bait being used*

breaking strains of line work better with different size spools. Generally, the lighter the line, the smaller the spool.

Some of the older models of multiplier include a level line system within the reel's frame, which lays the line on the spool evenly. This is linked to the gearing of the handle with the line lay running backwards and forwards across the spool several times at each turn of the handle. Whilst this system undoubtedly lays the line on the spool evenly, it is generally frowned upon by seasoned shore anglers as it reduces casting distance. With practice, the angler can lay the line on the spool cotton-reel fashion with the aid of his thumb.

Older models also have a front strengthening bar in the frame, which can actually restrict the caster's grip on the spool during the cast. The bar prevents the caster's thumb from clamping firmly on the reel's spool – purchase on the spool when casting compression is applied is thus reduced, leading to premature release of the spool. Conversion kits can be bought to replace the offending level line and front bar, and this partly solves the problem, whilst special solid aluminium one-piece frames are also available for some models. Fortunately there are now lots of models produced with one-piece frames as standard and without line lays. Multiplier models like those from ABU Garcia were originally intended for game spinning, and it is only in recent years that models from companies such as ABU Garcia, Daiwa and Shimano have been purposely manufactured for the British beach-casting style of fishing. The Daiwa 7HT holds upwards of 300 yards (275m) of 15lb (6.8kg) breaking strain (0.35mm diameter) line and so offers massive casting poten-

● *Lay the line on cotton-reel fashion with the thumb*

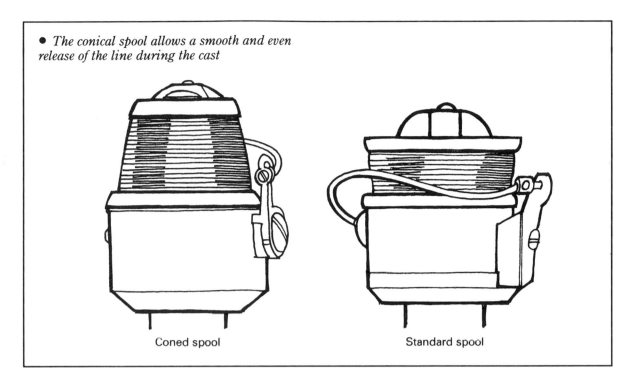

● *The conical spool allows a smooth and even release of the line during the cast*

Coned spool   Standard spool

tial; whilst the Shimano Speedmaster II gives a very fast retrieve and a similar line capacity. The ABU 6500C – the C denotes ball-bearing races – remains one of the classic beach-casting reels used in the UK. Amongst more recent innovations is the ABU Syncro drag system which offers the shore angler pre-set drag settings; these are ideal when large fish are the target.

Fixed spools

The general design of fixed spool reels for sea fishing has improved in recent years, like that of the multipliers, with designs based on sea angling requirements. The Shimano Biomaster incorporates a special line-lay system and long-coned spool which has greatly improved the casting potential of the reel. Line is laid across the spool rather than straight around it, and this prevents coils burying themselves under each other. The longer-coned spool allows line coming off the spool to do so steadily, without being reduced so rapidly that it catches the lip of the spool – thus casting distance is unhindered. Other improvements include stronger gears, drags and bale arms. Points to look out for when choosing a fixed spool are that the drag system allows the spool to be locked down tightly when cast; and bale arms that do not snap shut during the cast. Several models have self-load bale arms which cure this problem. These improve-

ments in design will eventually produce fixed spool reels which get a lot closer to the multiplier's performance. The new breed of fixed spool is expanding, although it has yet to reach the cheaper end of the market. In the main it tends to be a big version of the fixed spools used for freshwater fishing. There are a few popular models which are suitable for beach casting but, as with most tackle, you get what you pay for, and the most expensive models are the best.

Most of the Continental anglers use fixed spool, yet it is worth noting that England's first attempt to win the CIPS World Sea Angling Championships in Holland in 1990 resulted in a clear victory for England, with Scotland runners-up. Both results were totally attributable to the superiority of the multiplier over the fixed spool in distance terms when having to contend with strong onshore winds.

Reel maintenance

Care of your tackle is important, and whereas rods need little maintenance other than an occasional wash in soapy water, reels are another matter. Both multipliers and fixed spools will be damaged by salt water and spray if left in a damp tackle box for long periods, and both models also require regular internal maintenance if you are to get the best results from them. It is essential that reels are washed after a trip to the beach. Warm soapy water is sufficient, and an old toothbrush is ideal to remove sand and weed from the reel casing, with a rinse in clean water to finish off the job. Shake off excess water, then dry the reel with a towel and leave it to dry in the air.

Internal servicing should be carried out every three months or so. Most of the main manufacturers offer a reel service if you are not up to taking the reel apart yourself. The basic requirements of a service include cleaning out any salt deposits that have entered the reel casing, and oiling bearings etc. A once-a-year service might also include washing out bearings, but generally keeping them well oiled will allow the reel to perform well enough. Beware of removing grease and oil from the internal working parts of the reel with solvents – the reel may look nice and clean, but in fact oil and grease offer a great deal of protection from salt water. A light engine oil is all that is required for oiling bearings. Certain makes of reel oil make extravagant claims to the effect that they add casting distance, but this is only feet and inches which may matter on the tournament field but not so much on the beach. It is better to have an oil that stays inside the reel to protect it from corrosion than one that is dispersed from the bearings after one cast.

Line

The variation available in monofilament line is enormous, not only in makes, but also in colours, breaking strains and prices. As the line is the main link with the fish, it is important to use the best – and therein lies the angler's dilemma. What is the best? Talk to each and every angler and opinions differ, and my choice would not be the same as another angler's. However, there are several rules and observations about line that are important, and these will be detailed as well as my own preferences and the reasons for them.

It is a fact that all lines come from just a few factories, be they American, German or Japanese. The same line is spooled in different colours on different spools under different brand names. Hence anglers argue about different lines which are very often in fact the same.

The two basic differences that do exist are between the cheaper soft lines, and the pre-stretched and more expensive low diameter lines. Low diameter lines are favoured for distance (tournament) casting, though remember that the smaller diameter line with the same breaking strain will probably not withstand the rigours of fishing as well as the larger diameter will. So it may

be a bad investment to use the smaller diameter expensive lines, as these may suffer breakage more easily from sand, rock or beach stones. In fishing terms, it may be preferable to sacrifice a few yards' casting distance for the added strength gained by choosing the stronger, more rugged makes of line for fishing.

Line colour may not be that important, although the current trend towards dayglow high visibility line does help the angler. Crossed lines and line tangles are easier to untangle when the lines are bright colours, whilst their greater visibility means that lost tackle is much easier to find – this is particularly important with leaders on the casting practice field, as bright-coloured ones can be found easily if snap-offs occur.

Some say that line colouring weakens monofilament slightly, though I myself am not an advocate of this theory. Personally I prefer the German makes of line, and usually choose those from the Bayer factory. Olive, black, green, white and orange are my favourite colours; I never use blue line although many highly successful anglers do – the choice is yours.

Bright-coloured lines do not seem to put the fish off, and in fact the reverse is sometimes the case. Anglers using bright orange Stren 50lb (22.8kg) bs (0.70mm dia) for terminal rig bodies have actually found that results improved, especially for dabs and flounders which may well be attracted to the baits by the bright-coloured line.

For shock leaders Du Pont's Stren takes some beating for quality, whilst Drennan Greased Weasel is one of the new breed of low stretch, low diameter, low memory monofilament lines currently available.

Amnesia line from America is another favourite low memory line ideal for hook snoods. It does not coil or twist up easily, and if it does, then any coils can be run out of the line without damaging it. The most economical way to buy your reel main line is in bulk, and most of the main line manufacturers have bulk spools available. Buy a set length spool of line and you may well either not have enough to fill your spool, or have some over; a bulk spool overcomes this problem, and the reel spool can be filled to the required amount without wastage.

The variation in opinion regarding different lines almost certainly results from the different use to which anglers put their line. Used for just one day trip, the cheaper sort may prove adequate. Problems arrive, however, when you try to use these lines for weeks on end. If the line must last, then buy the better quality one; but whatever your

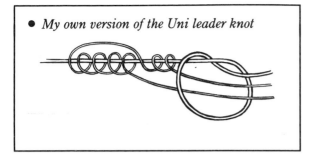

- *My own version of the Uni leader knot*

choice, keep a close eye on it because any line can quickly become damaged in use.

Line breaking strain will inevitably relate to the venue. So on a snag-free beach and when casting distance is a priority, the choice would generally be 12lb (5.4kg) to 15lb (6.8kg) bs (0.35mm dia). A compromise in a stormy or weedy sea where a stronger line may be required is 18lb (8.1kg) to 20lb (9kg) bs, though remember that a bigger diameter means a reduction in casting distance. For fishing over rocks or snags, 25lb (11.4kg/0.55mm dia) to 30lb (13.6kg/0.60mm dia) line would be used, whilst even heavier line may be required for bigger fish such as conger eels or when fishing over really rough ground.

When using lines under 30lb (13.6kg) bs, a short length of casting shock leader is required to take the shock of casting up to 8oz (226g) of lead. As a general rule the shock leader bs should be 10lb (4.5kg) for every 1oz (28.5g) of lead used, eg 50lb (22.8kg) bs (0.70mm dia) for 5oz (150g) leads.

Remember to extend the bs of the leader through to the terminal rig. The length of the leader should allow at least six turns around the spool of the reel.

Hook snood breaking strains can vary from 10lb (4.5kg) to 30lb (13.6kg) depending on conditions, with 25lb (11.4kg) bs a good all-round size, able to cope with line twist produced by small fish and the damage done by sand, stones, mussels and so on. Ultra-light snoods from 15lb (6.8kg) and under tend to twist around the body of the rig, causing tangles, and are not always practical.

Hooks and leads

Hooks are available in a thousand patterns, each the product of a particular angler or the answer to a particular angling situation or fish species. The basic hook shape has not changed since prehistoric times, yet the list of hook designs has been added to annually. Small wonder shore anglers have problems in selecting which hook to use. Yet despite the enormous range available, local preferences often dictate that tackle shops stock only a small selection, usually described as 'best-sellers'. A typical example of a 'best-seller' is the popular and dreadful stainless steel, beaked hook with bait-holding barbs at the back of the shank. Some anglers know no better than to use this prehistoric pattern, and don't seem to realise just what advances have been made in hook technology in recent years: yet you only need inquire at the largest tackle dealers or via mail order firms to find out the full range of hooks available. Indeed, there is a hook for every conceivable shore angling situation.

In recent years a new breed of hook has arrived: the carbon steel, chemically etched pattern. These

- *A nice codling in the net; note the fixed-grip wired lead*

are much lighter, stronger and sharper than all the older hooks, and bring enormous advantages, especially to the shore angler. Smaller hooks are always much sharper, with needle points which penetrate fish flesh more quickly and deeply; and lighter hooks are sucked more easily into a fish's mouth. Furthermore the strength of the latest carbon steel patterns is superb. A 14lb 14oz (7.7kg) cod landed during a recent competition from my local pier was taken using a Drennan chemically etched Aberdeen size 4. In the early days such lightweight models as the Kamasan Aberdeens experienced a certain brittleness, but this problem has now been cured with improved tempering techniques; the Drennan/Kamasan models in particular are far superior to non-chemically etched hooks of the same patterns in all departments, especially strength. In the past, the coating process involved tumbling the hooks in a vat which dulled the point; nowadays the chemical etching process means that hooks retain their sharp point when being coated with black, blue, gold or whatever. Chemically etched hooks are infinitely superior, and many anglers (including myself) use them exclusively.

The most important factor when choosing a hook model, pattern or size is that it should relate to the bait size which will be used, and not just to the fish being sought. A large bait on a small hook will mask the hook point and hinder penetration; similarly a small worm on an over-large hook will work inefficiently.

Other considerations include using soft wire, long shank hooks for flatfish: these are easy to remove without damaging those smaller fish which you wish to return, and are more suitable for worm baits; or using short shank hooks for crab or fish, as these offer better bait presentation.

There is a standard sizing for hooks which most manufacturers use, although when the same sizes are compared they do seem to vary tremendously between different companies. The sizes used for sea angling range from size 6 (small) for flatfish and small species, to 6/0 (large) for such species as conger and tope. For shore angling the required range is smaller, from size 2 to 3/0, thanks mainly to the stronger, chemically etched, carbon steel patterns.

Present-day fish stocks mean that it is much more practical to fish the middle-of-the-road sizes – around 1/0, 1 and 2 – with the 1/0 capable of landing virtually any fish hooked from the shore with the exception of tope or conger.

Don't always expect a hook straight from the box to be the ultimate fish-catching pattern; there are certain improvements that can be made to some models. Offsetting the point is a popular means of improving on a hook's catching capabilities, because it increases its hooking dimensions. Try the following test: run a straight-shanked hook between your finger and thumb – the point will find it difficult to stick in. Now offset the hook's point and try the same test again – the hook cannot fail to stick in. This small but effective adjustment, done with the aid of a pair of pliers, gives a hook 25 per cent more hooking efficiency. It also helps it retain its position, and helps prevent mini-barbed patterns from coming unstuck.

Of the various means of attaching hooks to line, the eyed model is most popular. Spade ends are available in some patterns but are far from popular amongst sea anglers, especially when the hook needs to be passed through a delicate worm bait. Whipped hooks are sometimes employed for this task when harbour ragworm are the bait for fish such as flounders. Whipped hooks have little other advantage, and in fact the eye and knot on the standard eyed pattern help to retain the bait's position during casting. A compromise is the Mustad Sea Match Blue and Nordic bend patterns which are ultra-fine wire hooks with mini-eyes.

There are several different finishes available to hooks, ranging from black to gold. All prevent hook corrosion and are not really important in terms of their colour. Personally I use a hook only once, and prefer to discard it for a new one each trip to the beach.

Having chosen a pattern of hook there is no reason to use this one exclusively for every situation – the thousands of different patterns exist to help you overcome the small problems caused by bait size etc, and if three different baits are being used on a rig then three different patterns of hook can equally well be used: provided they are all chemically etched.

Leads

Having cast your tackle out, it is important that it stays in position on the sea bed. Strong lateral tides create pressure on the line which can easily tow a lead along the sea bed. This can sometimes be used to advantage with a rolling lead used to seek out feeding fish, but on most occasions the best results are obtained when fishing from the shore by ensuring that the lead stays where it is cast. This is particularly apparent when fishing in surf or a weedy sea during gales when strong tide, swell and weed on the line can soon force tackle back on the beach

● (Above) *Mixed coloured whipping also provides efficient rod grips (see page 8)*

● (Below) *Bulk spools are the most economical way to buy line (see page 9)*

or well downtide. The shape of the lead and the addition of wire spikes help the lead to keep its position; a good shape also makes it streamlined to cast and comfortable to retrieve. Bomb and torpedo shapes are the favourite, whilst cone and pyramid shapes have a place in certain conditions.

● *Crude but efficient fixed-grip leads for strong tide*

Also important to results is the fact that very often a fixed lead will act as a buffer for fish taking the bait, thus setting the hook. Other improvements to the basic lead include grip wires which snap out of the anchor position (Breakaways) to help in retrieving the lead, and plastic vanes which help the lead to plane off the bottom and over snags when retrieved. As with hooks, the shore angler can make use of all the various shapes, patterns and styles to add versatility to his fishing.

The leads used for shore angling range from 4oz (113g) to 8oz (226g): most efficient and popular is the 5¼oz (150g). This weight of lead suits the average angler's casting ability, whilst still offering maximum distance; over 6oz (170g), the effort to cast long distances relates to the angler's size and power. For juniors, small anglers, or those over retirement age, the lighter weights between 4oz (113g) and 5oz (150g) can drastically improve casting distance in ideal conditions. Leads most often used to combat very strong tides or to cast into gale-force winds are 6oz (170g) to 8oz (226g).

Swivel or Breakaway wires are used for average tide conditions, whilst fixed wires are employed for extremely strong tides. How the wires are bent to grip in the sand and mud dictates their efficiency – the best are the type of lead with wires coming out of the lead's nose. The addition of a short length of

copper wire around the wires adds grip whilst also preventing hook snoods from tangling with the wires.

Long tail wires are popular but have little practical value in adding grip, although there may be some benefit in stabilising the lead during its flight

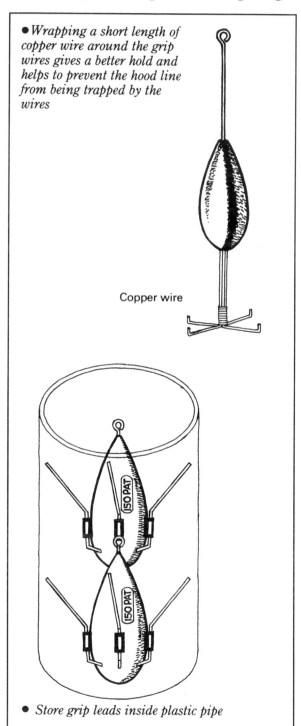

● *Wrapping a short length of copper wire around the grip wires gives a better hold and helps to prevent the hood line from being trapped by the wires*

Copper wire

● *Store grip leads inside plastic pipe*

when cast. Lead lift vanes or fins either fitted on the line above the lead or permanently to the lead assist retrieval. These are particularly effective when fishing over snags; they also take the hard work out of the retrieval of fixed wire grip leads, which would otherwise bump and trundle over stones and rock.

Amongst the other types of leads available are the bait-holder and swimfeeder designs. These have several practical uses, with the Intaki bait-holder particularly effective for long-distance casting with delicate worm baits such as harbour ragworm. These are stored on the hook, inside the capsule, and released on impact with the water. Fins added to the device give it lift, keeping it away from snags etc during the retrieve. Swimfeeder leads in general are not that effective, although they are a means of casting delicate baits and dispersing scent and small bait scraps close to the baited hooks.

The storage of grip leads inside the tackle box is a problem for the angler as the wires can easily spike an unwary finger. An excellent method is to store them inside a short length of pipe.

Tackle accessories

Tackle boxes

Fishing tackle is expensive, and so a major consideration once you have purchased your rod(s) and reel(s) is something to put them in. A rod holder is essential to keep rods and so on together, besides making it much easier to carry them to the venue. Wrapping or tying a collection of rods and rodrests with string will quickly damage them, with varnish scratched and rings broken. Rod holdalls come in a variety of sizes, and there are many purpose-made

for the long tip, short butt rod combination. Lightweight plastic tubes stored inside the holdall help to keep rod tips apart and give added protection.

As far as tackle boxes are concerned, choose the biggest box possible. If you take everything you need to the beach it must help your results as well as keep your muscles in trim, lugging it along the shingle. The large plastic Shakespeare or Riva boxes are ideal; they are rugged, and also 100 per cent waterproof which is essential in order to keep corrosive salt water away from delicate tackle. This make of box also has smaller, custom-made boxes and trays which fit inside the main box, to store hooks, line, swivels, scissors, elastic cotton, beads, booms, tape, plasters, lead lifts, starlites, spare rings, etc, etc.

A tackle box is essential for several other reasons, one of which is to provide a base to which to anchor your umbrella (more about that later). Also, the biggest boxes do away with the need to carry lots of bags and buckets: put the lot in one box and it is dry and to hand, and unlikely to move when the wind is blowing and the brolly is tied to it. The only disadvantage is that anglers tend to fill their box to the brim and then complain that it is heavy; in fact most use a rucksack for those far-off venues when the tackle load needs to be kept to a minimum.

Umbrellas

Umbrellas have grown in popularity in recent years, just as the other types of angling shelters have, too. Used on beaches where there is limited tidal movement between the low- and high-tide marks, they offer shelter on the coldest winter night and make fishing more enjoyable when bites are few and far between. Unfortunately there is not a purpose-made umbrella for sea fishing and most are designed for freshwater fishing – and the salt spray soon makes a mockery of these. The Beach Buddy is the best of the specially designed shelters. An important point to consider when buying a brolly is the size – 45in (115cm) models are more practical in strong winds, as any bigger, and your shelter is likely to blow away in the first force six gale.

Rodrests

Rodrests come in various designs, from the one-legged monopod to the tripod. In recent years

● *The umbrella is now standard equipment for the shore angler. Anchor it with luggage straps*

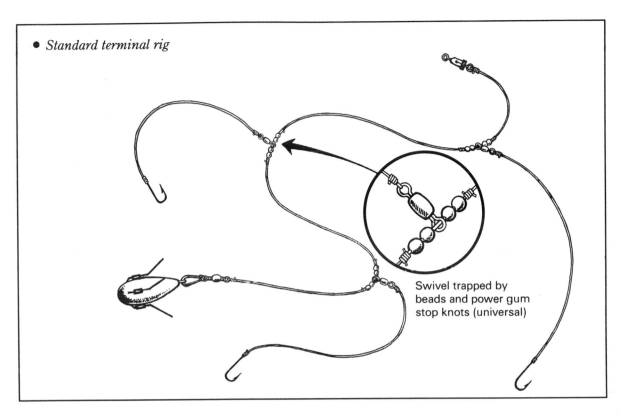

- *Standard terminal rig*

Swivel trapped by
beads and power gum
stop knots (universal)

custom-made beach tripods in aluminium have
become state-of-the-art items of tackle. Double
heads, trace clips, clamped legs, butt buckets and
even a bucket hook are all standard fitments. The
neck-straining, monopod spike rodrest has gone
out of style, as it cannot be used on the increasing
number of promenades to be found on our coasts.

Lights

When fishing at night the angler has several
options as regards illumination. The paraffin and
petrol pressure lamps are all highly efficient, with
lamps of 500 candlepower transforming the beach
at night to virtual daylight. However, the paraffin
models in particular can prove troublesome and
messy at times, and many anglers have turned to
electric head-lights. The head-lights designed for
pot-holing and fishing have become really sophisti-
cated and powerful; Petzl and Spelio Technics are
two of the top models. Ex-miners' lamps are also
rugged and reliable, although somewhat bulky.
Most of the head-lamps work off rechargeable
batteries on a 4½-volt to 6-volt system. By way of
additional aid to sight and bite indication is the
range of light sticks available, including the Starlite

- (Left) *A tackle box provides a dry padded seat*

which can be fitted to the rod tip or even the terminal tackle to attract the fish to the hook.

Clothing

Modern weatherproof and thermal clothing is
superb. In my youth these were unknown, and
the part where trousers and jumper were meant
to join was always cold: now, one-piece thermal
undersuits and oversuits are available in Space Age
materials, and suits are actually waterproof as well
as being lightweight and warm. Most anglers find it
best to wear a thermal undersuit beneath a separate, light waterproof oversuit. This way the body
temperature can be controlled more easily than if a
waterproof and thermal one-piece suit is worn.

Warmth also stretches to the feet; even insulated
moon boots can be found in the range of footwear
available. However, warm feet and a warm head
mean the angler is happy and can remain alert during those cold winter nights – and that can only
mean more fish on the beach.

Terminal tackle

Whilst there are particular terminal rigs used for
different species or methods of fishing (these are
detailed in the appropriate sections), there is one

basic terminal rig design on which most are based. Factors which dictate a rig's design are that it should present the bait efficiently, be aerodynamically streamlined so as not to restrict casting distance or accuracy, and that it should not tangle easily.

The most popular and efficient rig is the monofilament paternoster, and this forms the basis for most of the rigs shown. The hook snoods are fixed to the body of the trace via small swivels. Mustad or Berkley 45lb (20.4kg) breaking strain are preferred, and these are trapped in position by micro-beads and stop-knots. The latter are made from IPG Power Gum which is particularly efficient for the job as it does not damage the main body of the trace when tightened. Using Power Gum stop-knots means that the snood position can be altered by moving the stop-knots up or down the line; in effect this makes the basic paternoster rig very versatile.

Stop-knots can also be made with 15lb (6.8kg) to 20lb (9kg) monofilament line, but when tightened, care must be taken that they do not damage the main line of the rig. Gluing stop-knots in position

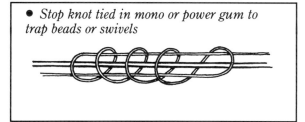

• *Stop knot tied in mono or power gum to trap beads or swivels*

with modern superglues is also far from ideal as initially this prevents snood positions being adjusted or moved, and because the glue breaks down in water. I would add that the ability of a stop-knot to slip position when under pressure from a snag can often lead to a hook-up coming free because of the sudden jerk.

An alternative system of trapping beads and swivels is the use of metal crimps of the type designed for use with plastic-covered wire. These produce a neat stand-off swivel although if crimps are applied too tightly the main trace line can become damaged, with potentially dangerous consequences. If using this system, ensure that the crimps are a close fit on the line, and close the crimps with a proper crimping tool. Rigs can be made up using crimps and telephone wire (see the section dealing with bait clips). A three-hook rig is constructed with three trapped swivels. This can then be converted to a one-hook or two-hook rig by removing hook snoods as required, whilst the

lower snood being made longer converts the rig into a two-up, one-down rig which is popular amongst pier and estuary anglers.

Attaching the terminal rig to the main line can be done via a purpose-made Quick Fit swivel (QF Dexter) or with a lead link, American snap, buckle clip or plain swivel. Pendulum casters should be aware of some makes of American snaps that will open under pressure, and should also ensure that swivels are of sufficient breaking strain. The use of a QF swivel means the rig can be changed without having to tie the a knot each time the rig is joined to the main line; thus rigs can be changed quickly whilst you are fishing. Match anglers change their rigs after each cast to save time – this involves pre-baiting a separate rig prior to reeling in the one that is already fishing. There are many advantages to this system which saves lots of fishing time, particularly as it means the angler can continue fishing even when rigs become tangled or damaged; the offending rig is simply removed and replaced.

At the lower end of the rig the lead is joined to the line via a lead link (Mustad Uni link, Berkley McHahon snap, American snap). Some form of link is essential at this point, as line tied direct to the eye of the lead can soon be damaged when retrieved over shingle and stones. This could result in a snap-off, with the lead endangering other beach users. On this point it is essential that swivels, lead links etc which are used on the body of rigs are of good quality and at least 50lb (22.7kg) bs. Mustad and Berkley offer the best quality.

The most efficient way to carry rigs is in a rig wallet. These are available custom-made with sealable, plastic see-through packets inside a waterproof wallet. Terminal rigs in various forms can be made up in the comfort of the armchair and then transported to the beach for use. A small label on each tells the angler what it is, and includes line breaking strain, size of hooks and so on. It is totally impractical to make up rigs on the shoreline, except when a rig may be required for a specific purpose.

Whilst the basic mono-terminal rig is suitable for most occasions, there are times when other items of terminal tackle may be preferred. Booms, for instance, are often the choice of pier anglers, whilst occasionally they also have certain magical properties when used for flounders. Most modern booms are made of lightweight plastic and can be fixed in position on the terminal rig with the same micro-bead/stop-knot method used for swivels. Metal booms are considered out of fashion, but they have their uses especially if required to fish baits hard on the sea-bed in strong tide; the fact

● *Quick-fit swivel and other line links*

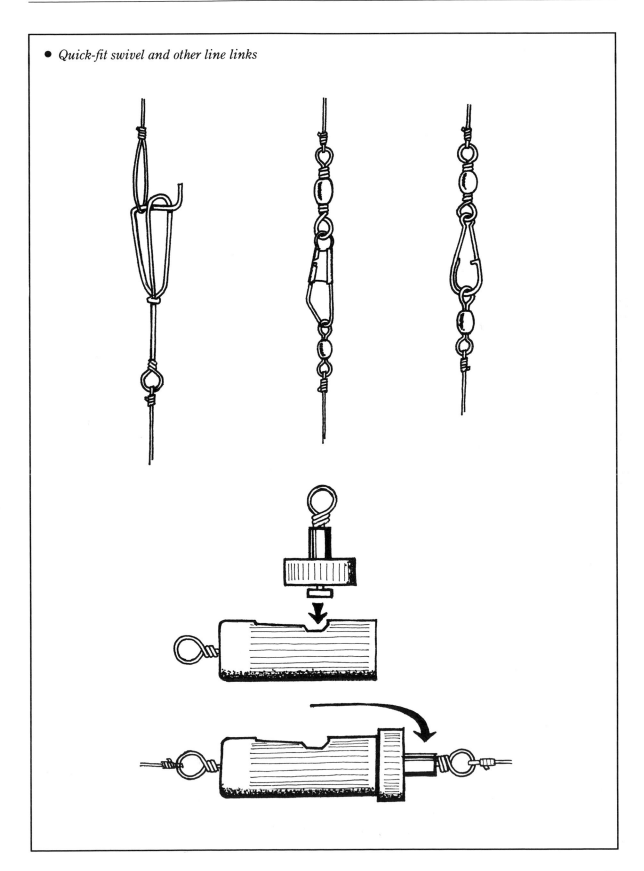

● *Time for some illumination (see page 21)*

that they glint and shine underwater may attract species of flatfish.

There is a host of sundry terminal rig items, including sliding booms and all manner of plastic concoctions. The terminal tackle industry is a minefield of items which derive from the plastic moulding revolution, and much of which are rubbish. Keep your tackle simple, the complications are not needed to catch fish. For instance, many beginners fall into the sliding boom trap, reasoning that if the fish can pull the line through the boom he will not feel the lead and will therefore eat the hookbait without fear. In fact, fishing with the hook snood fixed to the line causes the fish to hook itself when it meets the resistance of the lead and tide, and this is particularly the case when using wire grip leads.

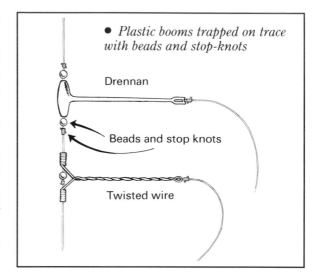

- *Plastic booms trapped on trace with beads and stop-knots*

Drennan

Beads and stop knots

Twisted wire

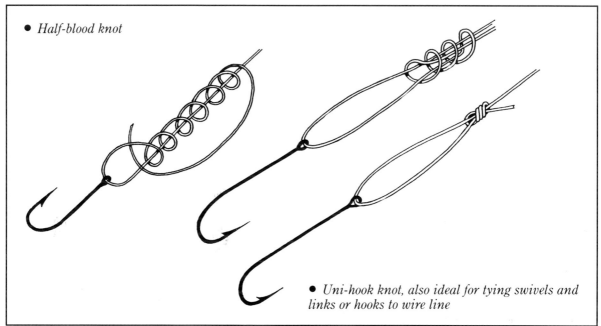

- *Half-blood knot*

- *Uni-hook knot, also ideal for tying swivels and links or hooks to wire line*

Knots

There is no need to be conversant with a long list of knots to make up terminal rigs. The various strengths of different knot designs are often quoted, but the differences are too small to have much effect on success or failure. It is far better to concentrate your efforts on tying a proper knot than to construct a complicated knot incorrectly and damage or flatten the line in the process. Care should be taken when pulling a knot together. Wet the line with saliva and this will prevent friction causing heat damage. Also tension the knot slowly,

easing each strand or loop into position.

The half-blood knot is the best knot for tying hooks. In its tucked form it adds a bait-securing spur of mono to the hook, although the basic half-blood is as strong a knot as the sea angler needs for use with 15lb-plus (6.8kg-plus) bs lines. Five turns are sufficient, with ten turns required for lighter lines. The Uni knot is also efficient for tying hooks, swivels etc, whilst the variation used for tying leaders is ideal for shore casting as it streamlines the knot thus easing its passage through the rod rings. For the ultimate in leader knot strength for shore tope, conger or even sharks, a double Grinner knot is most efficient.

2 Casting

THE SEA IS VAST, AND CONSIDERED FROM THE shore the angler has a very limited range in which to fish. He can improve his chances either by moving along the shoreline or by learning to cast further out. Piers, rocky outcrops and similar vantage points offer an easy way to reach deep water, and within reason, some fish are available to all anglers, even those with limited distance-casting skills. Obviously those who do learn to cast long distances have the advantage, in that the area of sea which they can cover with a baited hook is larger; and this ability is particularly advantageous during a gale or storm. Those extra yards often make all the difference in the worst conditions, in particular being able to get your tackle clear of the breakers. Whilst others must continually re-cast because sea, wind and tide have dislodged their tackle, the long-distance caster can continue to fish unhindered.

In recent years distance casting with sea angling tackle has become a sport in its own right. Regular tournaments and competitions have idolised distance casting to such an extent that it has dictated shore-angling fashion, and to many is the ultimate goal in shore angling. There is no denying that long-distance casting catches a lot of fish – yet sometimes it may be better to control your casting ego and drop short on occasions, even though this ability may be harder to master than learning to cast long in the first place. Many fall into the distance-casting trap – their tackle and fishing is geared to maximum distance for every occasion, and they fail to appreciate the real advantages that being able to cast long can bring.

Casting styles

There are several different casting styles, and these have evolved as sea anglers have given more thought to the physical aspects of launching a lead into the air with rod and reel. Distances have improved dramatically as anglers have found how to increase the amount of compression put into the rod by using different casting styles. Other improvements in distances have come as a result of the advances in tackle technology, especially rod and reel designs. Tournament casting has undoubtedly played its part in improving distances on the beach by making anglers aware of what is possible with the correct gear and technique. The tournaments have also brought to sea angling a very important asset: the casting instructor. Paying to learn to cast is now accepted in the same way as the golfer seeks out the help of the Club Professional. This is by far the easiest way to learn to cast long distances, and in the long term is far less costly than trying to teach yourself.

The overhead thump

The most basic casting style is the overhead thump, the teach-yourself style adopted by a majority of anglers; it is capable of distances of 100 yards (91.4m) with relative ease. The main pitfall of the overhead thump is that it does not give the caster

• *The pendulum cast. Note the body position and the long drop between lead and rod tip*

● (Above) *Slimy but obliging, the eel is a common catch in many estuary areas (see page 37)*

● *A powerful reel-up-the-butt cast*

● (Above) *Weed on the line (see page 36)*

the full opportunity to impart power to the rod and lead because of the short arc in which the rod travels. The frustration provoked by the lack of distance achieved is also the major cause of a jerky action, which results in the reel tending to overrun and birdsnest.

The layback and South African style

Although these two styles differ slightly, both see the lead stationary before the cast. In the layback cast, the caster leans back, coiled like a spring. This cast advances the overhead thump because it involves a larger movement of body and arms, with the rod coming overhead at 2 o'clock to the caster's body, thus creating a bigger, smoother arc which makes overruns less likely as well as increasing distance. The late Leslie Moncrieff gave us the layback cast, and it was the forerunner of the great advances made in distance casting in recent years.

The South African cast involves increasing the length of the drop between the lead and rod tip. The lead is placed on the ground in an arc behind

• *Rock fishing at Ballyreen in Co Clare, the scene of some of Jack Shine's shore shark captures*

the caster; the same 2 o'clock casting angle is employed. This style increases the compression put into the rod and the lead travels in an even larger arc than with the layback style. Again, it is a smooth and easy-to-control cast.

The pendulum cast

The most forceful of the present styles of casting is the pendulum cast and involves the lead being swung, in pendulum style, behind the angler with the lead travelling in excess of a 180-degree arc during the actual casting stroke. The build-up of compression imparted to the rod by the pendulum swing increases the total compression of the rod, thus increasing the casting distance.

A product of the tournament field, the pendulum cast allows very long casts to be made with relative ease once the swing and casting movement have been perfected. As in the South African style, the pendulum cast sees an increase in the length of line (drop) between the rod tip and the lead.

There are two intermediate styles of pendulum cast that are also used, and these are linked with rod length. Most anglers use a rod of around 12ft (3.6m), with the reel some 24in (61cm) from the butt. The pendulum cast with this rod style requires perfect timing, as the arc in which the lead

● *The pendulum arc*

● *A pier cod*

employed in the future, and the distance ceiling of 300 yards (275m) is likely to be exceeded. One of the biggest advantages of the long rod pendulum cast is that because the rod and drop are longer, the lead travels in a wider arc than when using the other style. It therefore travels more slowly, which gives the caster more control over both rod and reel. Whilst timing is important, the long rod, reel-at-the-butt pendulum style is more forgiving and less likely to result in a reel overrun. In practical angling conditions it is also kinder on hookbaits.

Whatever type of cast the angler chooses, there are obvious dangers should the line break. Casting leaders are therefore essential to all those shore casting with light lines: and never forget that a wayward lead could kill! Bright-coloured shock leaders are preferred for practice casting on the field where leaders may be lost.

Joining the shock leader to the main line can be done via several knots. Most anglers prefer the strength of the Uni knot, and I have shown in the diagram my variation of that knot. Ensure that when pulling all knots tight they are wet; this prevents damage through the line burning, and saliva is the ideal coolant. Both the Grinner knot and the blood knot are especially suitable when fishing for very large fish when the leader knot may be subjected to extra strain. However, both of these knots are more bulky than the Uni knot, which is also streamlined in the direction of the rod rings thus helping to achieve smoothness in casting. Remember to place the shock leader knot on the side of the multiplier reel away from the side you thumb the reel to avoid line burns. For fixed spool reels, the leader knot should be placed near to the lip of the spool.

● *The Grinner knot is ideal when a strong leader knot is required*

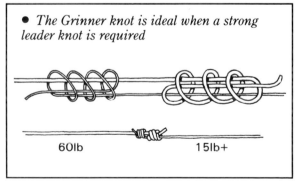

60lb   15lb+

Tackling up to cast

Learning to cast efficiently and without birdsnests or tangles is just as important, if not more so, than learning to cast long distances. On the tournament

flies is relatively small – one mistake in the timing of the swing and casting stroke can spell disaster. This style is also notorious for spraying bait around the vicinity as the lead is cast whiplash fashion. It is the most difficult of the pendulum casts to master, but is more often chosen because of the comfort of fishing with the reel in the up-the-butt position.

The other style of pendulum cast involves longer rods and produces greater distance more easily, and is far more practical for fishing. The length of rod is increased up to 15ft (4.6m), with the reel place at the butt. Lighter materials like boron and Kevlar make it likely that even longer rods will be

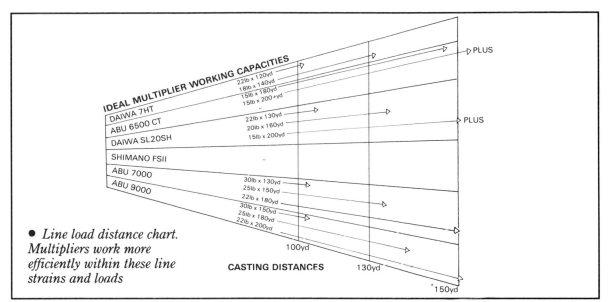

IDEAL MULTIPLIER WORKING CAPACITIES

DAIWA 7HT
ABU 6500 CT
DAIWA SL20SH
SHIMANO FSII
ABU 7000
ABU 9000

22lb x 120yd
18lb x 140yd
15lb x 180yd
15lb x 200+yd

22lb x 130yd
20lb x 160yd
15lb x 200yd

30lb x 130yd
25lb x 150yd
22lb x 180yd
30lb x 150yd
25lb x 180yd
22lb x 200yd

PLUS
PLUS

100yd

CASTING DISTANCES

130yd

150yd

● *Line load distance chart. Multipliers work more efficiently within these line strains and loads*

field snap-offs are common in the quest for extra yards, but on the beach they mean lost fishing time. After all, who wants to spend most of their time on the beach undoing tangles or replacing lost terminal rigs? Thus it is important that the tackle is correct for the job. Reels should be loaded adequately as well as being free-running, with spool float adjusted correctly.

One of the biggest pitfalls to smooth long-distance casting is that reel spools are over-loaded with line. This problem applies to both fixed spools and multipliers. Mostly to blame is the assumption made incorrectly by anglers that the more line the reel has on it, the further they will be able to cast. This is a long way from the truth, especially when using multipliers.

All reels work best with a particular size line and load, and the tolerances are narrow – step outside these and you risk lots of casting problems.

Line load should be governed by the weight of the lead used, the number of hooks and type of bait, and the wind force and direction. All of these factors affect the speed of the lead and this is crucial. In perfect conditions with a plain lead cast downwind, the lead is simply skied: the wind does the rest, and a fully loaded multiplier will unload its line. As the lead slows, the diameter of the line on the spool decreases, thus less line is fed to the lead. Cast the same lead towing two baited hooks into a headwind and the lead will slow dramatically so that it cannot pull the line off the spool as fast as the spool speed: result – one birdsnest.

For the best results with a multiplier, ensure that the line load is able to cope with the conditions and bait load. This is especially important during strong gales. A small model multiplier loaded with a limited amount of line will feed the line off to the lead speed giving a smooth, tangle-free cast. Field casters who cast great distances with the wind to the side or behind, quickly find that a skied lead into a headwind spells disaster. Low and flat hedgehop style is the way to sneak extra yards into a strong wind.

The fishing cast

Whilst the pendulum cast may be responsible for long distances over grass, the full-blooded style is totally impractical in the average shore-fishing situation. Strong head-on winds, an uneven beach, promenade walls behind the angler, or simply lots of other anglers or people, all these render the pendulum cast either difficult or dangerous to execute. Anglers have adapted the style by shortening the length of line between rod tip and lead, and by lessening the swing. The end product is a very effective but stubby pendulum cast. Using such a style enables the angler to cast from any position and achieve reasonably long distances. It is, therefore, much more practical to concentrate on perfecting such a style than to concentrate totally on the more ungainly full pendulum.

An additional skill is being able to cast to the same spot regularly. The most forceful casts tend to ruin accuracy and spray leads in all directions. By casting to the same spot, a fish feeding zone can be created, with fish lining up to feed on a continuous scent and food source. This is particularly effective for certain species, and most effective in competition fishing.

- *Plaice (see page 147)*

- *A pollack from the kelp (see page 149)*

- *A steady pull – but mind the line on the rocks (see page 41)*

3 Weather and tides

PLANNING PLAYS A LARGE PART in successful shore angling, not only from the point of view of tackle and bait, but also in selecting the best times and tides to fish. It is not very efficient to fish at just any weekend and in all-night-long marathon sessions in the hope that sooner or later you will collide with a shoal of fish. It works on occasions but wastes a lot of fishing time and during winter can be cold and boring. Being more informed about venues, fish behaviour, tides and the effects the weather can have, not only helps the angler to catch more fish but makes the fishing much more fun. So often you hear anglers say 'You should have been here yesterday', or 'Last week the fish went mad'. With a little thought and planning you could have been there yesterday or last week. Several very basic facts affect angling success, and finding the peak times to fish is not difficult. A set of tide tables provides the basic information concerning the times of high and low water plus the height of the tide.

To determine the best times to fish, an understanding of how fish react to weather and tide is necessary. Most species of fish encountered by the shore angler are travellers – with the exception of those like wrasse which take up almost permanent residence, most move from one venue to another, taking advantage of weather and tide. They will capitalise on the results of a storm, when shellfish or worms may have been washed from a sand bar into the surf or when coloured water provides cover equal to darkness. Fish are almost always more active during the spring tides when extra water movement and a more powerful tide may aid a journey inshore. Just watch how fish activity in an aquarium increases when you switch on the air pump and filter. In the sea, strong tides mean movement amongst the bait fishes too, and they put pressure on other forms of sea life which must cling to their habitat or be eaten.

The tidal movement of the sea is governed by the gravitational pull of the sun and moon. Every fortnight both planets combine their gravitational pull and tidal movement is at a maximum; these are called the spring tides (nothing at all to do with the season). When the gravitational pull is at its weakest, the tides are described as neap; thus one week brings spring tides, the next neaps and the next springs and so on. Spring tides are those that rise the furthest and then retreat the furthest, often uncovering rarely seen sandbars and suchlike. These are obviously the best tides for digging and collecting bait. Spring tides are also the fiercest, those most likely to require wired grip leads to hold bottom.

DAY		MORNING		AFTERNOON	
		Time	Height	Time	Height
1	Mon	04 16	6.7	16 21	6.7
2	Tues	04 51	6.7	16 21	6.6
3	Wed	05 26	6.6	17 27	6.5
4	Thurs	00 03	6.4	18 03	6.4
5	Fri	☾ 06 43	6.2	18 45	6.2
6	Sat	07 35	6.0	19 42	6.0
7	Sun	08 46	5.9	21 01	6.0
8	Mon	10 00	6.0	22 21	6.1
9	Tues	11 12	6.2	23 34	6.4
10	Wed	** **	***	12 17	6.5
11	Thurs	● 00 42	6.6	13 14	6.6
12	Fri	01 40	6.9	14 06	6.8
13	Sat	02 32	7.2	14 54	7.0
14	Sun	03 21	7.4	15 39	7.2
15	Mon	04 07	7.5	16 24	7.3
16	Tues	04 54	7.4	17 06	7.2
17	Wed	05 37	7.2	17 49	7.0
18	Thurs	☽ 06 21	6.8	18 34	6.7
19	Fri	07 07	6.5	19 23	6.4
20	Sat	08 01	6.2	20 22	6.1
21	Sun	09 01	6.0	21 34	5.9
22	Mon	10 14	5.8	22 59	5.8
23	Tues	11 30	5.9	** **	***
24	Wed	00 05	6.0	12 25	6.1
25	Thurs	00 55	6.2	13 09	6.3
26	Fri	○ 01 35	6.4	13 47	6.5
27	Sat	02 12	6.6	14 22	6.7
28	Sun	02 46	6.8	14 56	6.9
29	Mon	03 21	6.9	15 29	6.9
30	Tues	03 55	6.9	16 02	6.9
31	Wed	04 27	6.9	16 31	6.8

● *Tide table, showing spring and neap tides*

With the aid of a basic tide table the angler can immediately discover the best dates to visit a venue by looking for the spring tides. This is not an infallible method of gaining the best results from all shore venues, but most do fish best during the strongest tidal movement during the fortnightly spring tides.

A complete tidal cycle occurs every twelve hours: this means that every twelve hours there is a high tide; low water occurs approximately six hours later, high water occurs again approximately six hours after this and so on. Double high tides and other tidal anomalies occur in some areas and are caused by large land masses like islands or headlands, where a giant eddy may distort the tidal movement.

High tide is generally seen as the ultimate time to fish from most shore venues. A scouring flood tide brings the fish inshore, with three hours either side of high water usually offering the best fishing. Some venues experiencing a strong ebb also fish best at low water and only local experience can help you discover this fact. At night the high tides which occur between 8pm and 2am are often the best ones to fish; the night hours offer the added bonus that fish travel close to the shore feeling safe under the cover of the darkness. Fishing from most venues between 2am and 5am is not normally very productive, although there are exceptions, with certain species which feed at these times. A notable exception to the early hours' activity is sole, whilst dawn often signals activity from bass and the ray family.

Weather conditions are crucial to fish behaviour, with wind direction being one of the most reliable forecasters of fish activity. An onshore wind nearly always signals good fishing, and as mentioned previously there is one obvious reason for choosing a storm shore in preference to a lea shore even though the latter is the most comfortable to fish. Some wind directions, notably east, tend to make shore fishing difficult in certain areas. That old saying 'When the wind's in the east the fish bite least' has a ring of truth, whilst 'When the wind blows west the fish bite best' is also very often right. One school of thought maintains that barometric pressure affects the behaviour of fish in respect of wind direction.

Certain species prefer clear water, whilst others only feed in daylight. There are not many generalisations to be made, although the few given here may help the angler to decide which species to set his sights on in certain conditions. Plaice are notable as daylight feeders who prefer calm, clear water conditions. Flounders feed mostly in daylight

in any water clarity. Mackerel and mullet feed best in clear water, and both feed in darkness – this fact is not generally known. Cod and bass love storms, with bass preferring the biggest surf, and cod a pea-soup sea.

Facts about the venue

Selecting the best times and tides to fish will undoubtedly bring rewards, yet there is one very superior time to fish and that is during or just after a storm or gale. Being able to drop everything and go fishing is not possible for everyone, but those who *can* rush to the beach as a storm subsides will vouch for the fishing. Unfortunately for most of us, to get there several tides later is invariably too late; and if you live inland then the problem is greater, and the importance of good information about, for example, how a venue is fishing is even more acute. Local information can help when selecting a venue, but beware the advice of tackle and bait dealers who may have something to gain by exaggerating

● *Fin-perfect, this flounder fell to a bunch of small white ragworm*

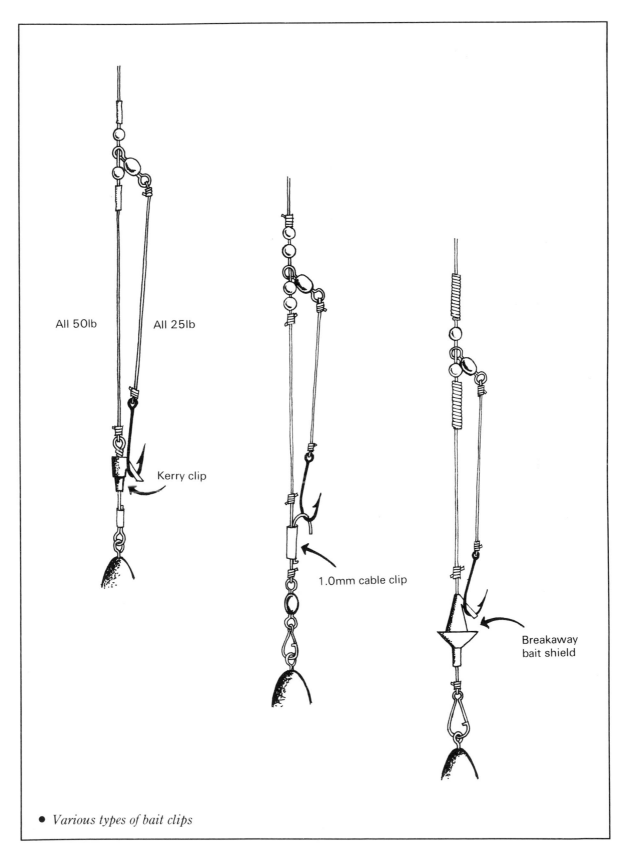

All 50lb   All 25lb

Kerry clip

1.0mm cable clip

Breakaway
bait shield

● *Various types of bait clips*

the catch stories. Similarly the angling press reports are weeks old. Whilst the phone-in fishing lines may be more up-to-date, there is no substitute for a friend on the ground. Contact with a local angler can be invaluable to determine what beach is fishing, where the current hotspot is on the pier, and what bait is the best. This is a definite short cut to learning by trial and error, and is well worth the occasional pint in the local pub or angling club.

Fishing in a storm

Whilst storms and gales blowing onshore invariably offer the best fishing for the shore angler, they involve fishing into the worst possible conditions he can encounter. A wind of force eight and 20-foot surf can make a mockery of sea angling tackle. Cast out and tackle and line are swept, weed-laden into the surf-line or beach, or even buried in the shingle. At its worst a gale can be unfishable, and then the angler will have to wait until the wind and sea subside.

However, the angler who can fish during a gale will inevitably catch fish, and nothing is more satisfying in sea angling than to catch fish whilst others around you cannot even cope with the weather.

The basics of the technique needed to fish into an onshore gale firstly require the acceptance of the limitations the wind and sea impose. You won't be able to cast as far as if the wind is behind you, therefore the reel line load required will be less. Your casting style will have to be adapted to get under the wind, and your terminal tackle will need to be more streamlined to combat its force. Lastly your lead, once cast, must stay put where it lands. This means a total change in your tackle set-up: try to fish with the gear you fish with in normal conditions, and you are doomed to failure.

The first necessity is to reduce your bait size. This can be done by using one hook instead of two or three, and if you can get away with two small baits rather than one large one, that may suit the species you seek. Use the size of bait and number of hooks most suited to each individual situation. Bait clips greatly assist the angler fishing into a gale, as these pin the baited hook closely to the terminal rig. The most effective terminal rigs for casting into wind are the wishbone rig and pennel rig. Whilst these rigs each present hookbaits in a different manner, both place the baited hook(s) very closely behind the lead and this adds to the rig's aerodynamic shape, thus aiding casting distance.

The leads to fish in storms should be the same as those used in strong tide, with the fixed-wire type essential. Leads with the wires coming from the nose are the most efficient, whilst short wires grip better in hard mud or sand than long springy ones. The latter are ideal for rocks or soft mud. Breakaway leads with swivel-grip wires can be made to grip the sea-bed better by the addition of an elastic band around the wires.

It is essential when casting distance into wind, or indeed when a side-on wind is encountered, to cast low and flat. A punch style for such conditions can be mastered with practice, with the emphasis on getting the lead flat over the waves with a limited loop in the line following it. A large bow of line following a high cast encounters wind resistance, not only halting the lead's flight but dragging it off course.

Once you have cast well clear of the breakers, the problem is to prevent the line from being grabbed by them. This is the one time when a monopod rodrest is most useful, to place the rod tip as high as possible above the waves.

Weed collecting on the line linked with strong wind or tide can also serve to drag tackle downtide. By casting slightly uptide, the angle of the line between rod tip and lead allows the weed to run up the line to the rod tip, rather than create a bow in the middle of the line and so increase the pressure on the lead's hold. Weed on the line is a problem when it meets the leader knot and then becomes jammed in the tip ring. There is no real answer, save to ensure that your rod has reasonably sized rings which allow small amounts of weed to go through where it can be removed at the reel. A weed-laden leader knot jammed in the tip ring during a gale means that a big fish is likely to be marooned in the breakers where the backwash will put the hookhold under severe pressure.

Other ways to solve this problem include using a longer-than-normal leader so that tackle is kept out from the breakers whilst the weed is removed from the knot. Another alternative is to use a stronger line, thus doing away with the need for a leader knot. However, heavier line does tend to catch the tide because of its bigger diameter, and holding bottom in a gale using heavy line can prove a problem. Perhaps the ultimate way to solve the problem is to use a tapered leader; this allows a small knot to be used between leader and main line which is less likely to catch weed in the first place.

Bite detection during a storm may be difficult, but the rhythm of a heavy surf is regular and so any rod-tip movement that deviates from that rhythm should be given attention.

4 Estuary fishing for flounders and silver eels

WHERE THE RIVER MEETS THE SEA there is also a confluence of angling techniques, with anglers able to employ both sea- and coarse-fishing methods in their pursuit of several estuarine species. The mullet, for instance, can be fished for with coarse angling gear, and this can be used fairly high up into the estuary. On the other hand flounders, bass, coalfish and eels can provide more basic sport to sea tackle, the estuary providing a more sheltered environment than that of the open sea or for those not prepared to specialise in the shy and sometimes elusive estuary mullet.

For the majority of sea anglers, estuary fishing involves fishing the shoreline at the mouth of the larger rivers, although the river proper is often the scene of some excellent sport. In Britain this might be on the Thames, Humber, Severn or Tyne, where sea anglers fish the river bank in sight of the opposite side, and here a certain merging of tackle and methods has evolved. The volatile nature of the open sea makes fishing light both impractical and less effective, but inside the river estuary the sea angler can scale down his tackle and still be able to fish successfully.

There is no need to fish ultra-light for sea fish in estuary conditions in order to catch them, but it can be more enjoyable for the angler when the environment allows it. A carp rod, 10lb (4.5kg) bs line and 2oz (57g) lead, represents the lower limit of estuary gear, whilst standard beach tackle will suffice and indeed is necessary when casting distance may be important or larger fish are likely.

Most estuary areas contain large sources of bait – worm beds, peeler crabs and shellfish in the mud, sandeels and lots of other bait goodies; the sheltered environment enables such life forms to thrive, and the threat from predatory sea fish is less because there are not many species which will actually swim in the estuary water, often a mixture of salt and fresh. As regards estuaries, the saying is 'Plenty of bait and few fish', and invariably those areas around the coast which are close to, or run up to estuaries have poorer fishing than the open sea beaches. The amount of freshwater travelling down the river into the sea certainly has a great effect on the fish present the nearer to the estuary you fish. Indeed, a river estuary in spate in winter is often not worth fishing, and it is not until you get many miles away and the freshwater is dispersed and diluted that the sea species can be found. There are, though, two species which exploit the estuary environment and thrive in it, and these are the flounder and the eel. Both are particularly adept at adjusting the salt tensions in their blood, and this enables them to survive in salt, brackish or virtually freshwater conditions and thereby feed on an exclusive and otherwise untapped food supply. This versatility also makes the flounder our most common sea fish: you find him everywhere.

There are other estuary species which are less resistant to the changes in the salinity of the water, and these range over a larger area of the estuary and are greatly affected by, for example, rainfall. Some of the northern rivers such as the Tyne and the Wear have large coalfish populations, and big shoals of young coalfish travelling into the estuary mouth provide continuous sport for sea anglers. Also, the estuaries of some southern and Irish rivers offer fishing for rays, with the best results in times of drought or low rainfall. The mullet is, of course, a major estuary species, and there are three types: the large-lipped grey which prefers the edge of the estuary, and the smaller thin-lipped and golden grey which make the journey up the river into freshwater. All can be caught with coarse angling tackle and methods and offer a challenge to the angler. Small baited spoons, float-fished bread and mud ragworm are the usual methods, with the river fish requiring a great deal of stealth and dedication to catch. (For more about mullet, see chapter 7). Another estuary species is the shad – the Allis and the Twaite – but these are found in very limited numbers and are both on the endangered species list, and are therefore no longer sought specifically by anglers.

Flounders and silver eels

The shore angler has a certain advantage when fishing for flounders or eels in an estuary as he knows that the fish will travel into the estuary with the flood tide and out with the ebb. Thus no matter where he fishes, sooner or later, and providing that he fishes long enough, the fish will pass by. In some river estuaries the fish travel into the river along one bank and out along the other, or they may travel close to one headland or point. A certain amount of local knowledge can therefore help the angler to decide which are the best times and the best places to fish. Moving around as the tide floods and ebbs is also a worthwhile practice, to get the best of the full tidal cycle. Moreover it is important to realise that both flounders and eels will travel anywhere where there is water, sometimes going to the water's very edge as the tide floods over a sandbar or mud bank, with only inches over their backs. Using human reasoning to choose a spot to fish – such as 'It looks likely that fish will prefer to go there', or because everybody else fishes there – is doomed to failure. Those who maintain they can 'read the beach', and who pin their faith in gullies and patches of seaweed, will find that success requires more factual reasoning. More success will be enjoyed by finding out the route that fish must take in order to circumnavigate groynes or sea walls, and fishing these places. Never discount any spot, as so often the least 'fishy'-looking places offer the most success – and remember that if you are on your own, the fish there don't have to be shared with another angler!

The top estuary bait for flounder and eel is the peeler crab, and the ultimate bait for flounders is a large, fat and juicy half-crab, especially in spring. Eels prefer whole small crabs, and a peeler about the size of a 2p piece is ideal. Flounders can engulf a large piece of crab, and don't underestimate the

extent to which they can open their mouths. In winter, ragworm and small wriggly harbour or white ragworm can prove killer baits, whilst a mixture of both peeler crab and ragworm can prove most effective – a single white ragworm added to a crab bait gives it another dimension: movement, thus offering both scent and movement in one bait. A small sliver of fish strip added to a worm or crab bait is particularly effective in some estuaries, notably those in Ireland where fresh mackerel is the best. Lugworm cannot be discounted, but it is far less effective for flounders than the baits mentioned above; indeed, it only enjoys majority success in general sea-angling terms because it is the most easily available.

The basic terminal tackle for fishing for estuary flounders should aim to spread the baits over as wide an area as possible. Using beach gear, a three-hook monofilament paternoster or flowing trace takes some beating. The body of the terminal rig should be as long as can possibly be handled with the rod you are using. Butt casters find that their extra rod length enables very long rigs to be used, which can be useful for estuary flounders in

● *Two school bass for the author*

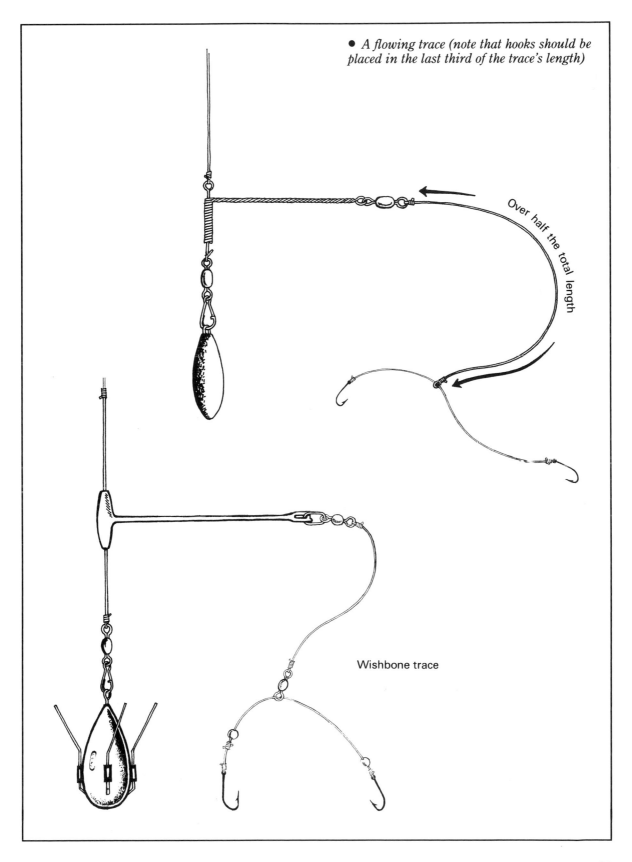

• *A flowing trace (note that hooks should be placed in the last third of the trace's length)*

Over half the total length

Wishbone trace

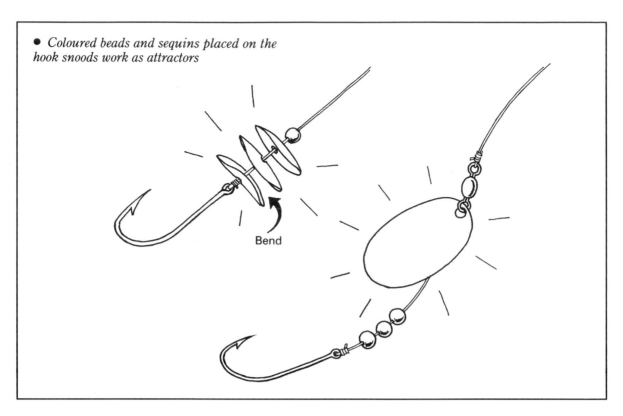

- *Coloured beads and sequins placed on the hook snoods work as attractors*

Bend

spreading the bait scent trail over a wide area of the current.

Snood lengths can be 15lb (6.8kg) breaking strain and above, since it is pointless to go lighter. Snoods should be as long as is practical, remembering that the lighter and longer the snood, the more likely it is to tangle around the body of the rig. Hook patterns are only significant in that they should suit the bait being used; this is especially important when using peeler crab baits. Use short shanks for crab, in a size to suit the size of the bait – the Kamasan B980 or Mustad 496 spade-end blue is my favourite for use with peeler, in sizes 4 and 2; whilst for worm baits, Kamasan Aberdeens in the same sizes are the sharpest, although the softer Maruto Aberdeens are easier to remove from a fish's mouth.

Long-distance casting is rarely required in estuary areas. These nearly always experience very strong tides which sweep both fish and food close to the bottom and onto muddy or sandy banks, so a 30-yard lob to the low tide mark is usually sufficient.

Flounders are inquisitive, and like most other flatfish, will respond to movement and colour. Beads, coloured sequins and spoons close to the hookbait all work well at certain times and in some estuaries. Don't underestimate ragworm: fished behind a silver or white spoon, they are an effective

means to combat bait-robbing crabs and will catch flounders in estuaries and harbours. They don't *always* work, but when they do, spoons retrieved slowly can provide an exciting way to catch these small flatfish. Moving the baits also works when bottom-fishing: use a plain lead, and let the tackle trickle along in the tide with just the odd tweak of the line to entice a fish; alternatively use a grip lead with wires or even a cone shape, and tweak it occasionally to send up a plume of sand or mud. Bite indication can be improved by placing the rod tip low to the ground, coarse-fishing style. The absence of large breakers makes this most practical.

The only difference between the methods and tackle to catch eels and flounders is that eels can soon make a mess of light line snoods and so stronger hook snoods are advisable. When catching flounders, it is just as well to leave a biting fish to take the bait completely into its mouth; indeed, such patience can sometimes result in two fish or more in one cast. However, leave an eel to take the bait and hook itself, and you risk your terminal rig returning in a ball of slime, minus the eel. Should you land him, he can prove a slippery customer to unhook and retain. A bucket with a sealable lid is ideal and totally necessary.

5 Rock fishing for wrasse, conger and cod

The venue and tackle

A MAJORITY OF SHORE ANGLERS never even consider fishing into rocks or kelp because of the inevitable loss of terminal tackle and line, preferring to fish the many clear, snag-free beaches. Hence one half of the coast of the UK remains comparatively unfished whilst the other half is fished heavily. As well as there being several different species which inhabit a rocky or weedy sea-bed, this is the one habitat which the commercial fishermen cannot exploit easily. As a result, whilst stocks of species found on open ground are in decline, many of the rock species remain prolific and within reach of the shore angler. So those who can come to terms with the inconvenience or cost of losing a few sets of tackle, very often enjoy some marvellous fishing, especially for the larger species like conger and cod. With the correct approach and gear, tackle loss can be kept to a minimum and it is surprising how few terminal rigs will be lost even to the most hostile-looking sea-bed providing a few basic rules are followed.

Fishing deliberately into rocks, kelp or a snaggy bottom requires different tackle and techniques from those used for fishing clear ground. There is no compromise between the two methods of fishing if you are to get the best out of each. The first step for the rock angler is to reduce his chances of hooking up, which means he will rarely use more than a single hook, other than a two-hook pennel rig used to present one large bait. He must then use stronger tackle, so that should he become snagged up he has a fair chance of pulling the rig free. 30lb (13.6kg) breaking strain (0.60mm dia) monofilament line is the first choice of many rock anglers, and this offers a good chance of pulling free from most snags without losing too much tackle, particularly if wire hooks are used. The Mustad Nordic bend 4447B, for example, is ideal, as its softer wire allows it to bend out of a snag rather than snapping or causing the line to break. Obviously the type of fish you seek also governs hook size and strength, so whilst a Nordic bend 4/0 may suffice over rocks for cod to 15lb (6.8kg), a stronger or larger size hook such as an O'Shaughnessy may be required for conger eels.

Retrieving tackle from rocks or kelp is made easier with this simple and basic combination of single hook and heavy line. With the terminal rig itself kept simple, the lead used should be as light as is practical, 4oz (113g) to 5oz (142g) normally being the preferred weight for rock fishing. Whatever reel is employed, it should be fully loaded with line to give maximum retrieval per turn of the handle. Most of the biggest fixed spool reels offer a rapid retrieve, whilst of the multipliers, the Shimano Speedmaster range and Daiwa SL20SHA are the fastest.

Having loaded the reel to its maximum, the angler should always make his retrieve by lifting the rod in one swift upwards movement – moving the lead around to 'feel' the bottom is tempting a hook-up. Similarly once the tackle is cast it should be left where it drops until the retrieve. Having lifted the rod, turn the reel handle speedily and without pausing. It helps if the rod and reel are placed comfortably; for the up-the-butt reel position it is most efficient if the rod butt is held firmly between the legs. For the down-the-butt reel position, tuck the rod butt into the hip; whilst a rod bucket should be considered for fishing really rough ground.

Position yourself as high as possible above the rocks – this will also help in the retrieve of tackle. Never walk down the rocks as you reel in, but stand your ground, high up the rocks, and reel as fast as you can. Experienced rock anglers develop a sixth sense as to when the tackle is nearing the sea-bed or a snag, and they can lift the rod quickly at that split second the lead touches. This is an especially useful skill when spinning slowly and close to the kelp fronds.

Amongst other aids that help keep tackle off the sea-bed are lead lift vanes: these either fit on the line or above the lead, or are an integral part of the lead. The former can be made from thick flat plastic, or can be purchased ready-made from tackle dealers, with the Breakaway version one of the best examples. Long-wired grip leads are used from some rock venues to prevent the tackle rolling or being moved around and snagged. Long wires spring out easily and thus help to avoid tackle loss. In severe conditions a weak link system can be employed – although it involves the loss of the lead each time it becomes badly snagged, it does ensure the hook and therefore any fish is retrieved.

Even if you do snag your tackle, it is not a certainty that it will be lost. Many anglers in this situation simply put the rod over their shoulder and heave until a break occurs. However, there are alternative procedures worth trying which might help to get the odd rig back. Firstly, you can change your position before pulling the line, thereby altering the angle of the line to the snag. Make sure you have a comfortable place to pull from and are not

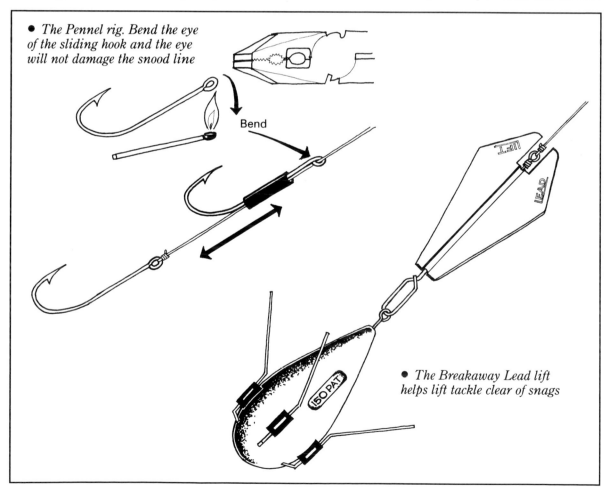

● *The Pennel rig. Bend the eye of the sliding hook and the eye will not damage the snood line*

Bend

● *The Breakaway Lead lift helps lift tackle clear of snags* off-balanced by a sudden break of the line. Allowing the line to drop slack sometimes releases a hookup; or you could try applying a steady and slow pull without stressing the line to breaking point.

The final option is to break the tackle out, but in this case be careful as you risk damaging the reel spool or the line itself. If pulling direct with the rod, wrap the line around the rod butt thus taking the strain away from the reel spool. Avoid pulling with the rod tip held high as this could break the rod. Also, try not to let the line touch any rock or suchlike, as this will cause a line breakage near the rod tip. Finally, if you put the rod down and pull on the line at the rod tip by hand, take care not to let the line slip suddenly through either your hand or a rag; going through your hand it can burn you,

whilst slipping through a rag will burn the line and cause a breakage. Grip the line firmly and apply a steady pull.

With these basic and simple rigs and methods, anglers can fish over rough ground or rocks anywhere around the coast. However, the various sea coasts which are classed as rocky are often very different in character, and in fact rock fishing itself is most diverse – the angler may be contending with steep granite or limestone cliffs which tumble into the sea, or the flat lava-like rocks such as those found on the west coast of Ireland, the chalk ledges of Kent, the deep kelp gullies of Cumbria or the potholed rocks of South Wales. All offer him a formidable challenge if he intends not only to get his tackle back regularly, but to catch fish as well.

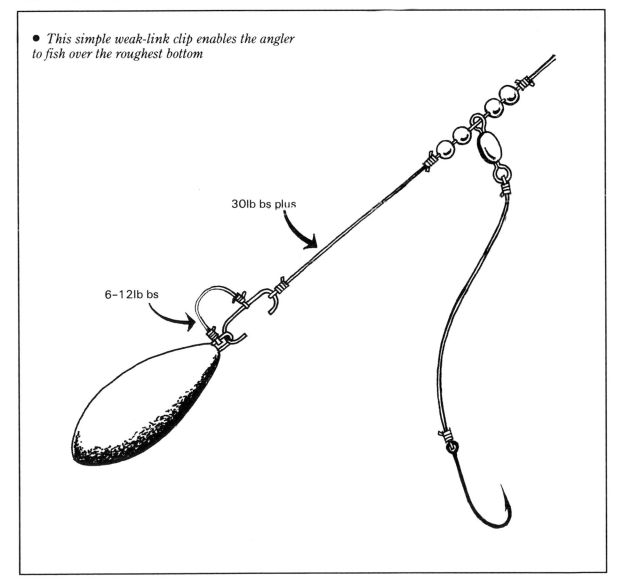

● *This simple weak-link clip enables the angler to fish over the roughest bottom*

30lb bs plus

6–12lb bs

A basic essential to rock fishing is the correct footwear: if you are going to clamber over hard, slippery rocks then this should not be neglected. Modern trainers give a better grip than most other types of shoe, whilst a leather-soled boot with support for the ankle is best for some areas of the coast. Some rocks are extremely slippery when wet, and smooth-soled shoes or pumps can be dangerous. In the north-east, anglers prefer to wear chest-waders for wading to far-off rock platforms, though there are obvious dangers in wearing these around slippery rocks and deep water, and personally I cannot recommend their use at all. Studded waders are often said to give the best grip, but on smooth rocks these too can be deadly. It is worth giving the matter some thought, and choosing the footwear which is best suited for the ground you intend to fish over.

There are dangers from the sea itself, too, for the angler fishing from a cliff rock position, particularly into Atlantic driven swell on the west coast of Ireland, England or Scotland, and rock anglers would do well to heed the warning that every seventh wave is a big one. The odd rogue wave in the course of a storm, or even in comparatively calm weather,

● A 6lb (2.7kg) ballan wrasse from the rocks of Co Clare

has drowned many an individual who has chosen to take up stance without due respect for the power of the sea!

Rock fishing for wrasse

There are three main species of wrasse found around the coast of Britain but only one, the ballan wrasse, is considered a big enough quarry by sea anglers. The other two, the corkwing and cuckoo wrasse, are considered mini-species, colourful but small. Wrasse are certainly pretty, but as an angling species their charm soon wears thin after the sixth is hauled from its rocky lair. They fight well but somehow lack the attraction of many of the other species, perhaps because they are regarded as poor eating or because the small ones can be hooked so easily.

Wrasse prefer the roughest, rockiest ground and survive on a diet of crustaceans and molluscs which they crunch and scrape from the rocks with the aid of a tailor-made set of forward pointing teeth. You cannot mistake the wrasse with its big rubbery lips and bright red, green, blue and brown colouring.

Because they colonise rocky areas in large numbers, wrasse are exploited by anglers and invariably the shoals from easy-access rock marks are quickly depleted or consist only of small specimens. Find a remote and difficult-to-get-to rock mark, and the wrasse can be as big as 5lb (2.3kg), with 8lb (3.6kg) a possibility from many of the most rugged stretches of coast. In fact catching the biggest specimens involves more rock climbing than angling skill, and should you dare to go where no other angler has been, then the wrasse record could be yours.

Wrasse can be sought with standard rock-fishing rod and reel, a single hook and a small lead, as casting is unnecessary. Float fishing is also a method worth considering, with a sliding float rig ideal. Simply drop your baited hook alongside the rock or beside an overhang. Wrasse love water turbulence and a white water hole between rocks is often an ideal spot to drop the bait. The bites are immediate and forceful as the wrasse seize the bait and dash off to the safety of their particular haunt in the rocks. Their comparatively small mouths and manner of grabbing the bait and swimming off fast gives the angler some exciting and often impossible bites to hit, whilst once hooked the fish quickly dive into crevices in the rock and are difficult to retrieve. Essentially this is the type of rock angling where the angler must hold the rod, strike, and reel in as quickly as possible once a fish is on.

● *The British record bass: 19lb (8.6kg), caught from Dover breakwater by David Bourne*

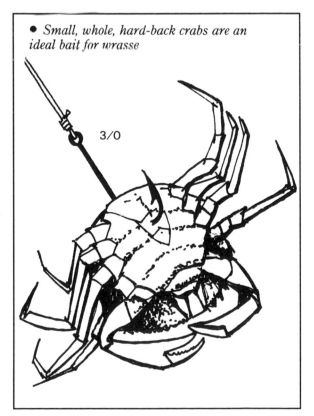

● *Small, whole, hard-back crabs are an ideal bait for wrasse*

3/0

The best bait for big wrasse is, without doubt, a whole shore crab, 1in (2.5cm) across the back being the ideal size. This is one time when hard-backs are better than peelers as the hard crabs withstand the attacks of small fish better than the softer peeler crab. Baited on a 3/0 Mustad Viking 79510 hook, the crab is impaled through its abdomen. If bigger crabs are used, the wrasse tend to bite off their legs and leave just the crab carapace, so sharp and strong are their teeth. Smaller wrasse up to 2lb (0.9kg) will accept ragworm, lugworm and shellfish, but rarely fish flesh. Wrasse fishing requires mobility – the angler should take only the minimum of tackle owing to the rock climbing aspect, and if a bite does not come from a spot within five minutes then he should move on. Wrasse fishing is to be enjoyed occasionally, whilst small wrasse are ideal for juniors and beginners to learn rock-fishing skills as they also frequent piers. For the majority of anglers, however, fishing for wrasse is unpopular since the exploitation of the shoals around some coastlines leads to so many unwanted fish being returned from high on the rocks to die on the surface of the sea.

Rock fishing for conger eels

Of all the rock species, the conger eel is the most formidable. It can grow well into double figures with an excellent eel from the shore being a fish weighing over 20lb (9.0kg). When small, the 'strap' congers are a nuisance as they peck and pinch at any bait. Once mature, they are muscle-packed predators that are difficult to remove from their lair. Congers tend to be found mostly in the southern and western half of Britain and nearly always from rough ground – rocks, kelp, holes in pier walls – in fact anywhere they can lie in wait for an easy meal.

For the rock angler there is no bigger quarry than the conger eel, and tackle and approach needs to be specific or specialised. Big congers are rarely landed on light gear or by an angler not fishing for the species without a great deal of good fortune. A conger will fight like a dog on the end of a lead – its head surges from side to side and its tail wraps around rocks and searches for leverage as it retreats to the safety of its lair. The small but sharp teeth will make short work of light monofilament lines, so the first essential of the terminal tackle is a heavy monofilament trace. A short length of up to 150lb (68kg) monofilament provides a bite trace which prevents the fish from biting through the hook length. Wire is not really required to combat the conger's teeth, although it was favoured in the past. The advantage of using monofilament is that eels and equally other species of fish, are not put off as they are by the stiffness of wire. A double-figure bass taking a mackerel head aimed at a conger is considered a bonus and never refused by the angler!

The rig itself can either be of paternoster or running trace design, with the latter preferred by most anglers. Basic rock gear is sufficient for conger fishing, although specialist anglers after big congers may prefer a more powerful rod (ZZiplex NG 1, Pro Am) or one with a soft action for casting large baits. Also necessary is a larger reel (ABU 9000/1000C) with a line capacity to suit the extra diameter of heavy line (30lb/13.6kg plus) and a ratio of retrieve and large handle to give added leverage against the bigger fish.

An essential piece of equipment is a gaff: try to land a large eel without one and all will be lost. Fixed-head gaffs are the best, as the screw-head type can become unscrewed when a big eel decides to spin on feeling cold steel. Gaff congers in the middle or in the area of the vent, though first of all be sure that you have a firm footing and have chosen a safe place to gaff from. Once landed, the eel can be consigned to a sack well above the high water mark; the hook or trace can be left for removal later if you use a line clip to disconnect it from the rig.

Congers will accept most baits although fresh fish is preferred, with a fresh mackerel head and entrails or flapper considered the best.

Bites should be allowed to materialise, and the conger given time to pick up the bait and manoeuvre it inside his mouth. A series of runs can produce some spectacular pulls, and the angler must decide whether to strike early to prevent the fish getting back to the safety of its lair and risk missing it, or to give the bite time to develop then find the fish deeply hooked and difficult to extract from its lair. By mounting baits hair-rig fashion with the hook well exposed, the fish are hooked forward in the mouth having been struck early. And if big congers are to be returned alive there are obvious hazards to removing hooks.

Congers are territorial and will take up residence in a small area of rock, only choosing to venture further afield under the cover of darkness or in coloured or deep water. A calm moonlit night during late summer is by far the best time to fish for the species.

Rock fishing for cod

Whilst cod are available the length of the coastline from both rocky and sandy shores, those which are resident amongst thick kelp and rocks are always the most attractive as they take on the rich orange and red colouring of the kelp fronds. Sand-caught cod lack this colour, and are an anaemic and pale creamy-green. The red or kelp cod are generally the smaller codling – fish above 15lb (6.8kg) are rarely taken by anglers because living inshore they will inevitably be caught before reaching such a size. The largest populations of red cod are found around the northern shoreline of Britain, particularly Cumbria and along the north-east coast of Northumberland and the east of Scotland. Rock cod in many other areas also adopt a dark or orange-red hue, but they lack the richness of those northern fish.

Fishing for cod in the rocks requires the simple and basic tackle already discussed, with a single large hook reducing the risk of tackle loss in the snaggiest spots. Long-distance casting is rarely required, so line breaking strain can be increased to around 30lb (13.6kg), with little need for casting shock leaders. This is not to say that on the odd occasion a long distance cast to a far-off gully with a lighter outfit will not pay dividends. However, the further the cast over snags the longer it takes to pull back in through them, with correspondingly increased chance of a hook-up.

The fishing position amongst rocks and weed is important, more so than when fishing over open sand or mud. The fish funnelled by the flooding tide along rock gullies or beside reefs take the same route whatever the tide and time of year, and successful angling involves placing your bait in suitable ambush. If your cast lands your bait on the top of the reef or on a rock in shallow water you may spend hours without a bite. Timing is also crucial to catching the fish, as they may pass by in a shoal during a short period at a certain state of tide. Learn their route and timing, and the shoals can be exploited.

Darkness is usually considered the best time to fish for cod from most venues, but they can be caught from some of the deep-water kelp forests in bright sunshine.

The best bait for fishing for cod in rock or kelp is undoubtedly peeler crab, with lugworm and mussel a good second. Fresh squid has some success in areas where other baits are removed quickly by shore crabs, but fresh peeler crab and lugworm are invariably most successful. It is noticeable that the bigger cod prefer lugworm to peeler crab or mussel, and that the latter is particularly effective for codling.

The most successful terminal rig for the rock angler after cod is the pennel rig. This involves the use of two hooks in one bait and is ideal for very large worm or crab baits because it puts a hook at either end of the bait. When using peeler crab, use a 3/0 hook as the base hook around which the bait is secured, and a 4/0 hook as the slider. The eye of the sliding hook can be bent by heating it for a few seconds with a match or lighter and then bending it with a pair of pliers. A short length of plastic cable insulation added to the hook and snood gives it a snug fit on the line (2.5mm twin and earth PVC cable insulation is ideal). The peeler crab is then cut into two halves which are mounted one above the other along the shank of the bottom hook and secured with the minimum amount of knit-in elastic. The sliding hook is then nicked into the bait so that it is held in position whilst fishing it hair-rig style. The biggest hook is the one that is likely to hook up, since it is at the unrestricted end in the front of the bait when it is taken into a fish's mouth.

The bigger cod feed positively, engulfing the bait into their large mouth in one go, and producing either a rod-bending run or a slack line which is difficult to miss. Small codling, on the other hand, pick up and drop a large bait, producing slack line-bites that many anglers complain they cannot hit when they strike. The key to success with this type of bite is to allow plenty of time for the fish to take the bait, which he will do eventually. In some regions of the coast a wriggly white ragworm added to the point of the hook when using both lugworm and peeler crab baits encourages the fish to take the pointed end of the hook, giving more likelihood of a contact on the strike.

Cod are not renowned for the resistance they put up when hooked, and it is their sheer bulk against strong tide which provides the 'fight'. The hookhold is most vulnerable when the fish is landed with swell and backwash from waves, both of which exert extra pressure on the tackle and thus the hookhold. When fishing from high rocks the angler needs either a hand gaff or, in extreme cases where he is high above the water, a drop gaff or net.

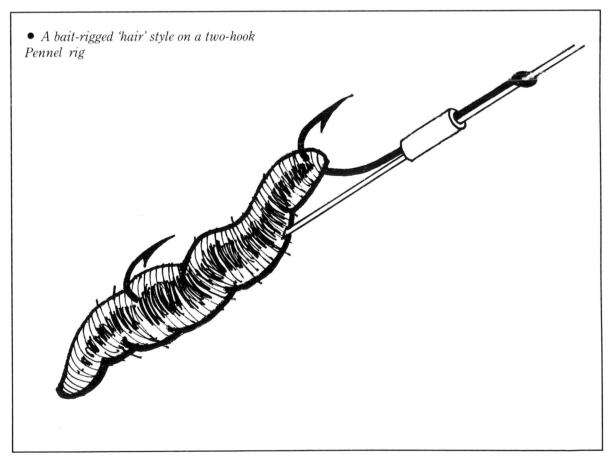

● *A bait-rigged 'hair' style on a two-hook Pennel rig*

6 Beach and promenade fishing for bass, cod, rays and flatfish

The venues and tackle

SEA DEFENCES OFFER THE SEA ANGLER an ideal platform to fish from, and in recent years there has been a dramatic increase in the construction of promenades, groynes and protective shingle banks as a consequence of more frequent storm ferocity and damage. A promenade around a cliff allows easy access to what may have been otherwise inaccessible fishing; it also means the angler doesn't have to move up and down the shingle with the tide. The installation of a bank of shingle gives access to deep water as well as providing a convenient, clean, sand- and mud-free place to fish from. Classic examples of each type of sea defence are Marine Drive promenade at Scarborough in Yorkshire, and the shingle beach at Seaford in Sussex. Both of these venues were improved dramatically by sea defence construction, offering easy access to a much wider area, and much improved fishing.

As well as the man-made sea defences there are many natural ones, and Chesil Bank in Dorset is one of the most famous examples. Continuous wave action over hundreds of thousands of years has built up a natural barrier of shingle and stones, whilst the east-to-west drift of shingle and the wind have graded the size of the stones in a unique manner. On the Kent coast, Dungeness Beach is another classic case of the sea and strong tides building up a bank of shingle, east to west, and at Dungeness the shingle 'point' grows approximately an inch a year. It is no coincidence that both of the examples I have mentioned are famous for their fishing, as they both offer access to deep water, strong tide and thereby fish.

Along with the shingle beaches – actually made up of stones and pebbles – anglers tend to classify any open shore-line as 'beach' and this includes long sandy stretches of strand backed by a small amount of shingle, sand hills or even promenade. All offer a similar type of fishing, generally over clear sand, mud or shale, because storms push the bigger stones or rocks up onto the shore-line or bury them completely. Such 'storm' beaches are popular with anglers primarily because they offer a clear, snag-free sea-bed and therefore tackle loss is kept to a minimum.

The storms themselves tend to have a significant effect on the fishing from such shores, with huge breakers, waves and wind-driven swell gouging shellfish, worms, crabs and eels from their homes in the sand. Even the smallest waves prompt a continuous stream of dislodged food items for fish, and despite looking barren, many of these flat, sandy storm beaches are a mass of burrowing creatures. A storm during the biggest spring tide can often smash a complete sandbank colony of razorfish or cockles to pieces, thus providing a natural groundbaiting effect to which the fish flock. During such times the fish can be as close in as the trough behind the main breaker, feeding at the base of the most powerful waves as these gouge out the sea-bed. In calmer times the far side of a sandbank or deep gully 100 yards (91.4m) or more offshore may be the place to find the fish, where a minimum of wave action will provide a food source.

Most storm beaches seem quite featureless, and give little away in the way of clues as to where the angler might find fish; however, there are a few things to look for. Groynes, concrete cliff aprons or promenade supports, for example, force the fish to make a detour, and the end of such an obstruction is always a hotspot. Pick the longest groyne and fish close to its end. Gullies and sandbanks can only be seen at low water, but their presence at high tide is often revealed by wave action and surf, whilst patches of coloured water may reveal mud or sand being disturbed.

Local knowledge as to the path, direction and timing of the arrival of the fish is very important, and you can rarely do better than to fish the proven hotspots – but remember, a crowded beach does not always mean the best spot to fish. It is often only

popular because of the close proximity of the pub or car park. Similarly lots of anglers means a smaller share of the fish, so fishing at the less sociable times on your own, you will receive the majority share of the fish available.

The clear nature of the sea-bed on sandy or storm beach venues has allowed anglers to fish with light line and therefore at very long range, and several techniques and methods have been devised for reaching those far-off sandbars and gullies. Rods and reels are as previously mentioned, and the only deviation from the standard tackle is perhaps a lighter outfit for bass fishing in surf (Daiwa PKS115 bass). There is a certain delight in fishing in surf and holding the rod, whilst the same outfit also allows the roving angler to travel light; this is especially helpful when fishing those venues with a great distance between the high and low tide-lines. Long rod, reel-at-the-butt enthusiasts may need a reducer in their rod butt to keep their reel out of the sand or sea. One alternative is to have two reel positions, with the reel being moved up the butt after casting. A tripod with butt cup also solves this

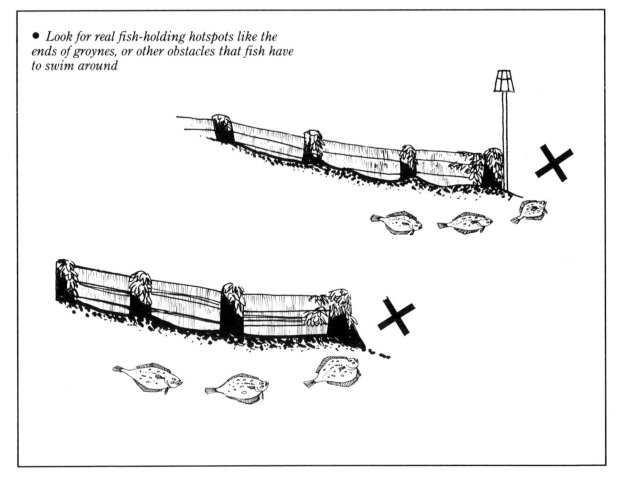

● *Look for real fish-holding hotspots like the ends of groynes, or other obstacles that fish have to swim around*

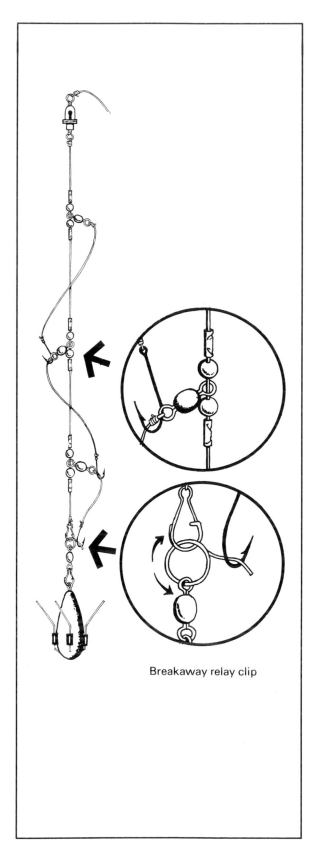

Breakaway relay clip

problem whilst doubling for promenade, beach or fishing from the water itself.

One item of tackle which has become an essential of beach angling is the large green umbrella, providing a dry and sheltered base for the angler to fish from. For use on sandy beaches, the best brolly is one with a tilt, preferably with a lock. Amongst other points to look for, choose a brolly where the extension pole is adjusted by a lever clamp, as screw and thread types soon become clogged with sand or corroded. In summer the brolly serves to keep the bait cool and out of the sun; it can be erected with ease on beach or promenade with a bucket of stones tipped inside the material to keep it in position. Brolly wings add to the size of the shelter and help keep the brolly secured.

Plastic-moulded tackle boxes are the best type for beach fishing; they provide a seat, and can be placed on wet sand in the complete confidence that your gear is safe even when a rogue roller surges up the beach.

Where terminal tackle does not have to be designed to avoid snags, more hooks can be used. A maximum of three hooks is acceptable in sea angling, and whilst many anglers only use a single hook, match anglers or those fishing for the smaller species often use two or three. Limiting the number of hooks only occurs when the angler wants to cast further. Obviously the fewer hooks and the smaller the baits, the less the air resistance of the complete terminal rig and lead, and the further it can be cast. Hook snood lengths also affect casting distance – try casting with long snoods and the baits swirl around the rig, helicopter blade fashion, as it is cast. Short snoods partly solve this problem, whilst the bait clip was invented and developed to solve it completely: the hook and bait are clipped to the body of the rig, thereby making it more aerodynamically streamlined.

There are many variations of bait clip available commercially, and the angler can also make his own clips from a few basic materials; 1.0mm twin and earth domestic lighting cable is ideal for use with 50lb (22.8kg) main line. In fact the standard design bait clip is no more than a small hook secured by a short length of plastic sleeving on the main line of the terminal rig. The baited hook is placed in the bait-clip hook which is then tensioned by sliding it away from the snood. Using multi-hook rigs, a bait

---

● *The Relay rig, invented by Nigel Forrest of Breakaway Tackle*

clip is provided for each hook or a relay system is employed. The theory is that when the bait hits the water after the cast it will fall free of the clip – in the relay system, one clipped-up hook releases the other two.

Improvements on the basic bait-clip design include the Breakaway bait-shield type which incorporates a streamlined plastic cup which sits in front of the baited hook when it is clipped up. On contact with the sea the cup tips and the line running through it forces the hook out of the clip. This is the most reliable of the bait-clip designs. Others which come in clip form include the John Roberts clips and the Paul Kerry clips both of which work reasonably well. There is another bait-clip idea which operates like a safety-pin, securing the hook even when the terminal rig line is slack. A small dissolvable pellet secures the safety-pin clip which releases the hook when the pellet dissolves on contact with the water. Fiddly to use but very efficient.

One of the basic problems with most bait clips, especially those that are home-made, is that of tension. If too tight they refuse to release the hook after the cast, if too loose they release the hook prematurely during the cast. Wind strength and direction can also greatly affect their efficiency. When used correctly, bait clips can add 30 per cent extra distance on a cast; they can also help the most delicate baits to stay intact during forceful casting.

Distance-conscious anglers tend to over-use bait clips, and there is a tendency for bait clips actually to cut possible catches because the presentation of the bait on the hook is altered by the use of bait clips. By pinning the hook and bait downwards on the trace, the bait is forced along or up the snood during the cast, and therefore ends up away from the hook point. This effect can be cured by the addition of a bait-stopper knot on the hook snood above the hook eye – a bead or stop-knot will suffice.

Clipping baits 'up' the rig also cures the problem, although this does lose the advantage gained by clipping 'down' which is to tuck the bait close behind the lead. Multi-hook rigs clipped 'up' tend to wobble when cast, owing to the baits being a long way away from the lead. Bait clips can be prevented from moving by the addition of a stop-knot above the clip. IPG Power Gum is the ideal material for stop-knots – being rubber, it does not damage the line and can be moved or adjusted with ease.

Bait clips can greatly help anglers to increase their casting distance, especially in strong onshore winds when hook snoods 'helicopter' and dramatically shorten the cast. However, the angler who learns to cast long without bait clips will inevitably have better bait presentation, and they should therefore be used sparingly for the best results, and not as standard on every terminal rig.

Another way to gain distance from flat sandy beaches is to wade, and a set of chest-waders can add both yards and fish. There are obvious dangers, such as being trapped on a sandbank by the incoming tide or falling over in deep water or mud. However, chesties are popular as they have the added advantage of keeping the angler completely dry even when not wading.

Remember that anglers wading can sometimes walk right past the fish they are after; they also pose a hazard for other anglers casting from the shore. If you wade, think about what you are doing and why.

Beach fishing for bass

Whilst bass can be caught from rocks, in estuaries and over sand, they are really a fish of white water and surf. The bass is considered the sea angler's only game fish, and is far removed from the mundane pouting, flounder or eel. From the shore this sleek silver torpedo is a fine catch indeed, and whilst not as great a fighting fish as its sheer beauty and classic surf environment would portray, it is a highly sought sea angling species. Unfortunately for the bass and for anglers, it is also highly prized by restaurateurs, its flesh selling for a high price with taste less important than the tag, 'sea bass'. In recent years the heavy commercial pressure of the monofilament gill net and that from anglers themselves has so decimated the bass shoals that it is considered under threat. Unlike many other species, the bass is relatively slow-growing; and because it is plate-sized bass, which have not yet reached breeding maturity, that are sought commercially, its future really is uncertain, with its reproduction cycle thus threatened.

Bass catches from the shore have declined in recent years, not only because of the pressure on the bass shoals but because of the greater distances that anglers can cast. In fact many often over-cast the species. Noted for swimming close to the shoreline, good specimens are often hooked by a short-casting novice or as a result of a reel tangle. Many very proficient anglers fish their whole life long and never catch a decent-sized bass – yet it is often the beginner's first fish, as small bass infest the inshore areas throughout southern England where they are called 'school bass' or 'checkers'.

Bass are found mainly in the south of England and Ireland, although they range as far as The

● *Hold spiky fish like this harmless sea scorpion by the mouth*

Wash on the east coast and south-west Scotland on the west coast. During warm summers their range is extended, with the Atlantic shoals travelling north, and on these occasions the number of small bass in particular increases. Bass feed on a wide range of food including small fish, sand eels, lugworm and crab. They are, however, very specialised in their feeding habits in particular areas and at specific times of the year. One bait will catch bass from one venue, whilst twenty miles away the fish will prefer another. One example is lugworm, an excellent bass bait from Sussex shores but less effective for bass from Kent shores. There, a whole peeler crab or a fillet of mackerel is more likely to be accepted.

Smaller bass will take most food items and this includes chasing sandeels in the surf; the bigger, more lazy fish prefer to scavenge and will often fall to large whole calamari squid or mackerel-head baits. This gives a clue as to where to catch the bigger bass which may have tired of the active surf and retired to exploit an easier food supply. One such example is the fish which holds the British Bass Record at Dover, a magnificent specimen of

19lb (8.6kg) caught by local David Bourne. The half mile (800m) long Admiralty pier is a mackerel hotspot. Anglers gather daily to land hundreds of mackerel and many of the fish are gutted on the pier wall, with the heads dropped straight into the sea. The pier area is the home of some big bass which feed on the mackerel heads as they are pushed to the pier end by the tide. Bass shoal in their class year, but the bigger fish are considered loners; the shoals of big fish are therefore naturally much smaller.

Catching bass from the beach invariably means fishing at short range. Even when fishing in a big Irish surf the fish are likely to be found inside the main breaker as they feed on the food the surf dislodges. A large lugworm bait cast into the white water will invariably get a response if the bass are around, and the bigger the surf the better your chances. On occasions the fish can be spotted inside the curl of the wave as it breaks, running the surf line in search of food. Fishing in surf is always best as the tide floods, with the fish following the ride in; dawn is a prime time at many venues.

Surf bass will also take shellfish and crab baits, with large baits preferred. Red edible-type crabs and velvet-backed swimming crabs are especially favoured as bass baits, preferably in their peeler or

• *A catch of codling for Kent angler Mick Wilson*

soft states. A large edible crinkly-back is the ideal large bait to aim at bass because it withstands the attacks of smaller bait-robbing species and other crabs. On a calm summer night, bass fishing from a steep shingle beach or promenade can involve no more than dropping a small live pout within feet of the water-line; a sliding rig keeps the pout in position in tide- or surface wind-drag. Takes are spectacular, ferocious and sudden at short range, and such tactics require the reel clutch to be set to allow the hooked fish to take line. Just the situation where the instant and pre-set drag systems like ABU Syncro drag are ideal – one touch of the drag-star and the fish is able to take line.

Some anglers believe that catching bass in such conditions requires stealth and should be carried out in darkness. Personally I have caught bass on live pouting under the glare of a paraffin pressure lamp whilst other beach users have been throwing stones in the sea. One minute the pout can be seen as it lies tethered close to the surface, the next it is gone in a flurry of spray with the rod lurching out of the rest.

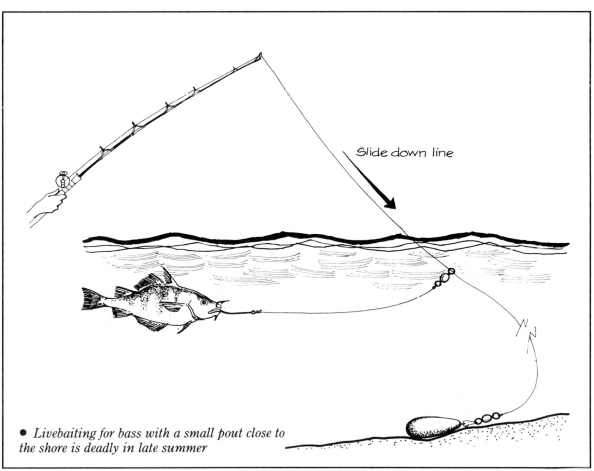

Slide down line

• *Livebaiting for bass with a small pout close to the shore is deadly in late summer*

Bass demand a degree of respect from anglers, not only because they may be considered marine royalty but because they can inflict damage to unwary hands or fingers when being handled. The sharp-spiked dorsal fin stands erect as a warning, but it is the less obvious, yet razor-sharp gill edges which are more likely to cause the damage. Small bass or other spiky species which are to be returned can be handled safely by gripping them in the mouth or grasping them firmly in a cloth. Unhook and return bass with great care: today's tiddler could be tomorrow's specimen.

Beach fishing for cod

The cod is the most popular and fished-for species around the shores of the British Isles. Its rapid growth rate and, as one of the biggest species, its sheer size, make it especially popular with shore anglers. Although it is generally considered a winter species, in some areas it is present throughout the year, whilst in many coastal regions the arrival of small codling in spring extends the winter cod season.

There are various populations of cod around Britain and Ireland, and these migrate between summer and winter feeding grounds and spring breeding grounds, with a degree of overlap. Predation on the fry of cod is heavy as these spend their early life on the sea's surface and are prey for herring and mackerel and other pelagic species. Thus water temperature, and very hot or cold summers tend to affect the breeding success of the species greatly, as these conditions dictate where the shoals of predators are when the cod spawn. However, the cod's rapid growth rate (it virtually doubles its size each year) allows it to overcome the years when there is a heavy fatality of fry, and the species tends to reproduce successfully in cycles every few years, notably following a cold winter. Marine science estimates that if every cod egg survived to become a mature fish the world would be knee-deep in cod within three years. Heavy commercial pressure has been blamed for its demise on several occasions, yet it has come bouncing back. In particular, gill netting, because it is so selective in the size of fish it catches, may yet put the species under threat. Like the bass, the cod cannot survive if all its immature fish, those that have not reached breeding size, are destroyed.

The angler fishing from a clean storm beach in search of cod is most likely to encounter fish under 6lb (3.2kg). These are classed as codling, and are found in large shoals which feed on virtually all marine life forms. Lugworm, white ragworm and peeler crab are three of the most effective angling baits for codling. As it grows bigger, the cod adds small fish to its menu to maintain its increasing food intake; it will feed on sandeel and lance, small rockling, gobies, pout, whiting and flatfish – in fact any species that swims slowly enough for it to catch and eat. It will also accept other marine food forms, including the favourite cod bait of many anglers, lugworm spiced up with a whole calamari squid.

Any cod into double figures caught from the shore is an excellent catch, whilst a 20lb (9kg) fish is the target specimen size of a lifetime for most shore anglers. However, your chances of encountering such a beast do depend to a certain extent on where you fish, and from many areas the chances are slim indeed. Codling therefore provide shore anglers with the bulk of their cod fishing, and the bigger fish are much rarer than many would have you believe.

Because codling have as large a mouth as cod, they can engulf almost any size bait. This makes it difficult to fish exclusively for the bigger fish by using large baits and large hooks, because a large bait is just as likely to catch a small codling of, say, 2lb (0.9kg). In recent years anglers have been happy to catch any cod at all, so the large bait approach with a single hook or twin-hook pennel rig aimed at catching any size cod or codling has become the standard approach. This method is totally necessary over rough ground (see the rock-fishing section p41) but is not as effective for catching cod from clear sand venues as is commonly thought. Also, a single large bait would seem to be the most logical when fishing for big fish, but again, is it that effective?

For many years I have favoured the three-hook small-bait approach as a means to catch cod from the clean-bottomed storm beaches. The method enables the angler to fish for any small fish, whilst at the same time the tackle also allows a bigger specimen to be hooked and landed. There are several advantages gained by the three-hook method. Firstly, a wider bait scent trail is created by using three baits, including different types. The use of three small baits and hooks allows small fish to be hooked, and in turn their struggles will often attract the attention of other and bigger fish, including cod. With a single bait, once this is taken by a small fish, the rig's effectiveness is over. Besides, catching

● *A 31lb (14.05kg) sting ray for the author in an Irish competition*

small fish keeps the angler awake and alert, which is especially relevant during a cold winter's night; it also provides a catch should the target cod not be tempted.

Finally, cod – like all other fish – eat whatever food crosses their path. It is a myth to think that they will ignore a small bait; more likely they will snap it up without a second look. A small bait readily taken is therefore engulfed deep into the cod's mouth quickly, thereby promoting a more secure hookhold. The modern carbon chemically etched hooks are much stronger and sharper than the old style ones, and are capable of landing very big cod indeed. A 1/0 Kamasan Aberdeen will cope with any shore-caught cod, as well as allowing the angler to catch dabs on the same rig. Oversize hooks such as 6/0s are not required for shore cod fishing unless you use the very large bait method of fishing, such as whole squid or livebaits.

If you have the time and patience to fish in this manner – with large bait – specifically for big cod, then the first essential is to ensure that the venue you choose to fish is capable of producing big fish. There *are* such venues around Britain: Balcary

Point in Scotland, Chesil Beach and Dungeness Beach in the south of England, Orford Island in the east, and Hinkley Point in the Bristol Channel, plus a few others. The technique for this sort of fish means using livebait – small whiting or pout are the best. Obviously it is impossible to cast small live whiting, for example, and so the angler has to fish a rig that catches the livebait after it is cast. A small hook baited with a small piece of worm rigged close to a bigger hook forms the basis of the livebait rig. There are obvious pitfalls: that a small fish does not take the bait, that you have no way of knowing whether you have a livebait 'on' or not, and that on occasions the bait turns out to be a 3lb (1.4kg) codling or a 2lb (0.9kg) flounder! Livebaiting is a technique which *will* take big cod, but it is hit-and-miss, and so it is best used on a second rod whilst the first fishes more conventional methods.

Beach fishing for rays

The opportunities to fish for members of the ray family from the shore are limited with only a small number of venues still capable of producing any

number of these fish. The west coast of Ireland in particular offers the best chance of catching thornback, undulate or painted ray, whilst in England the Essex and Hampshire coasts will produce thornback and sting ray. The south-west of England and Scotland are generally considered the best places to catch rays from the shore, with Devon and Cornwall offering some of the rarer species such as the spotted or blonde ray; and a notable southern venue for spotted and small-eyed rays are the front beaches of the Isle of Wight. An essential to catching rays is to fish from a venue they frequent. This may sound obvious, but there are many areas in the country where the occasional ray is taken: fish here, however, and you could be in for a long wait as the species might only be present for a few tides a year.

The thornback and painted rays in particular are found in large shoals, and generally if you catch one there will be more to follow. This lifestyle has led to their downfall, however, as both anglers and commercial netsmen have exploited their liking for company. In an effort towards their conservation it has become a common policy amongst anglers to return the small fish of the larger ray species, with the figure of 5lb (2.3kg) being the most often quoted.

Rays can be found on clear sand beaches, over mud, or amongst tangles of kelp where they feed on shellfish and crustaceans. They are not difficult to catch provided bites are allowed to develop. The ray settles on top of the bait and invariably a strike at this time will either foul-hook the fish or miss it altogether. Given time to take the bait, the fish will move off giving the most dramatic bite which can often pull the rod over. Rays have a reputation for being sluggish fighters and they behave rather like a plastic bag when hooked. Whilst reeling them in often does feel like this, some of the bigger fish such as the sting rays can put up a dogged resistance. They use their large body area to kite in the tide which produces powerful runs that always end when the ray surfaces. But with patience even the most dogged plastic bag can be landed, and the pleasure in catching rays from the shore, quite apart from their rarity, has to be in the beauty and the sheer size of the various species.

Sting ray

The sting ray is the only member of the ray family found in European water which offers any real danger to the angler. They carry a barbed spine, sometimes more than one, two-thirds of the way along

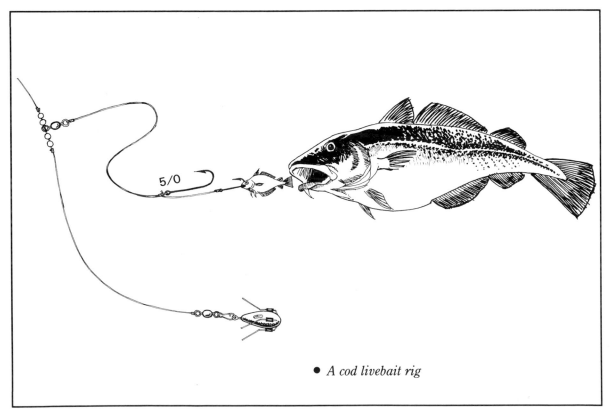

5/0

● *A cod livebait rig*

● *Thornback ray are child's play from Fenit pier in Ireland*

their whip-like tail, and this should be treated with great respect as the spine can inflict a nasty wound. Should you land a large sting ray and wish to weigh it or otherwise handle it, it is a good idea to tape up the sting by simply wrapping the spine with PVC tape. If the fish is to be returned, the tape can be removed.

Sting rays frequent shallow inshore areas in spring where they feed on peeler crabs, ragworm and fish baits. They are most often caught by accident, by anglers fishing for eels and flounders – it is not really practical to go sting-ray fishing except in just a few places with Park Shore and Sowley Sedge the top Hampshire venues, and St Osyth Beach in Essex the venue which holds the British Shore Record for the species. The sting ray's large size offers an interesting angling challenge, as the present British record at 53½lb (24.26kg) is well below the maximum weight attained by the species. Obviously the angler landing a sting ray is advised to gaff the fish rather than grab its tail or head as is the manner in which the other rays are landed, because the tail and spine will lash out and can pierce a

wader. Stingers are squat and dumpy and therefore very heavy for their size, a point worth noting when you attempt to lift a gaffed fish.

The other rays

The thornback, and the small-eyed or painted, are the most common members of the ray family found around the British and Irish coasts. There are also the undulate ray, cuckoo ray, blonde ray, sandy ray, spotted ray and a few rarer rays such as the eagle, electric, marbled or bottle-nosed.

Both the small-eyed and the thornback rays frequent sandy and rocky bottoms; the thornback also likes rugged, kelp-covered sea-beds. All the common species are harmless compared with the sting ray, but they do possess small thorny spines; these are most pronounced in the thornback, giving this ray its name. Treat the thorns with respect and handle rays with some care.

Rays will accept mackerel, herring, ragworm, peeler crab, lugworm, squid and many other baits – but top of the list are sandeels. Thornbacks in particular have a liking for fresh sandeels, but they will also take frozen. Of interest is that dogfish often prove a pest when fishing for rays with frozen sandeels – but switch to fresh eels, and the doggies lose interest. They *will* accept fresh sandeel, but not as avidly as frozen.

Frozen sandeels can be transported to the beach in a food flask. Remove one from the flask to allow it to thaw slightly before baiting up. Used this way, frozen sandeels are not wasted and can be returned to the freezer after each fishing trip. A large sandeel of 6in (15cm) is not the easiest of baits to cast from the shore, and this is one time when the use of bait clips on the trace can help the angler reach

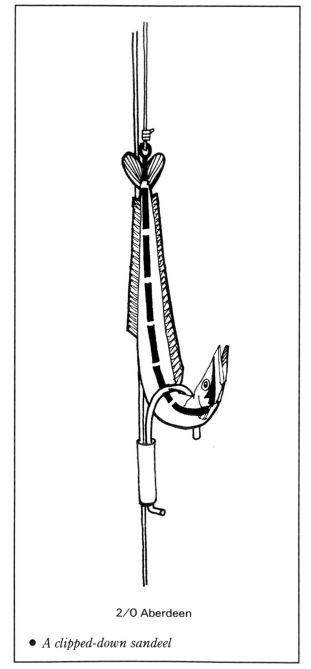

2/0 Aberdeen

● *A clipped-down sandeel*

● *Beware the clamp-like grip of the ray's mouth*

those distant rays. When the thornbacks are feeding under your feet in the kelp fronds, bait clips are not always required for distance, although they do help present the sandeel in position on the hook. There are many variations of baiting sandeels which involve cutting off the head and tail of the eel, but the most efficient means to mount it on the hook is to thread the hook through the eel, tail first, as for a lugworm. Allow the eel to curve around the bend of the hook, and then trap the eel and hook bend under the bait clip. The hook size will need to suit the size of the sandeel being used, with a 2/0 or 3/0 long shank Aberdeen model ideal in most cases. You will need to use slightly larger bait clips for sandeels than you would normally use for worm baits; using stainless steel, 18-gauge wire adds strength when using large sandeels. Baited in this manner, the eel will stay in position under the most extreme casting pressure. In most cases a single hook rig with bait clip will be adequate for ray fishing at long distance, whilst from rocks and suchlike where the fish may be close in, multi-hook rigs can be used.

There is another method of reaching the far-off rays in shallow estuary areas where the tide retreats over a long distance: use a large reel loaded with upwards of 500yd (457m) of line. The baited terminal rig is laid on the sand and then as the tide comes in the angler walks back paying out line and leaving the bait to fish at enormous distances from the shore. This technique obviously gives the angler only one effective cast per tide, but it has been responsible for the capture of some big fish including members of the ray family, particularly in the Bristol Channel area where it is often used. All the rays have strong jaws but they lack teeth which makes it unnecessary to use wire traces. They can still, however, inflict damage to unwary fingers with their clamp-like grip, so remove hooks with care.

Beach fishing for flatfish

Flatfish have a certain charm. They do not grow big and cannot be described as sporting in any shape or form, and yet thousands of sea anglers seek to catch them regularly. Their popularity may be influenced by their undoubted eating qualities, although the fact that they are common around much of the coast has a lot to do with their attraction. Sea anglers have the flatties to fall back on when the cod, bass and other larger species do not turn up – and who can argue that few fish can beat a 9in (23cm) dab for taste?

The species of flatfish most likely to be encountered by the shore angler include the flounder, dab, plaice and sole. The larger turbot and brill are caught occasionally, with some of the western Irish strands regularly producing turbot; although in the main the species are mostly boat-caught. Lemon soles are rarely caught as they have tiny mouths. The only other flatfish is the halibut and this has been caught from the shore but is a rare beast indeed preferring the deep, cold water of northern climates.

The different species of flatfish are often confused, and most of the identification problems are between the plaice, flounder and dab. The sole has a pronounced hook-shaped mouth, whilst its overall sole shape is a certain giveaway to its identity. Identification points to look for between the other species are that the flounder has a pronounced square-cut tail and bony tubercles at the base of its anal and dorsal fins. The plaice and dab both have rounded tails, whilst the plaice has bright orange or red spots and the dab a pronounced curve in its lateral line.

All the flatfish respond to small hook, small bait tactics and there are not really any hard and fast rules to follow to catch each particular species. Fish for one and you may well catch another, and isn't that just part of the attraction of flatfish fishing? A golden rule is that bites should be left to develop,

and there is no need to strike at all. In fact one hooked flatfish will sometimes attract another, so it is a case of sitting on your hands when a flatfish bites and not being tempted to grab the rod. On many occasions the bites are not detected and a surprise flatfish is landed. One tip to detecting bites is to place the rod tip low when possible; a small pebble balanced on the tip ring serves as a bite indicator should you fail to spot a small movement or if you are required to leave your rod for any reason.

Long shank hooks between size 4 and 1 are generally preferred for flatfish, with Tony's Tackle Blues an established favourite. The three-hook monofilament paternoster is the most often chosen and effective terminal rig, with a long snood preferred on the bottom swivel close to the lead. Booms provide an excellent way of fishing effectively with light line. Even the old-fashioned metal Yarmouth and spreader-type booms still prove popular. Whether it is the metal that shines or the weight of the boom that keeps the bait on the seabed which makes metal booms so effective is not clear. It could even be some form of magnetic field that booms produce in water. Whatever the reason, metal booms do have a magic on occasions.

The flounder

The flounder is the most common of the species of flatfish, and in fact is the most widespread of British shore fishes. Most of those caught by the shore angler average between 12oz (340g) and 1lb (450g), with the biggest likely to be encountered from the open beach around 3lb (1.4kg). Much bigger specimens are taken in the river estuaries where the British record approaches 6lb (2.7kg). Flounders can be found everywhere including estuaries, harbours, storm beaches and even rocky shores. Not so famed for its eating qualities, the flounder of the estuary has a muddy and unpalatable taste, although fish of the open beach and surf are often a different matter.

From many beaches the flounder frequents the inshore line between sand and stones, and a short cast will often produce fish; it is no coincidence that long-distance casters rarely catch many flounders. Another likely hotspot is the end of a groyne or breakwater which the fish have to circumnavigate on their travels.

Flounders will accept most of the worm baits but have a preference for small wriggly white ragworm, red ragworm and peeler crab – a large half of peeler oozing pungent yellow juices is the ultimate flounder bait in spring. A sliver of mackerel added to

● *A winter flounder from the beach*

other baits can also prove effective for flounders in many areas, especially from the Irish surf strands. Here, the flounder will often be found in the famed third breaker within easy range of the poorest caster, whilst those who wade may well wade past the fish. Flounders can get so close to the shoreline that anglers have actually caught fish on their spare-baited traces which have inadvertently been allowed to dangle from their rodrest in 6in (15cm) of water.

A three-hook terminal rig is most effective and in surf the longer the trace, the wider spread it gives baits. This is one time when longer, light line snoods increase catches with the baits allowed to flutter in the breakers as they tumble onto the sand. One of the best rigs for surf fishing for flounders is a rig designed by England International Dave Andrews which uses blood loops and superglue to produce a tangle-free terminal rig which includes long snoods. Alternatively the basic three-hook mono rig previously shown is ideal, with the snood lengths increased. Flounders sometimes eat all three of the baits on a three-hook rig,

so making up the rig so that hooks are well spaced apart helps to prevent this.

Flounders are renowned for responding to the movement of the bait, and will in fact chase a baited spoon in many areas of the coast. The method works particularly well where crabs may remove a static fished ragworm bait quickly. Silver, gold and white-coloured metal and plastic spoons all have their followers, and this method of fishing should not be discounted as an alternative.

Movement can also be added to baits by using a plain bomb lead and allowing it to roll around in tide and surf. This method is preferred by many match anglers who fish regularly for flounders.

The plaice

Because of the commercial pressure on the plaice it is not as common nowadays as it once was, although some areas of the coast, notably the Solent, experience an annual spring migration of plaice following spawning which brings large plaice within range of the shore angler. Plaice have a preference for calm clear water and are rarely encountered from the shore when the sea is coloured up. They also rarely feed at night.

Clearly identified by those big orange or red spots, the plaice is an angling favourite both for taste and the fact that it is the biggest of the shore-caught flatfish. Most shore specimens weigh around the 1lb (0.45kg) mark, with the biggest reaching 5 to 6lb (2.3 to 2.7kg).

Top baits are lugworm, king ragworm and white ragworm, with peeler crab taking plaice in spring from many venues. Bright yellow or red beads placed on the hook snood definitely increase catches and the plaice, like most of the other flatfish, seem inquisitive when it comes to bright colours and movement. Bright dayglow sequins are particularly effective for plaice, flounders and dabs and these have the added advantage that they do not restrict casting distance like beads do. Simply thread the sequins up the hook snoods and bend them in opposite directions to each other; in my experience the red, pink, orange and silver work the best.

The dab

The smallest and most obliging of the flatfish, the dab, is fairly common from sandy shores where it will feed come bright sunshine or darkness. Sometimes confused with the plaice, the dab is a sandy colour and occasionally has small orange flecks on its back; a distinguishing feature is the curved lateral line behind the gills. A dab of 1lb (0.45kg) is considered a specimen; most of those encountered by anglers range from 8in (20cm) to 10in (25cm). The species has a definite liking for lugworm, with stale lugworm often having the edge over fresh. A three-hook paternoster is the favoured rig, whilst my favourite method of catching dabs is tipping lugworm with a small piece of white ragworm.

Dab fishing is a fun way of fishing for the pot, whilst many a big cod has been caught by the angler fishing with a tiny bait for dabs.

The sole

The sole most likely to be encountered by the shore angler is the sole-shaped Dover sole. The lemon sole is in fact not a sole at all, and more accurately should be called a lemon dab; it also has a small mouth and is rarely caught. Noted for being a nocturnal feeder, the sole feeds avidly during darkness and the first light of dawn. It is also active on some venues when the tide changes direction. Again it is not a big fish, with a 2lb (0.9kg) sole being a superb specimen, but it is rare enough to be prized when it forms a part of the catch, however small.

Sole seem to feed on some beaches and not others, even if these are in close proximity; the sole beaches are therefore usually well known. The best method to fish is to use two rods, one fished at short range and one at long range. Sole have a particularly small mouth, and the hook sizes preferred are size 2 and below, with lugworm and small king ragworm the top baits. Plastic whisker booms such as the Drennan or Avis booms allow light lines to be used and are ideal for sole fishing.

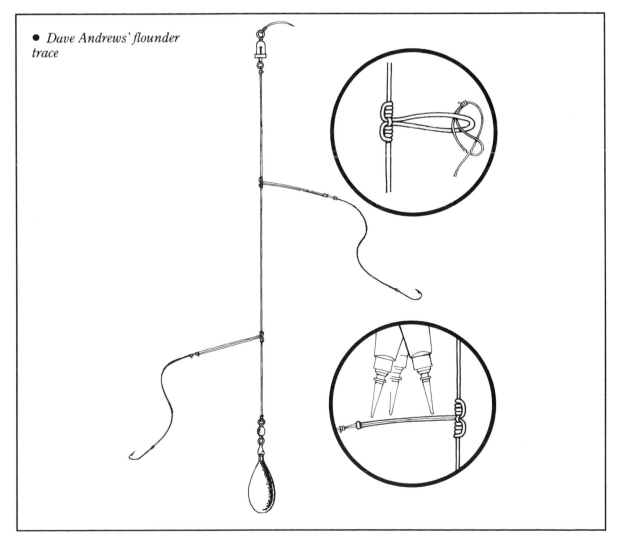

● *Dave Andrews' flounder trace*

7 Pier fishing for cod, whiting, pouting, pollack, mullet and mackerel

• *Fishing in deep water from the comfort of the pier*

The piers

A PIER ATTRACTS ANGLERS LIKE A MAGNET, and the chance to get out to sea and over the fish without the need for a boat always proves popular, especially amongst beginners. The biggest advantage a pier offers is that there is no need for long casting, with deep water within any angler's range, whether it is with an overhead thump or simply by dropping tackle alongside the wall. The pier offers comfort as well as safety, whilst the camaraderie that results from so many anglers fishing in close proximity is a great attraction in itself.

There is always a temptation to head for the very end of the pier. Logic has it that the further out from the shore you travel, the better chance you have of catching fish, and to an extent this is true. There are exceptions to the rule, however, and it may be better to avoid the end of the pier if you are a beginner as this is most likely to be crowded, and where the tide is probably at its strongest.

Piers offer the angler different fish environments and various species of fish all within easy reach; they are therefore a great place to learn different angling skills and techniques, and the ideal place for a junior angler to enjoy his apprenticeship. There are two main types of pier, the piled pier and the walled pier. Tackle and tactics for each are different, and both are a mixture of those used for beach and promenade fishing, so here it seemed better to discuss the ways to fish the venue, rather than fishing methods for each particular species.

Fishing from a piled or stilted pier

The fun piers of the 19th century are dotted around the coast, and although many have fallen into disrepair and been reclaimed by the sea, a few survive, notably in the most popular holiday resorts such as Blackpool and Hastings. These piers are the classic picture-postcard venues with deckchairs, candyfloss and Punch and Judy, and are often frequented by the holiday angler out for a day's fishing whilst the rest of the family is catered for. During the evenings and winter months they prove a popular venue for more serious angling, and most have a club which organises events and competitions.

The construction of these piers is such that a framework of wood and metal is supported on piles driven into the sea-bed. They are usually low to the sea, so the fishing is relatively easy. The powerful lateral tide experienced on walled piers is absent, as the tide meets little resistance from the piles or stanchions. Casting is usually unnecessary, and many species of fish can be found around the pier piles: bass, pollack, mackerel, garfish and mullet swim behind the piles out of the tide, and the maze of underwater and fallen framework found under some of the oldest Victorian piers is also home to conger eels. Other species swim close to the pier, though what these are depends upon the nature of the sea-bed – most piled piers are built on clean sand and therefore have a reputation for producing flatfish.

The tackle needed to fish most piled piers does not need to be heavy, and to a certain extent even coarse-fishing gear will cope; this can be used to fish between the pier piles, whilst more conventional shore-fishing gear is required for casting out from the pier.

Bottom fishing from a piled pier

The main problem that anglers encounter when bottom fishing from piled piers is related to the

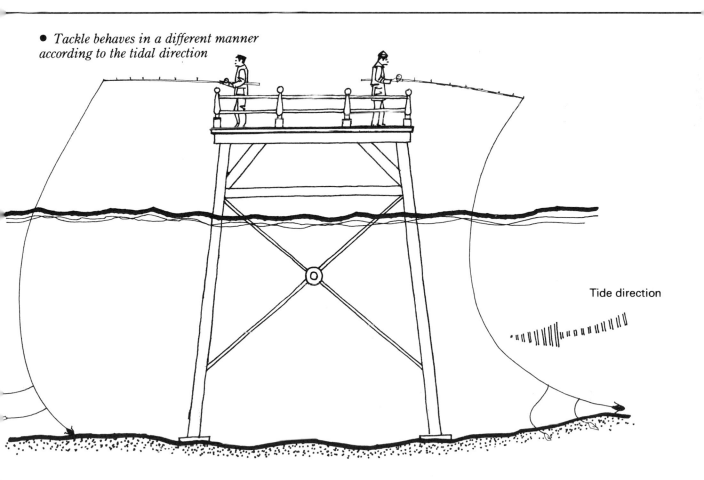

● *Tackle behaves in a different manner according to the tidal direction*

Tide direction

tide, because bait and tackle are presented differently, depending on which side of the pier you cast. Many anglers do not realise that the reason one side of the pier fishes best at high water and the other side at low water is because of the behaviour of the tackle in the tide, and not because the fish favour one side or another. If you fish into the oncoming tide, your baits and line are forced into a bow onto the sea-bed. If you fish with the tide, your baits and line are forced into a bow towards the surface and away from the sea-bed. Most of the bottom species of fish do feed on the bottom or within 6in (15cm) of it, and they will not take a bait 2ft (0.6m) off the sea-bed. The whiting is one of the few exceptions, and will occasionally take a bait which is higher off the bottom. To ensure that baits are hard on the sea-bed the angler can employ a different rig for fishing from each side of the pier; a flowing trace is favoured for fishing downtide, and the standard monofilament paternoster for fishing uptide. Alternatively, when fishing with the tide, if you allow the line to bow downtide the baits will eventually end up being close to the sea-bed. A compromise rig often preferred by experienced pier anglers is the one-up and one-down paternoster; this mixes both flowing trace and mono-paternoster, therefore covering either option.

Fishing between the piles

Perhaps the greatest sport to be had from the piled pier is by fishing amongst the piles and stanchions. The most efficient method is to fish a static line in midwater or just under the surface. Float fishing can be employed from some piers, but the tide makes this impractical from most, as the float can easily become snagged around the stanchions and so on under the pier. More control is achieved simply by dangling the rig alongside or behind a pile. According to the weight of the lead used, the angler will either fish straight down the side of a pile or – with a light lead – the tackle will be pushed under the pier with the tide.

Small wriggly white ragworm, harbour ragworm, fish strip and bread are the favoured baits, and the species most likely to be encountered include pollack, bass, mullet, mackerel, scad and garfish. Small ragworms are best for pollack and these should be fished in bunches, hooked through the head so that they wriggle. Fish strip is ideal for mackerel or garfish, and if using a three-hook rig, bait the top hook with a long narrow sliver of mackerel or garfish cut from the belly of the bait fish. Mullet will take steamed bread flake, whilst small

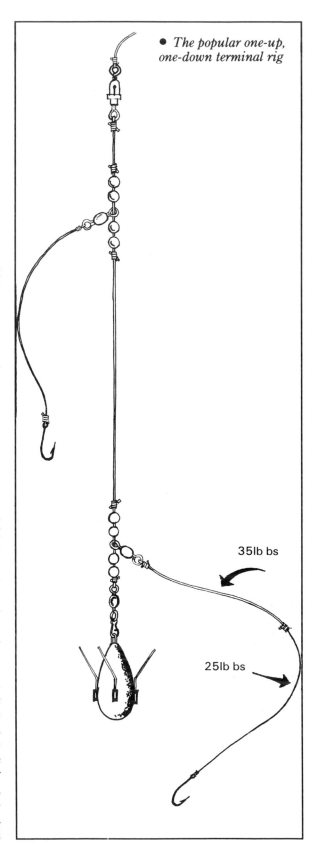

- *The popular one-up, one-down terminal rig*

35lb bs

25lb bs

● *A 6lb (2.7kg) mullet for Ian Dixon from Dover breakwater*

white ragworm and fish-based bread pastes work in some areas. Again, the hooks nearest the surface are those most likely to tempt a mullet, and so they should be baited accordingly. Food scraps are less likely to work from piled piers for mullet – scraps are more commonly found inside many harbours and estuaries, and it is here they will be more effective with the species. To catch mullet may require a more refined approach in some coastal areas; I have included them as they often do turn up when fishing this technique.

The terminal rig should be made up as long as is possible to handle with the rod used, as this allows a greater variety of depths to be fished, from the surface down. Booms or a straightforward monofilament paternoster are the preferred terminal rigs. Booms help to keep hook snoods apart and tangle-free from the body of the terminal rig when fishing in slack water. Some anglers who specialise in catching pollack and mullet use custom-made rods long enough to hang the rig away from, or angled under pier piles; these are held by a special rodrest fixed to the pier railings. Hook snoods can be as light as 6lb (2.7kg) breaking strain, to a maxi-

mum of 15lb (6.8kg) breaking strain, and these allow the bait to be presented naturally. Size 4 or 6 hooks are ideal, with the strongest patterns preferred as the odd bass may occasionally come along (Kamasan B-980).

Bites can be ferocious, especially those of pollack on a short line, pulling the rod over. In many instances fish have to be bullied out from behind the piles and it pays not to let them have too much line, so beware of fishing with the reel drag setting slackened. This is the type of fishing you should do in attendance of your rod, as bites can be sudden and end with tackle snagged and fish lost if you are not there. Moving the baits occasionally can prove deadly, the slight movement of the bait enticing the pollack to take. Finding and remembering the feeding depth is also important, and this can be done either by counting the reel handle turns up from the bottom, or marking the reel spool or line with tape or an elastic band. This method is very effective at night, with pollack coming to the surface. A Starlite chemical light-stick makes it easier to judge accurately the depth at which the rig is to be fished.

A net bag full of bread, fish waste, even cat food, and suspended by a rope under the surface can serve to attract mullet, pollack and the other

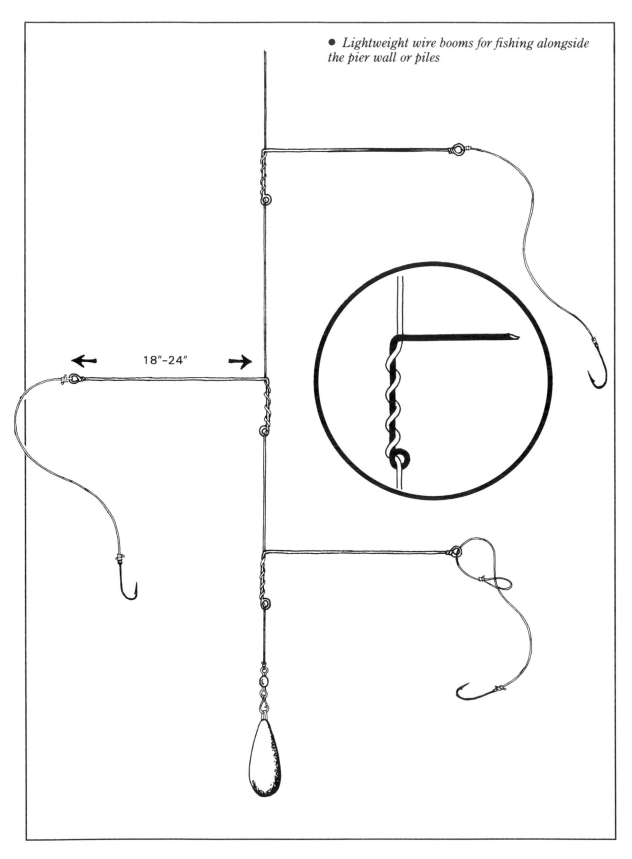

● *Lightweight wire booms for fishing alongside the pier wall or piles*

18"–24"

species, whilst loose feed will work in some tideless harbours. Ensure that the mesh of a bait net does not allow too much of the groundbait to escape – just a scent is needed. Also, watch for the tide rubbing the net against barnacles and suchlike, which will hole the net. An ideal groundbait sack is a standard onion bag, using two – one placed inside the other – where strong tide is encountered and there is greater risk of damage.

A landing net is essential for pier fishing, either the drop variety or a hand net if there are steps available. When using a net for landing mullet it is advisable to land them away from the groundbait source or fishing area. Alternatively use two rubby-dubby sacks placed some way apart. That way after each fish you can change positions.

It is possible to use techniques from both of the previous methods of fishing, thus giving the angler a chance of catching the bottom and midwater swimming species at the same time. This entails fishing a baited rig cast out onto the sea-bed, and then sliding a float rig down the line. Clip the rig onto the main line using an American snap-lead link, or the wire of a Breakaway lead lift which is even better. This method is an ideal way of catching mackerel and garfish which swim close to the surface, but care should be taken when using a sliding float rig that it does not interfere with other anglers, as in strong wind the technique can cause tangles as the float drifts over other lines. The same techniques can also be employed, less the float, to spread baited hooks over a wider area of the sea-bed, thus fishing out from the pier as well as alongside the piles during the same cast.

Fishing from walled piers

Walled piers, breakwaters or harbour arms are usually built as coastal protection or to provide a safe haven for boats and watercraft. They are therefore more permanent than piled piers, as well as being better maintained. Most are basic as far as amenities are concerned and consist of a long high wall with a lighthouse situated at the end. Customs, docks and commercial fishing restrict some areas on piers, notably the pier head where anglers' lines may prove a hazard to boats, or the inside wall where boats may dock. These walled piers are less

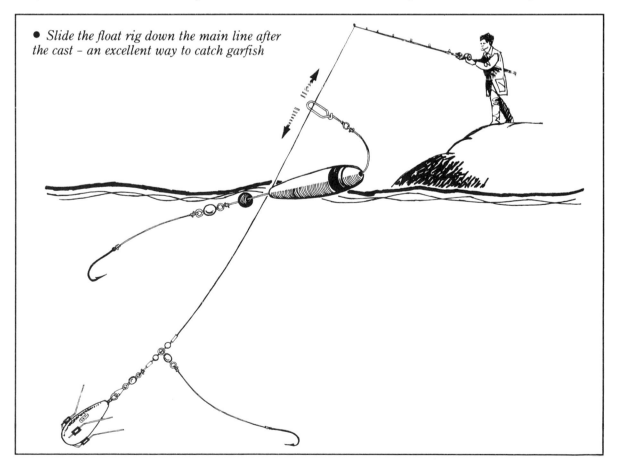

● *Slide the float rig down the main line after the cast – an excellent way to catch garfish*

likely to attract promenaders than the amusement piers and generally anglers have such places to themselves, often free of charge. In many cases angling clubs have obtained a lease from Harbour Authorities and you can fish the pier for a small fee.

Bottom fishing from walled piers

Many of the ideas and techniques for fishing alongside the piles of piled piers for pollack, mullet and scad can be applied to fishing close to the wall on walled piers. However, walled piers differ greatly when it comes to bottom fishing, because when the tide meets the solid wall it is funnelled along its length, and this creates a strong lateral movement which is difficult to combat, especially during the high water and spring tides. The first necessity is to hold the bait and rig in position, and this can be done with a fixed-wire grip lead. The snap-out Breakaway lead used on the beach does not give enough grip to combat the strongest tide, although placing an elastic band around the wires does improve their performance. Purpose-made fixed-

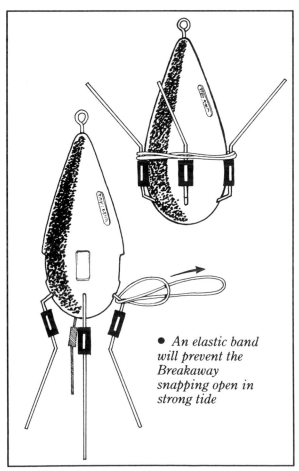

● *An elastic band will prevent the Breakaway snapping open in strong tide*

wire grip leads are the most efficient means to beat strong tide, and the type of lead with the wires coming out of the nose is the best of all. By winding a short length of copper wire (1.0mm twin and earth domestic electrical cable) around the wires, the business end of the grip lead is several inches away from the weight of the lead and this, along with short stiff wires (18-gauge stainless steel) aids grip in the strongest tides. Most standard patterns of fixed grip lead can be equally improved by bending the wires so that they grip below the lead. This alters the centre of gravity of the lead and aids grip, on the same principle as adding a chain to a boat anchor to force it to dig into the sea-bed.

A smaller line diameter also serves to reduce tidal pressure on the line and therefore the lead. When fishing from piers over a clear sea-bed, lines of 15lb (6.8kg/0.35mm dia) will allow the lead to hold bottom far more efficiently than heavy, large diameter lines.

Overcoming strong lateral tides also requires a degree of co-operation between anglers. Should one angler cast uptide in an effort to overcome the tide, he will cast over other anglers' lines which are bowed downtide. This can cause tangles and arguments which need not happen if anglers uncross lines as they cross, rather than waiting until the tide drags tackle downtide or anglers tangle each other's lines when they reel in.

The basic technique for beating strong tide is to cast slightly uptide and then let the lead sink and a bow of line develop. So often the angler stops the flow of line as the lead hits the water, which results in the lead dropping to the sea-bed downtide and much closer to the pier wall. You must take care to cast further than your uptide neighbour so that your lead will move outside his; failing that, you must take your rod over and back under his. At the same time, keep an eye on where your downtide neighbour casts; if he casts, short, then take your rod under and back over his and then back to its position. Anglers grouped together can also improve their chances by all reeling in at the same time. The make-up of the terminal rigs for fishing for cod, whiting, pout and flatfish from a walled pier in strong tide is basically the same as that previously described for beach and promenade fishing. Again, the decision rests with the angler as to whether to fish one large bait or two or three small ones.

There are variations on the monofilament paternoster, with a general opinion that fishing for bigger fish or from a high pier wall requires longer hook snoods to allow big fish such as cod to get the

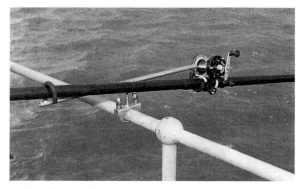

● *A pollack rodrest*

bait into their mouths. Use short snoods and the fish get a mouthful of trace line. That is the theory, although I don't totally subscribe to it myself. Long snoods do give the fish time to take the bait into their mouths before a bite registers on the rod tip, and this can sometimes be an advantage in that the angler does not strike prematurely. On the other hand, short snoods are favoured when fishing with sand eel for such species as dogfish, as they betray the slightest bite. Long snoods are ideal for fishing with a single hook, paternoster style, or with a short flowing trace, but it is important when fishing multi-hook rigs to keep snoods to a suitable length

to prevent them tangling with each other. Remember, what a rig looks like on dry land is not as important as how it behaves underwater.

Strong tide will force the rig and baited hooks close to the sea-bed if it is cast out a reasonable distance from a pier wall. If you are fishing at short range in deep water, high up on a pier wall, it is important to ensure that your baits are on the bottom. Increasing the length of the hook snoods when fishing hooks up the line, paternoster style, helps the situation, with the longest snood placed at the top of the terminal rig.

The ideal terminal rig for pier fishing is one including a short boom close to the lead; additional snoods can be placed paternoster style above the boom if required. The boom ensures that the lower bait is fished hard on the sea-bed, and is ideal when fishing at very short range. Both cod and whiting will sometimes only accept a bait nailed close to the sea-bed, and the combination of one boom and one snood above is a most effective terminal rig for fishing in very strong tide, especially when there are dramatic changes in tidal strength. The length of the boom snood need be no longer than 3ft (0.9m), with a swivel placed at the end of the boom to protect the line from breaking when small fish spin up. The boom also serves to keep the line clear of the

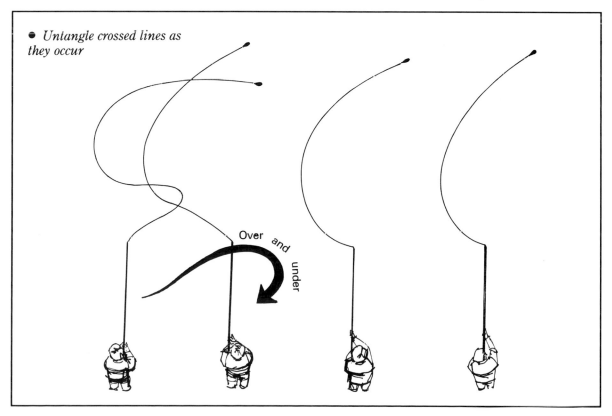

● *Untangle crossed lines as they occur*

Over and under

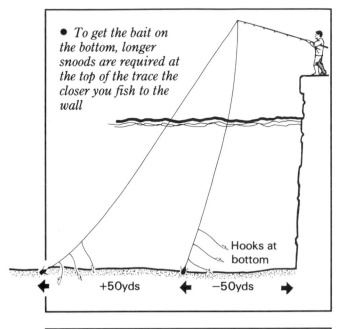

● *To get the bait on the bottom, longer snoods are required at the top of the trace the closer you fish to the wall*

Hooks at bottom

← +50yds ← −50yds →

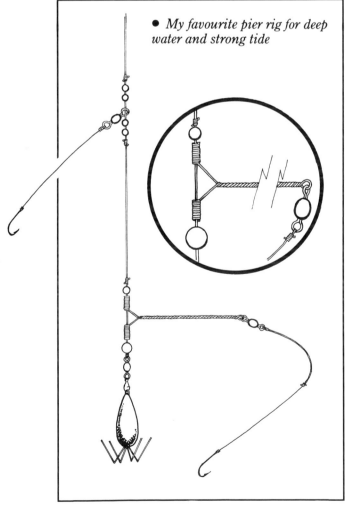

● *My favourite pier rig for deep water and strong tide*

fixed grip lead. When using long-wired leads you can prevent the line being damaged by the grip wires by increasing the strength of the snood line for the first 8in (20cm) from the boom with the aid of a blood knot.

Fishing in strong tide has an added bonus: because of the tidal pressure on the fish to maintain their position, they need to attack the baits on the move. They therefore dart in, grab the bait and invariably hook themselves, and there are none of the frustrations of missed bites that can be experienced in tideless conditions. Bites are often registered by the fish pulling the lead out of the sea-bed – and of course the fish is then already hooked.

Because of the lateral tides produced by most walled piers, when the fish swimming up the tide meet the pier, they are then forced around it. This produces hotspots where fish are congregated by the tide; these can either be in the form of an eddy close to the end of the pier, or at the start of the pier where the tide first meets the wall. A build-up of sand or shingle in these regions, or excess rocks from the building of the pier, can force the fish to pass in a set place or at a set distance, making ideal ambush points. Casting distance, direction and being able to hold bottom are therefore much more crucial to success when fishing from a walled pier.

Strong tide poses a danger to tackle because it can pull an unsupervised rod over or along pier walls and railings. A luggage strap is ideal for securing rods to railings, whilst from a wall the rod should be placed low, with no more than a third sticking out over the wall. A short piece of plastic hosepipe, split and placed over the rod blank, or half a rubber ball complete with rodrest V cut into it, protects varnish and rod rings from damage.

Gaffs and nets

An essential item of tackle for fishing from a pier is the landing net. Gaffs may be considered barbaric but in some sea-angling situations they remain unbeatable, especially for landing large conger eels, sting rays and other unsociable species. They can be used from some piers where access via steps is available but remember, on rocks or pier steps, when the tide retreats it leaves a treacherous trail of slippery weed and this poses a lethal trap for rubber-booted or excited anglers.

Most piers have a resident net owned by the local club and placed, for example, in such as the pier cabin. Failing that, you either take your own or rely on another angler to have one – bearing in mind

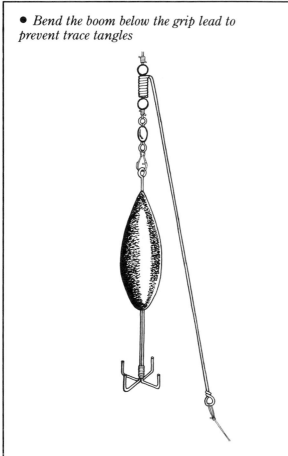

● *Bend the boom below the grip lead to prevent trace tangles*

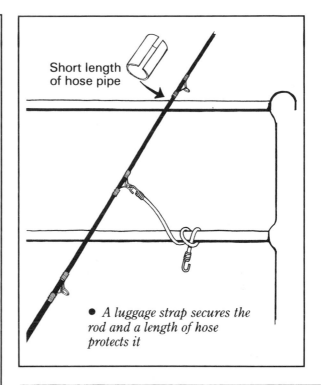

Short length of hose pipe

● *A luggage strap secures the rod and a length of hose protects it*

that serious big fish anglers would have their own net.

There are a few simple rules to follow when netting big fish. Firstly, calm down – many large fish are lost because the would-be captor and netsman are in shock, panic or just plain excited. Unfortunately, only practice makes perfect, though a few lost fish are generally enough to instil experience in a netsman; from many piers, however, it pays to enlist the assistance of the local expert. A good netter will make sure he is positioned so the fish can be drawn into the net; he will also take his time and net the fish first lift. Aborted swipes usually end up with the tackle snagged in the net and the fish lost.

The following points should be looked for when buying or making a net: it should be sufficiently heavy to combat strong tide – a brick or a bunch of leads can be used to add weight to a net. Square nets are also less likely to roll along the pier wall in strong tide. Ensure that the mesh is not too large or too shallow, as this may allow the fish to escape. Make sure that the net has sufficient rope for the

● *Safely in the net. Note the square sides, which prevent the net from rolling along the pier wall in strong tide*

venue, and lay the rope out before starting to fish instead of leaving it until a big fish is hooked to find the rope in a tangle. A few strategically placed knots in the rope help when lifting heavy fish; and finally, a rope sprayed white close to the net makes it easier to see in the dark.

I am a great fan of the drop gaff. This a treble-headed gaff placed at the end of a rope, and these were popular some years back. Their biggest advantage is that the angler can land a fish himself from a pier wall, promenade or rocks with a drop gaff; a net is to heavy and cumbersome to allow this. Barbed drop gaffs are also far more effective for large conger eels which can climb out of a net.

● *Untangle the landing net rope before you need it*

Fishing for mackerel from piers

Mackerel are occasionally taken on bait whilst fishing for other species from the pier, but they are more deliberately fished for with feathers and lures. The technique is generally frowned upon by serious anglers, with mackerel considered as a legitimate angling target only when they are needed for bait. However, thousands of anglers fish for mackerel from piers during the summer months when they are an easy target for the holiday angler or novice.

Feathering is the most effective technique to catch mackerel which, when shoaled up and feeding on the small whitebait and brit, work themselves into a frenzy, grabbing anything that moves. Feathered lures work well, but even bare silver

hooks or silver paper wrapped around a hook will take fish in this situation – huge bags can be caught by the novice with ease, simply by dragging six bright lures through their midst, sink and draw. The greed promoted in us by such easy fishing means that anglers catch many more fish than they can carry home, and on occasions dead fish are dumped back in the sea. Hence the unfortunate reputation that feathering has gained amongst the majority of anglers. This is a pity because the mackerel is one of the speediest fighters in the sea, and on light spinning gear he has few rivals. A single lure on a light spinning outfit fished from the pier at dusk is a fun way to catch mackerel for bait or for the pot.

There are a few points worth noting about feathering for mackerel: first, a warning about the commercial mackerel feathers on sale. Most are tied with inferior knots and in line which is too light. A snapped-off lead poses much danger on a pier crowded with mackerel anglers, and my advice is to buy ready-tied feathers with care. Failing that, you can make up your own or retie the commercial sets using stronger line.

● *The late Vic Naylor (the mullet man) fishes Ramsgate harbour*

Some of the dayglow designs are very effective, but they do tend to fall to pieces after catching a few fish. I prefer to tie my own feathers and use trout lures for the job. These smaller and more deliberate designs will catch pollack, whiting, bass, lance, coalfish, pout, scad and mackerel, and they bring a new dimension to feathering. The most effective flies include Jack Frost, Appetiser, Missionary, Zonkers, Whisky, Dog Nobblers and Cat's Whisker. These lures can be purchased in hook sizes ranging from 6 to 12, and although they are a little on the small size for mackerel, they are ideal for several other species. Alternatively if you know a fly tier, get him to tie the lures on bigger hooks such as 1s or 2s. The lures can be made up on rigs of three or four with 4in (10cm) snoods. There is no real need for sets of six, as a rig full of mackerel is difficult to pull up the pier wall.

Fish the lures 'sink-and-draw' – lift the rod and then reel in as you lower it down again. The speed of the retrieve and the depth to which the lures are allowed to sink, gives the angler the means to search the different levels of the water for fish. Another method which works on occasions is to creep the lures slowly along the sea-bed. A heavy lead improves the standard sink-and-draw feathering technique, as it increases the speed of the lures as they sink. Thus fish are attracted to the lures both as they are lifted and as they sink.

If you are filling the freezer with bait or simply catching mackerel to eat, a coolbox and a couple of ice packs keep the fish fresh. Gutted as they are landed and transferred to the coolbox, they will arrive home fresh, and will also keep in much better condition if being used for bait in the future.

● *The sink-and-draw retrieve used when feathering for mackerel*

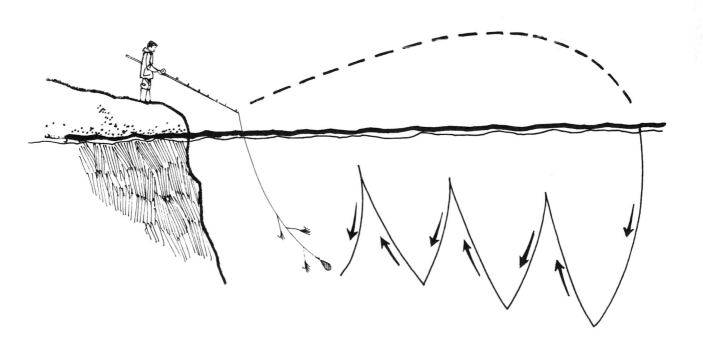

8 Float fishing and spinning

BY FAR THE MOST EFFECTIVE way to catch fish around the coasts of Britain and Ireland is to fish a bait directly on the sea-bed. Occasionally, however, when conditions and species allow, spinning or float fishing may bring better results. Both allow the angler to fish with light tackle and permit a lot more mobility than when he is bottom fishing, with all the tackle that that requires. Like all the techniques already mentioned, float fishing and spinning are alternative methods; they have their days, even though they are totally ruled out for much of the time by the hostile nature of the weather and sea conditions. Both techniques may be more fun than bottom fishing, but they are so often impractical in terms of results – if you can spend hours spinning in the hope of catching a single bass in a month, then good luck! For the majority of anglers it must appear common sense to bottom fish when conditions dictate, and then to float fish and spin when conditions allow. That way your chances of catching fish are increased, and whilst fishing is not totally about catching fish all the time, fishing without much success just for the sake of the method is surely foolish.

Float fishing

Float fishing has various advantages for the sea angler, the most basic being that it allows him to fish a bait at a fixed depth between the surface and the sea-bed. A float allows movement to be imparted to the bait via the surge of the waves, and float fishing allows the bait to be drifted slowly and deliberately with the tide. Perhaps its biggest attraction is in watching the float itself as it bobs and then suddenly disappears under the waves as a fish takes the bait.

Because of the great depth of the sea it is not possible to use a fixed float very often. The exceptions are when fishing for garfish or for mullet inside harbours and estuaries, within 6ft (1.8m) of the surface at short range. When there is a need to fish deeper or to cast the float, then the sliding float rig is required. The float is cocked when the stop-knot hits the top of the tube inside the float. The knot can be tied using Power Gum, in the same manner as the stop-knots used for terminal tackle. By altering the position of the knot on the main line, the depth the hook is fished can be adjusted.

Floats come in a variety of designs, and the sausage-shaped sliding float with a tube running through its length is the one most often preferred. Don't worry about large floats scaring the fish – they don't know what a float is; in fact I have had pollack trying to eat mine, whilst garfish often play leapfrog over them. Bigger floats are easier to see and cast, and also act like a brake when a fish takes the bait, thus helping it to hook itself. Most of the dayglow colours are fairly visible even at 100 yards (91m) and black is excellent in bright sunshine. Also, when there is a need to cast long distance, I have adopted the use of a loaded sliding float: by placing the lead required to cock the float inside the float, it then tows the trace and hook-length behind it and is less likely to tangle. Using the standard bulk shot or bullet-lead system results in the trace tangling when forceful casting is employed.

Sliding floats can be used to catch pier and rock pollack, and are also most useful for fishing for wrasse over rough ground. The float allows the bait to be fished just above any snags, and if a fairly large float is used, both the pollack and wrasse – once hooked – are prevented from returning quickly to the safety of the rock or kelp. English anglers fishing in Clare in Ireland developed the method: they used cistern ballcocks as large floats to catch big pollack from the thick kelp fronds of Blackhead at Lisdoonvarna.

Float fishing for garfish is possibly one of the most enjoyable ways to float fish from the shore. Garfish swim very close to the surface and the bait needs to be fished no deeper than 6ft (1.8m), with

3ft (0.9m) often deep enough. The float rig can be constructed like a one-up, one-down bottom terminal rig. This aids casting distance with more than one hook and prevents hooks tangling. Best baits are fish strip, with garfish belly strip a deadly bait for other garfish. Garfish often signal their presence by leaping out of the water, and will do this when hooked as well as running the float under. What a shame these acrobatic little fish do not grow bigger. Mackerel can also be caught using the same float set-up, whilst in strong tide the rig can be made up as a terminal rig and then slid down a bottom-fishing line.

Spinning

Spinning is the ideal method for those who like to fish with light tackle and wander over rock and

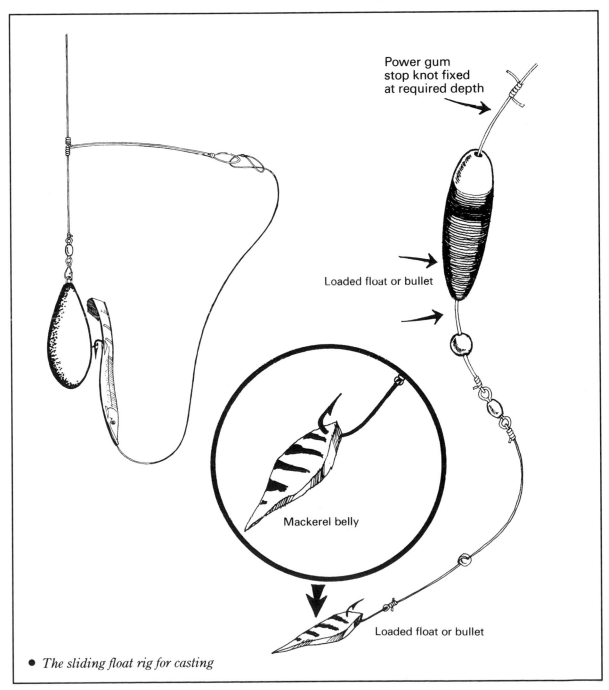

Power gum
stop knot fixed
at required depth

Loaded float or bullet

Mackerel belly

Loaded float or bullet

● *The sliding float rig for casting*

sand. Around each corner is a fresh swim to cast into, and the method allows small fish a sporting chance when hooked on a relatively light rod and line, as compared with the average beach outfit.

There are various British species that will take a lure or spinner, and these include the bass, pollack, mackerel, coalfish, scad, garfish and on occasions cod and mullet. However, this is generally only around the south and west of the UK and Ireland, and then mostly in gin-clear water. Spinning from the shore on the south-east and east coasts is much less effective for 90 per cent of the time.

Spinning requires a rod capable of casting up to 3oz (85g). There is a host of models designed for freshwater spinning and these are ideal; alternatively a carp or heavy feeder rod is suitable. The fixed spool is the reel which is most often preferred, and this is the one occasion when this model of reel outshines the multiplier at sea. They are compact and easy to cast from an awkward stance, whilst their drag control is always more accurate and easier to get to than the multiplier's. This is somewhat of an irony, since most of the small multiplier reels used by sea anglers for beach casting were originally designed for spinning. Fixed spool reels most suitable for sea spinning are those rated for 8lb (3.6kg) to 12lb (5.4kg) line loads, somewhere between a large freshwater reel and a small sea reel. Look for long-coned spools which aid casting distance; some of the latest carp-fishing models from Daiwa and Shimano are superb.

Lures come in a variety of forms ranging from a solid metal pirk, spinner or spoon to leaded plug, feathered lure or a rubber eel. If the lure or whatever is sufficiently heavy, it can be cast without adding lead; whilst the lightest lures or eels will require the addition of lead to the trace in order to achieve any distance. Pollack will not shy away from a lure close to a lead but bass are much more fussy, so if a lead is to be added to the trace it should be as far away from the lure as possible. One alternative is to place a small barrel lead inside the lure. It may be difficult to obtain some of the smallest leads since the ban on the sale of lead weights for coarse fishing, but the substitutes are now nearly as good as lead.

Amongst the most deadly of the lures for bass and pollack is the Redgill, with the 6in (15cm) sandeel look-alike the most effective for shore fishing, particularly because it can be cast more efficiently than the bigger eels. There are several other rubber eels based on the original Redgill pattern, and all have proved equally good. These are available in many colours with the brightest blue,

orange and green colours favoured for pollack and the naturals for bass; nor should black be underestimated. The main advantage of Redgills, apart from their enticing wiggly tail, is that the range of colour changes can often induce shy or wary pollack to take, as they have a very short memory.

Spinning for pollack from rocky areas amongst the kelp fronds is exciting stuff. The secret is to trickle the eel slowly over and among the kelp. Takes are tremendous, and a big pollack (4lb/1.8kg plus) takes some stopping on his initial run. A spinning rod may not be powerful enough in many cases where big pollack are encountered, and a light beach blank may bring better results. Alternatives to Redgills for this technique include live and frozen sandeels, and big ragworms spun very slowly through and above the kelp. When spinning with Redgills, a long trace will put the eel well back from the lead, and another trick is to knock a panel pin into the lead and then hang the Redgill on it – this aids casting. It also prevents the Redgill from snagging in the rocks during the cast, which could result in a lead or hook in the ear!

Spinning for bass is best done without the addition of lead on the trace above the lure. For this reason some anglers prefer plugs, and the range of surface, diving and popping plugs is tremendous. In particular there are plugs for pike and American black bass, although some of the most outrageous of these are to catch anglers and not fish; but some are effective enough to make them a worthwhile lure to use. The basic problem with plugging or spinning, especially for bass, is that the casting distance is limited by the tackle which has to be used. A maximum of 80 to 100yd (36 to 71m) is obtainable, and far less in strong wind. Long casts not only allow the angler to cover a great deal of ground, more importantly they also increase the attractiveness of the lures to bass and pollack. Both species, like trout, will follow a lure for some way before attacking it and short casts will eventually frighten the fish. Ideal places to spin are, for example, rocky headlands and outcrops, where the angler has a vantage point to reach the fish and effectively spin over maximum distance.

The other species which will take a lure, with the exception of mackerel, are most often caught by accident when spinning for bass or pollack. Codling sometimes accept feathers or a spinner, whilst scad, coalfish, herrings, shad and others are not really fished for but are occasionally caught. Thin-lipped mullet, on the other hand, will take a small, baited Mepps spinner in some estuary and coastal areas at some times of the year.

9 Bait

BAIT IS THE ANGLER'S MAJOR LINK with the fish, yet it is surprising how many anglers totally disregard its importance. Angling efforts enjoy success when a number of small but essential factors coincide, and this includes fishing in the right place at the right time plus a degree of luck. The attractiveness of the bait is an important contributing factor, and it is here that the angler can most effectively influence his results. Different baits bring different reactions from fish: some are ignored, some are seized on sight, and fish can be attracted to the hook by a bait's scent or movement or simply because of its attractiveness as a fish food.

For the shore angler it is most noticeable that as fish numbers and size have fallen, the fish have

● *Mixed baits: peeler crab, lugworm and mackerel*

become more fussy about what they eat. That large chunk of frozen mackerel which has been in and out of the freezer for countless trips loses its appeal to fish that do not have to compete so heavily for food. When fished from a boat, a lesser bait may well be seized as fish fight for it, but from many shore marks it will be ignored, simply because there are fewer fish and therefore less competition for food. During a recent trip to Iceland I fished from a pier where dabs carpeted the bottom. Every cast resulted in three dabs, and baits used were rotten squid and herring; even some obscure experimental ones – would you believe banana skin! – were taking fish non-stop. The truth was that there were so many fish it was a case of their eating the food regardless, and tasting what it was afterwards.

In a few places around the British coast the shore fishing is still like that, although for the most part it is now a case of tempting the fish with a variety of the most attractive offerings rather than just bait. Cocktail baits such as small wriggly ragworm, juicy lugworms or the very scented peeler crab have taken over from plain fish baits or frozen squid, especially in many of the hard-fished areas. This is not to say these baits won't catch fish, but if you want to enjoy success you will need to concentrate on providing the fish with more attractive foods.

The change in the reaction of fish along the shore-line to different baits is linked to the drop in the number of bigger fish. The food intake of a specimen fish is large so he cannot be too discriminating about what he eats. A small fish, on the other hand, can, and who can blame him for picking a strawberry instead of a potato? This may be a humanistic interpretation, but in times of plenty fish are just as fussy as we are about what they eat.

The variety of baits available commercially is limited, with most dealers selling the baits which are easy to obtain and to store, or those which are the most profitable. In the past this has meant that dealers have concentrated on lugworm, king ragworm, frozen fish and squid, and because there were few alternatives these became the popular sea-angling baits. Ask an angler what he considers the best sea-bait and he will invariably say lugworm – but the fact is that if the majority of anglers use lugworm then it will be certain to feature in the majority of catches. However, it is not the most effective sea-bait by a long way, with peeler crab or sandeel close to being the most versatile of the shore baits.

Some anglers, notably those who fish in competitions, have realised the potential of other baits when the fishing is hard. White ragworm or snake whites, mud or harbour ragworm, string ragworm, rockworm, clams, razorfish, queen cockles and of course peeler crab, are just some of the baits which on their day have proved more effective than the lugworm and rotten herring alternatives stocked by the tackle shop. Imagine what an angler with a variety of these baits can do in competition with other anglers. It is the strawberry amongst the potatoes again, and just about the most exciting angling experience when *you* are the one using the strawberry as bait!

The angler's problem is in obtaining the strawberries, and in fact there is little alternative but to go out and dig or collect your own bait if you want the most attractive or effective varieties – although in recent years the shortage of fish in

some areas, and the demand for a supply of better quality bait, has led to improvements. Some dealers do offer good bait, although for most this is simply a means to get you into their shop to buy other things. However, peeler crab, for instance, is now regularly stocked by many tackle shops, coming daily from the south-west of the country by train. Some dealers also sell white ragworm or harbour ragworm, though in the case of the former these are only available during the longest spring low tides.

Anglers collect and store their baits in a fridge. This means that bait collected during the spring tides can be stockpiled, and will be available for use during the neap tides.

Going out and collecting your own bait has several advantages, quite apart from providing a variety of the best baits available. The exercise helps to keep you fit, whilst there is an overall feeling of satisfaction when you are fishing, a feeling that you have worked for any result you may obtain. Perhaps the biggest advantage is that the angler who digs his own bait is less likely to waste it by throwing it away after each trip. Careful storage means there is always bait at hand, and this is especially useful when you decide at short notice to go to the beach, the opportunist trip which so often brings results.

● *The fridge salad tray is ideal for storing peeler crabs – if you're allowed to!*

Forks and spades etc

The basic digging equipment when collecting bait includes boots, a fork, bucket and tide table, though as you become more experienced the equipment may become more refined. Waders, for instance, allow you to kneel in the sand or wade to a sandbar. A flat-tined potato fork is the most successful tool for digging common lugworm, whilst a small lug spade or worm pump may be required for the deeper black lugworm. For ragworm, a thin-tined fork is required if you are digging amongst stones, shingle or mussel beds. As for buckets, a selection of sizes – the buckets that fit inside each other – allows the digger to segregate different types of worm and so on.

For the bait-digging élitist, a special bait fridge is the ultimate way to provide a continuous and unlimited supply. Fridge freezers too tatty to be seen in the kitchen can be picked up cheaply and kept in the garage where they provide a home for the digger's collection. Cat-litter trays provide a stacking method to store worms of all types; the salad compartment is ideal for peeler crabs; whilst the freezer compartment can be used to freeze crabs and fish – it is advisable to store these in small numbers so that only enough for each trip need be thawed out.

Cocktail baits

Mounting several baits together on a hook is an effective way of enhancing the attractiveness of an offering. There are no hard and fast rules about which baits go with what, and anything is worth trying – combining scent, movement, colour and texture offers a diversity of bait choices. Use the scent of one bait to attract fish to another, and never be afraid to experiment. A favourite combination of mine is peeler crab and mackerel strip; I once used this from an Irish strand to take 100lb (45kg) of bass, ray and dogfish in a night!

Frozen baits

Frozen baits have an effective role to play in shore angling – the likes of squid, sandeels and peeler crab can be frozen and used with some success, and frozen peeler crabs and sandeels are even superior to fresh on occasions. However, tackle shop frozen baits such as mackerel, lugworm and peeler crabs are often of very poor quality and of little use as bait; they are only a stopgap, simply a means to be able to fish. Bait is so important to results that it is

● *The author digs some fresh lugworm*

essential to use the best possible at all times if the priority is to catch fish; though if you wish just to sunbathe, or to fish simply to pass the time of day, then by all means use poor quality frozen baits.

Alternatively you can freeze down your own bait; the rules are simple enough. Treat bait as you would your own food, and only use frozen bait that is still within its freezer life. Peeler crabs, for instance, freeze down very well and come out of the freezer slightly softer than fresh crabs. They break up in water more quickly, and are especially effective as bait for coalfish and codling because their scent disperses so rapidly. The secret is to freeze them when they are just about to peel, and to freeze them live or having died only in preparation; tackle shops invariably freeze crabs that have died, and these come out of the fridge as a black mess.

My method of freezing crab is as follows: first, completely remove all the crab's shell and carapace, including the lungs and internal shell where possible. Wash the crab thoroughly under the tap, to aid removal of obstinate shell particles, then wrap it in tinfoil and place inside the freezer on a steel tray. Sandeels can be frozen singly also by placing them on a pre-frozen steel tray. Transport them to the beach in a food flask, and those that remain unused can then be returned, still frozen, to the freezer.

Some of the commercial freezer bait firms offer good quality bait with Ammo frozen sandeels having an excellent reputation. Other baits, including black lugworm and shellfish, come out of the

freezer in better condition if prior to freezing they are first sealed by blanching. This is done by pouring boiling water over them and then wrapping them in foil, plastic film or plain newspaper, and freezing. Remember to freeze bait down in small amounts to avoid having to thaw out huge amounts. Once thawed, bait should not be refrozen.

The lugworm

Lugworms are one of the most commonly used sea-fishing baits, not only because they are widely available but also because they are a convenient shape and size. What bait fits a hook better than a lugworm? It is almost as if it were tailor-made for sea fishing. Lugworms also keep for up to a week, with little effort other than to wrap them in newspaper – small wonder that bait dealers find them the most convenient bait to stock in bulk.

There are two basic types of lugworm, although biologists continue to tell us that the lugworms found around the coast are all the same. Anglers, however, know that there is the very tough black lugworm, sometimes called yellowtail, gullys or by other localised names; and the more common soft or blow lugworm. The two types are very different, though both have their place in the angler's bait armoury.

● *Common lugworm and a lone razor fish*

• *Codling on frozen peeler crab and calamari squid (see page 86)*

Black lugworm leaves a yellow iodine stain on the fingers after use and is preferred by anglers after cod; two or three of these large lugworms comprise just about one of the juiciest worm baits the angler can choose to use. They are dug from their burrow, which goes straight down in the sand, with the aid of a small spade; a cut-down border spade will suffice. In some areas they can be dug trench fashion with a flat-tined potato fork, but in most cases they need to be dug or pumped singly. Black lugworms have the habit of gutting themselves when they are removed from their burrow – without this confined space to squeeze down, the pressure the worm exerts tends to burst its skin. However, they can be kept from doing this by handling them gently and storing them in sea water. Gutted black lugworms wrapped singly in newspaper make excellent bait for small flatfish such as dabs; use them when they are a week old, and especially when they are 'sticky'.

Black lugworm are found at low tide extremes and are best sought during the spring low tides. Their presence is shown by a single cast which varies in shape in different areas, but in most cases is a neat circular swirl of sand rather than the uneven heap cast by the blow lug. Dark muddy casts usually signify that the worm is deep, whilst sandy-coloured casts show the worm to be shallow.

Common or blow lugworm exist anywhere around the coast where there is sand or mud. They live in an often shallow U-shaped burrow marked by a cast and blow hole, and can be dug with a fork with relative ease; dig between the cast and hole in the centre of the U. Soft lugworm come in a variety of sizes and colours ranging from black to red, and as their name suggests they are much softer than the black lugworm. This softness gives them a certain quality as bait and they are ideal for small fish, especially flatfish.

Blow lugworm are inevitably full of sand or mud when freshly dug, and this gives worms from various venues different scents or flavour. Not that I have tasted them, but I have found that some worms do not work as effectively as others as bait, even when fresh, and can only put this down to the flavour of their mud or sand content. By leaving worms in sea water for a short period after digging they will clean any sand or mud from their bodies. Also, worms which are tanked for a long period can lose their flavour, and are not always as good for bait as when they are fresh. Blow lugworm will keep for a week stored in dry newspaper in a fridge.

To make it easier to dig lugworm from waterlogged areas of sand, the water can be drained by digging a U-shaped moat, the open end seawards. Allow several minutes for it to drain, whilst also ensuring that water cannot enter the moat. As the sand dries, the worms tend to come to the surface and digging them is easier; and, as with all types of worm and shellfish, the trick is to keep the hole small and neat. Take many small fork- or spadefuls of sand rather than a few large ones.

For worms which are deep, dig two lines one spit deep and then dig another spit deep over the first line. Keep the sand and water from filling the hole as you go. By digging late in the low tide period, you will find that the sand has drained and the worms are nearer the surface. So many diggers wear themselves out because they rush to the sand as the tide retreats and dig when the worms are still deep. As the tide retreats to its furthest, the worms come nearer the surface, but by this time the digger is exhausted. This is especially relevant when digging black lugworm, which tend to be deeper when the tide first recedes. They rise in their burrows as the bottom of the tide is reached and it begins to return, and again, this is the best time to dig.

Lugworm can be dug straight into a bucket, and sea water helps them to purge the mud and sand from their bodies. During the warmer months, warm water will cause the soft lug to 'blow', hence their name. A freezer pack of the type used with coolboxes added to the bucket's water will keep the worms cool. Another good idea is to place the worms inside a bucket which in turn is placed

● *Place a freezer pack in the water to keep worms cool. The hole in the lid keeps the rain out*

inside a bigger bucket containing water. Any breeze will quickly cool the water and keep the worms fresh. A lid on the bucket with a hole cut in it keeps out the rain.

Worm pumps

Worm pumps have been around for many years and are used in Australia and America to suck worms, shellfish and crustacea from the sand for bait. They

● *Digging a moat to drain off excess water*

have limited use in the UK, although have proved effective for black lugworm. The pump is placed over the worm's burrow and then operated – some effort is required to suck up worm and sand, with several short pumps proving more effective than one long one. Pumps are not the easy way to a bucketful of lugworm as the manufacturers would have us believe. The bait pump requires almost as much effort and skill to operate successfully as a lug spade. The performance of the commercial pumps available can be improved by soaking the pump washers in corn oil, which greatly improves suction.

Freezing lugworm

Because they are 80 per cent water content, none except the black lugworms freeze down very well. Black lugworm can be frozen wrapped singly in newspaper and will catch dabs and small fish, although they are considered no more than a stop-gap bait.

The ragworms

King ragworm

There are several varieties of ragworm used for bait by sea anglers; the most common is the largest, the king ragworm. Fully grown, this worm can reach 3ft (0.9m) long, although at this size its use as bait is limited to the larger species of fish. However, segments of the large worms can prove effective from some deep-water venues, and they do possess a strong scent which is particularly effective when pieces of the large worms are used in cocktail fashion with other baits.

Large king ragworm can be trench dug, but in most cases need to be dug singly. Their presence is revealed by a small spurt of water coming from the mud when someone's foot falls close to their burrow. Large king ragworm have a fearsome set of pincers which can give a sharp nip if you let them. Most often shore anglers prefer the smaller king ragworm, with worms up to 6in (15cm) long suitable for all manner of species. These small king ragworm are relatively easy to dig and are available from bait dealers in most areas of the coast, especially where they are common. They prefer estuary mud, and are usually dug trench fashion in shingle, shale or mussel banks in shallow, sheltered areas. This can sometimes be a messy business when they are to be dug in thick black mud, and the

worms should be allowed to swim in clean salt water for a short period so they can purge themselves of mud. They can then be stored in popper weed, sand, shredded newspaper or vermiculite loft insulation material. The latter is popular with bait dealers as it dries out the worms and keeps them alive, providing they are stored in a cool place. Ragworm can be successfully tanked and kept alive in a fridge for long periods, and they are the easiest of the marine worms to keep with the least effort. Store them in a cat litter tray with minimum sea water. Don't overcrowd them, and remove any dead or dying worms as soon as possible. Ragworm can be fished singly or in bunches – mounted on the hook by the head, they offer a wriggling mass of tails which species like plaice and flounder cannot resist.

For several years cultivated ragworm have been available to sea anglers through tackle dealers. These worms offer excellent value: being used to artificial conditions, they can be stored in the bait fridge for long periods with relative ease. It is debatable whether they are superior or inferior to ragworm from the wild, but the technique does make ragworm available to anglers in areas where they are not naturally found.

As with all tank-stored ragworm, the water content of the worms tends to make them green and slimy. Placed in dry newspaper twelve hours before they are to be used, they take on that tough, bright-red ragworm characteristic.

White ragworm

A favourite of competition anglers, the white ragworm has a deserved reputation for catching small fish. It is also a very useful bait in hard-fished areas, and in clear water where a white's wriggly tail adds the dimension of movement to a bait's scent. White ragworm are found in various sizes, and this includes the largest pearly-coloured snake whites and the small wriggly cat-worms dug in sand. Tube worms indicate exactly where to dig whites: find tube worms' close to the low tide extremities and you will invariably find white ragworm as well. Whites prove effective for plaice, and in some areas dogfish and codling have a liking for snakes, but in general they are a cocktail or tipping bait used to spice up other baits, or to add the attraction of movement to baits such as lugworm. The addition of a white ragworm to the end of a large lugworm bait aimed at codling can often entice the fish to take the ragworm-baited

- *Snake white ragworm (white magic)*

- *A giant king ragworm, ideal bait for bass*

end of the bait, which the angler ensures is the end of the bait containing the hook.

Whites can also be kept in the fridge, in the manner already discussed for king ragworm. The addition of a ½in (12mm) layer of coral sand, available from most aquarists' shops, enables them to survive for months, and this method is also ideal should the worms need to be transported by car over a long distance. Before baiting with white ragworm, squeeze out the worm's tongue. This makes threading the hook through the worm easier, and allows eyed hooks to be used rather than the whipped variety.

Harbour ragworm

Harbour ragworm, sometimes called muddies or maddies, are the smallest and least significant of the ragworms and tend to be used for bait to catch the smaller species of fish. They are ideal for estuary flounders, pier pollack or mullet, whilst for the angler fishing in flat, calm, clear conditions they offer the addition of movement to a bait.

They can be dug with a fork in harbours and river estuaries, and are most often found in thick black mud – the sort it is easy to get stuck in, so be care-

ful. They can be stored in green weed or dry newspaper, although are difficult to keep alive for more than a couple of days other than by tanking them. Harbour ragworm are a useful addition to any angler's bait bucket, especially for those fishing from piers or where the fishing is hard. Cocktail six muddies to any bait and immediately it will receive attention, maybe from only the tiddlers, but then sometimes even a small bite or fish is enough to keep the angler interested.

Rockworm

The rockworm is a species of ragworm found in chalk rock. It burrows into the chalk and lives in a sand-filled burrow close to the surface. These worms can be collected by breaking up the chalk with a small hand-pick or fork, or simply by turning over rocks, and they can be kept alive in green weed, sand or shredded newspaper.

Rockworm migrate in large numbers, and are a

● (Above) *Collecting edible peelers and softies (see page 86)*

● (Below) *Peeler crab, a deadly parcel of scent and juices (see page 86)*

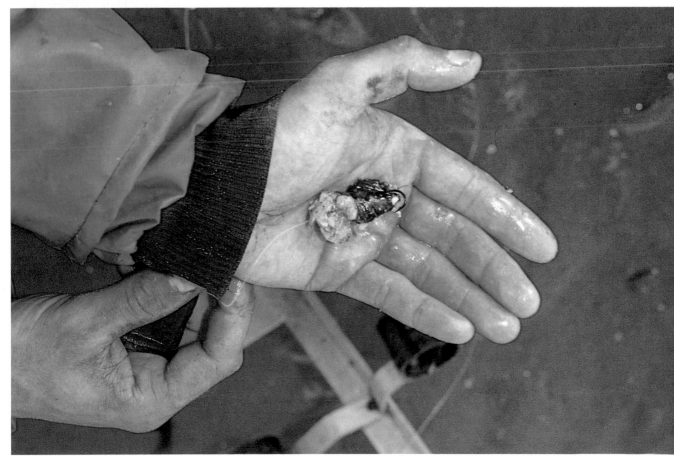

spectacular sight to behold at night when they swim en masse. One of the biggest advantages of using rockworm is that – unlike many of the other ragworms – they are tough. Hook one through the head, cast it out and retrieve it an hour later and it will still be wriggling if it has not been eaten. They are ideal for dangling alongside pier walls for pollack and bass, and are an excellent clear-water bait for wrasse and flatfish. A similar species of ragworm equally as tough as the rockworm is the one found inside hermit crab shells. Another worm found in chalk when digging rockworm is the flat-worm. These can be used as bait but they are deli-cate and break up easily, and are therefore less suitable for casting.

String ragworm

The string ragworm is a rarer species of ragworm of which I know little, except that it makes a superb and tough bait. The name 'string' is my own label for these worms, as they resemble a long thin piece of string when fully extended. Like rockworm they are tough and keep alive well, so are ideal for bait. I search for mine amongst tube worm in the same ground as I find white ragworm, and although strings are few and far between they are highly prized.

Seamouse

The seamouse is a member of the marine worm family. Often found washed up on the beach after storms, it has a very limited quality as bait except when specialised bait is required for large fish, as it will remain on the hook under the attacks of the tiddlers.

Peeler crab

Without question, peeler crab is the most versatile of the sea angling baits and ranks alongside the sandeel as one of the top fish-catchers. Most fish will accept crab because it is commonly found around all the coast. In its normally hard state, the crab is a poor bait for all but wrasse, smoothhounds and a few other species; its tough external shell is hard to crack and contains very little nourishment. This is not to say that most sea fish do not eat small hard crabs, but they do so with the crab alive and running free, in a natural envi-ronment that the angler can rarely imitate. How-ever, regularly during their lifetime crabs have to shed their shell in order to grow, as do all other

crustaceans, and it is at this time that they are most effective as bait.

Shell-shedding is prompted by the need to grow, and is induced by rising water temperatures during spring and summer. In the south-west of England and Ireland where the Gulf Stream raises the water temperature, crabs peel virtually all the year round. Elsewhere they can be found between April and November, depending upon seasonal tempera-ture fluctuation. The crab first grows a new shell underneath the old one. This is soft, but it swells to a larger size and hardens quickly after the old shell is shed. During the time of shedding their old shell, the peeler and soft crabs are particularly vulnera-ble as not only do they lose their armour plate but their mobility as well. They are also a most superior bait at this particular time. As they begin the shedding process, the crabs travel inshore to hide amongst mud, weed, sand or under rocks, inside groynes and so on, as close to the high-tide mark as possible and away from the shoals of fish which arrive to feast on them during the spring mass moults. Totally soft, including internally, the old shell and lungs are discarded completely, and the crab emerges helpless and jelly-like. For support the crab needs water or mud, which is why crabs about to shed their shell are always found in soft mud or rock pools, a point to remember if you are collecting crabs for immediate use.

Collecting peeler crabs

River estuaries and sheltered, shallow, muddy or rocky areas are favourite places for collecting peelers. They do not peel where they are likely to suffer in storms, such as open beaches, and in any numbers whilst inside an estuary they will hide in old rat holes in the mud or in the soft mud against groynes or sea-walls. In some instances they will cling to seaweed six feet up a sea-wall, and when seeking peeler crabs it pays to investigate even the smallest stone or hiding-place. Collect the peelers in a bucket, and watch out for damage to your hands and fingers when crabbing, as small barnacles on rocks and groynes can cause injury without you realising it until later. Garden gloves are ideal for lifting rocks, which should be replaced whence they came. Remember, if you leave rocks all scattered about they will be of no use to the crabs, and so on your next trip you will not collect many peelers.

In some areas of the estuary, anglers place crab traps in the mud. These include drainpipes, ridge tiles and old tyres, and offer the peeler an inviting home within which to stay for the moult. Regular inspection of the traps can yield a regular supply of peelers.

The spring moult is almost totally of cock crabs; as the hens can only mate when they are soft, the cocks rush to peel so as to have the pick of the hens. The cock crab protects the female during the period she sheds her shell and mating takes place just after she sheds. Most anglers are of the opinion, myself included, that the juicier cock crabs are a better bait than the hens. However, during mid-summer hens may be the only peelers available. They tend to be smaller than the cocks, and are particularly preferred by eel anglers for use whole.

Once a crab sheds its shell it is known as a softy or crinkly – within hours the shell hardens, and as this happens the crab rapidly loses its effectiveness as bait, except when used whole for large fish like bass. When the angler collects peeler crabs they will be in many different states of peeling; there will be crabs just showing signs of starting to peel, crabs about to burst out of the shell and crabs that have already shed. The secret of getting the best out of peelers is to manage the crabs you collect by promoting those which show the first signs of peeling, and slowing down those about to shed. This is done with the aid of a fridge. Obviously if crabs are best used when they are just about to shed, using temperature to halt or speed up the peeling process will result in a larger number of crabs in the ideal state. This is when the crab is showing a hairline crack at the back and sides of the top of its carapace. If you press the sides of the crab under the legs there will be a slight give if the crab is ready for use as bait.

Crabs ready for use can be stored close to the freezer compartment at the top of the fridge, whilst crabs showing only the initial signs of shedding can be placed in the salad compartment at the bottom. Crabs just starting to take on the characteristics of a peeler can be promoted by storing them outside the fridge – a large polystyrene box, damp newspaper and seaweed or hessian sack constituting the ideal method by which to move on the peeling process. A regular swim in sea water will also help to promote peeling – though beware of the crabs suffocating when all the oxygen in the water is used. If you leave them for a long period of time use an air pump and stone.

Crabs stored inside the fridge can be placed in shallow trays and covered with wet kitchen tissues – face-flannel material soaked in sea water is ideal. This keeps them from drying out, as the shedding process is not halted totally by the low temperature, but only slowed. The wet flannel stops the crab from going crinkly. Periodically add a small amount of sea water to the tray, though ensure this has been previously stored inside the fridge and is the same temperature as the crabs.

With a fridge, a regular supply of peelers in the ideal state can be maintained. Crabs *can* be kept alive for a month with careful handling – though before that time they will have reached the ideal state for use and will probably have been used!

Baiting with peeler crab

To get the best from peeler crabs, only those about to shed should be used as bait. At this time their internal skeleton is totally soft and their body juices most pungent. Fish can home in on those juices over a great distance, and they are crucial to the effectiveness of peeler crabs. Those anglers who have tried peeler with little success have invariably used crabs that were not ready for use and did not contain the powerful juices and scents of a ready-to-shed crab.

Baiting up is comparatively simple: first select your crab and kill it with a knife. Remove all the

● *A bucket of shellfish collected after a storm produce a flounder*

legs, all the shell and the lungs. You will have little trouble removing the shell of a crab in the perfect state for use. If the shell doesn't virtually fall off on its own, however, then the crab is of little use as bait. Depending on the size of the bait required, either cut the peeler into two halves, or mount on the hook whole. Scissors are ideal for cutting up peeler baits as they can also be used to trim baits into shape on the hook.

The most effective method of putting the crab bait on the hook is to thread the hook through the leg sockets of the crab, in one and out of the other. First take the hook in and out of the shoulder of the crab and then pull the hook through completely, needle fashion. An aid to this method is that the hook size should suit the distance between the leg sockets. For small crab baits used for eels and flounders, a size 1 or 2 short shank hook is ideal; my preference is either the Mustad Limerick 496 or the Kamasan B980. For larger baits, few hooks beat the Cox & Rawle Uptide pattern.

With practice, crab baits can be mounted on the hook perfectly efficiently, with no need to tie the bait on with elastic cotton, except when fishing with large baits or when other crabs are removing the bait quickly. If you do use cotton to secure the crab flesh to the hook, use the finest knit-in elastic.

Shellfish

There is a large variety of shellfish which can be used for bait. The most commonly used, especially in the north-east of England, is the mussel, where it is particularly effective for coalfish and codling. However, its potential is virtually untried in the many other areas of the UK and Ireland. Other shellfish baits include: the slipper limpet, an immigrant which has colonised many southern venues, and, amongst the natural inhabitants – razorfish, butterfish, cockles and clams. All of these have their uses as baits, though with the exception of the mussel, fish usually only feed in earnest on many of the shellfish when these are available in large numbers having been the victims of a storm. Then, the fish can become so preoccupied with feeding on shellfish such as razorfish that they will ignore all other baits. At other times the fish rarely encounter shellfish and this may be why, under normal conditions, shells are not always that good as bait. Perhaps the one exception is that of stale razorfish or rock clams, which on occasions can prove effective for tipping worm baits when fishing for codling and flatfish.

● *The clay/rock habitat of the piddock clam (see page 91)*

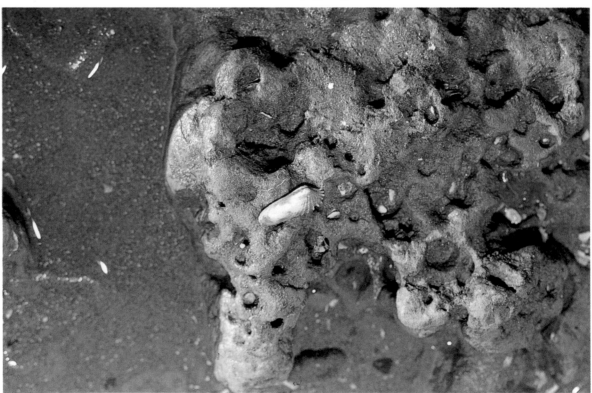

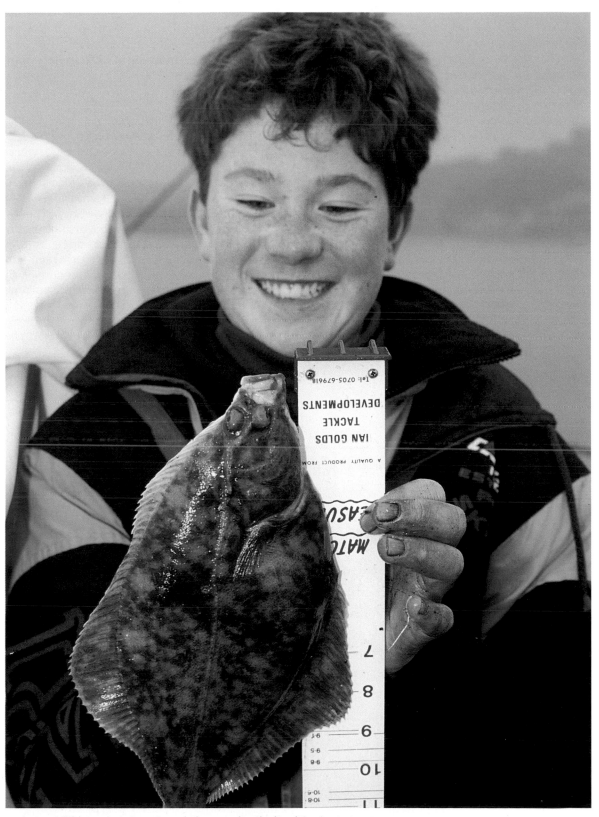

● *A goer! This one makes the minimum size limit with plenty to spare*

Mussels

The common mussel is an excellent bait for most shore fish, easily available and a bait that is easy to keep alive for long periods. When a large mussel is prised open, it will be found to contain an orange-yellow meat, and this can be tied on the hook with knit-in elastic. As a bait it resembles peeler crab, with similar qualities of scent and juices. Mussels can be collected all around the coast from groynes, sea wall and rocks; they are also readily available from the fishmonger or merchant, and this includes the deep-water mussels and the cultivated mussels which are generally larger. The last two types offer an attractive bait especially for rock fishing, and are equally effective fresh or frozen.

Gaining entry to the mussel's shell is best done using a blunt kitchen knife. Insert the knife blade in the mussel's hinge and twist – it looks easy when done by the expert, but takes time to master. The meat of the shellfish is scooped out with the knife and is then ready for baiting or freezing. Mussels can be kept alive and fresh in the fridge for two weeks or more.

Freeze mussels after first removing the meat from the shell, and then only in small amounts, perhaps six shellfish to a bag.

Razorfish

Razorfish are widely available and are usually found at the low tide extremities in sand, where they can be dug with fork or spade. Their shape resembles the old-style cut-throat razor, hence their name. As the tide goes out, razorfish can be found by looking for a small keyhole-shaped hole in the sand, the entrance to their burrow; a spurt of water often gives away their presence as they retreat. Once the sand is dry, they rise in their burrows and can be picked up from the surface by hand. You can also spear them down their burrows with a barbed spear, whilst the most effective

● *Razorfish, whelks, butterfish and lugworm*

method of collecting them and one that does not damage their flesh is to sprinkle salt down the entrance to their burrow. The razor, thinking the sea has returned, rises to the surface where you grab him – pull gently and his fleshy foot will eventually release its grip on the sand.

Small razorfish around 4in (10cm) long are the most suitable for shore fishing bait, and cut into short pill-shaped pieces are excellent for tipping lugworm baits. Large razorfish, especially the yellow-fleshed variety, don't seem to work so well, although bass and cod will accept them on occasions. Razorfish can be kept alive in a fridge for several days in a shallow tray containing ½in (12mm) of sea water. They are also an excellent bait to freeze, but you must blanch them first – that is, scald them with boiling water before freezing them. When they are slightly 'high' they can prove effective for small species of fish.

Butterfish

Butterfish or venus shells are found alongside razorfish, although they live just under the surface of the sand rather than down a burrow. Their presence is revealed by a small hole or lump in wet sand; once the sand is dry they rise to the surface and can be picked up by hand. During storms both razorfish and butterfish can be picked up along the shore-line at the water's edge as the tide starts to come in. The white tongue of the butterfish is an excellent bait for flounders, dabs, pout and codling amongst others, but butterfish also proves most effective, as does razorfish, when the sea is rough and shellfish are being washed out of the sand bars.

Cockles

The common cockle is not a very effective bait, although its larger relative the queen cockle is superb, especially for flatfish and cod. The meaty foot of the queen cockle is bright pink or red and can be used whole for codling or cut into small pieces to tip worm baits for dabs.

Whelks

The common whelk is occasionally used by shore anglers for bait to bulk up a large lugworm-based cod bait for rock fishing. It is extremely tough and will withstand the attacks of shore crabs. It has few other qualities, except that small pieces of whelk can be used to help retain delicate worm baits on the hook.

Limpets

The common shore limpet is shaped like a cone and will catch wrasse and a few other species, though in general it is a poor bait. The slipper limpet, on the other hand, is a most effective bait when storms are smashing the shells on the beach. The oval-shaped shells sit in piggy-back colonies attached to a stone or rock and can by parted by placing a knife blade between the pointed ends of the shells and twisting it. Slipper limpets are particularly common in the Hampshire Solent where they colonised the shore-line around Hayling Island. During storms the slipper limpet is a superb bait for bass and flounders; remove the orange foot with a knife and use it to tip-off lugworm and ragworm baits. The flesh can also be used in bunches, tied on the hook with knit-in elastic cotton.

Keep alive or freeze in the same way as razorfish.

Piddock clams

Chalk clams, rock clams or piddocks are found mainly in the south of England where they live in short burrows in chalk, clay or even petrified forest. They can be dug with a fork or small pick, and are one of the lesser-used sea baits. The chalk or clay rocks may be covered with clam holes, but you can discover which ones have a resident clam by tapping the rock – the clam shoots out a spurt of water as it travels to the base of its burrow.

The tough white meat of the clam is an excellent bait for pout, codling and flatfish, and is especially effective for tipping lugworm baits. Clams will keep for several days wrapped in dry newspaper and stored in the bottom of the fridge. I have not tried them frozen, but would suggest they be treated as other shellfish.

Gaper clams

The large gaper clams which can be dug in estuary mud are not commonly used for bait. I first came across them in Ireland a long time ago where they proved useful to bulk up large baits aimed at bass and conger – though after catching several big flounders using them on a 6/0 it was obvious that flounders like them as well. Clams are one of those baits to use if you are after big fish. Cocktail a clam with other baits, and wait; such a tough and large bait on a big hook will not be bothered too much by tiddlers. When using them as bait, dispense with the tough leathery foot and use the meat of the clam tied on the hook with knit-in elastic.

10 Angling rules and behaviour

A right to fish

VERY FEW RULES GOVERN SEA FISHING, and indeed the Magna Carta gave the public the right to fish from between the high and low water mark which extends around the entire coast of Great Britain. It would take an Act of Parliament to withdraw that right. Exceptions are Ministry of Defence land, including army ranges, and any shoreline privately owned, or where rights were given away, prior to the Magna Carta. Elsewhere you have a right to fish and local byelaws and suchlike introduced by councils are often not legal. Do not confuse this right with the right of access over land *above* the high tide mark, as this is land which is owned by an individual and is not Crown land, so access is only available with the permission of the landowner.

The increase in the use of the sea by other water sports enthusiasts is seen as an encroachment on angling; in the future, however, the word 'compromise' may be one we shall need to get used to.

Minimum legal size limits

The laws that govern sea anglers relate to the size of the fish that they can remove from the sea. These size limits are set by the European Community (EC) and the Ministry of Agriculture, Fisheries and Food (MAFF). The minimum fish sizes are for commercial fishery and many anglers consider it an injustice that they should include sport anglers. The law states that all undersized fish should be returned to the sea immediately after they have been landed.

Several of the angling organisations have their own set of minimum sizes; these are often above the MAFF sizes and are therefore only legally bind-ing in competitions. There are also local fishery limits as well as EC fishery adjustments for different sea areas from time to time. The onus is on the angler to be conversant with minimum size limits; the fine for taking undersized fish is considerable.

The fish should be measured from the tip of the nose to the tip of the tail. Special fish measures are

● (Left) *Fishing for bass amongst the kelp-covered chalk ledges of Thanet*

● (Above) *Deal pier, an ideal venue for beginners and the disabled*

made for competition anglers in plastic with a stop board at one end, and are readily available at tackle dealers for a few pounds.

Room to fish

A basic rule amongst anglers is that you do not encroach on another already fishing, and that you allow him plenty of room. However, nowadays crowded beaches are accepted as normal, with five yards (4.5m) an average distance between anglers. Over rocks, anglers fish much closer as they are

forced to congregate on single access points or rocky outcrops, so a degree of patience is required as tangles are inevitable. Pegged competitions place anglers at fifteen yard (13.5m) intervals, whilst many rovers have a five yard rule. Where distance-casting techniques such as the pendulum cast are being used, it is obviously sensible not to overcrowd individuals, whilst using potentially dangerous casting styles is also not compatible with venues such as crowded piers.

Litter

Litter is an age-old angling problem, and anglers are blamed for all manner of flotsam and jetsam that ends up on the beach. Whatever the arguments, anglers should dispose of their litter, especially that which is not biodegradable. Old line is always a problem, and large coils left on the beach are a danger to wildlife in particular. Burning it is the answer; if you put it in the waste bin it invariably ends up on the tip where it might trap seagulls. Alternatively wrap the unwanted line around your hand and then cut right through the loop; this leaves small harmless lengths which can be taken home or consigned to the bin.

Competition rules

The only other rules to which the angler must concede are those used when anglers fish in competition. The use of three hooks – which is common among all anglers – comes from the competition rules, whilst freelance anglers can use any number of hooks they like. It should be noted though, that specimen fish caught on tackle with more than three hooks will be excluded from many of the weekly or monthly competitions arranged by angling papers, local councils or piers.

Angling insurance

Membership of large organisations such as the National Federation of Sea Anglers includes a third party public liability insurance which gives the angler some protection should he be involved in an accident whilst fishing. Tackle insurances are available for as little as £20 per year and are ideal to protect valuable tackle against breakage, theft or loss.

● *Conservation competition fishing – Peter Green of the Irish Central Fisheries Board weighs a thornback ray before it is returned alive to the sea.*

PART II: BOAT FISHING

Ted Entwistle

Introduction

FOR SOME, THE CHALLENGE of sea angling from the shore is sufficient in itself. For others, the lure of far horizons, of off-shore wrecks and reefs, the likelihood of encountering large, powerful, more numerous and varied fish, coupled with the pleasure of just being afloat is irresistible. I have experienced this urge for thirty years!

Boat angling can take place from many craft, large and small, commercial, private and charter. The

fishing may be at anchor or on the drift, over rock, shingle, mud or a wreck. However, what is important is that the vessel and its equipment should be suitable for the sea area and the conditions likely to be met, and that tackle taken on board is balanced so that species likely to be encountered are fished for by sport-ing and productive means.

My contribution to this book aims to help you get safely afloat, find the fish – and catch 'em!

11 Tackle Basics

THERE IS A WHOLE RANGE OF TACKLE that can be used from a boat, but what the angler should seek is to use balanced tackle – that is, line, reel and rod that match one another in breaking strain, weight and flexibility respectively – and tackle which is appropriate for the type of fishing and species sought.

Rods

To help buyers match equipment, manufacturers market all but the most basic boat rods with an 'IGFA' rating. This stands for International Game Fish Association, and the accepted term came about because the IGFA is the world body responsible for administering line class records. Thus an IGFA 20lb (10kg) class rod is designed for use with line of similar breaking strain. In practice the IGFA prefix is often left off, and rods are referred to as just 20lb (10kg) class. Rod-makers do have differing views, and their products, though rated the same, may be more or less powerful than their rivals'. Remember that the rating is only a guide: the final choice is yours. Rod lengths vary, but most IGFA class weapons will be 6–8ft (1.8–2.4m) long.

The most commonly used and readily available line-class rods are: 12lb (6kg), 20lb (10kg), 30lb (15kg) and 50lb (24kg). The heavier 80lb (37kg) and 130lb (60kg) class are intended for tackling very large fish – bluefin tuna, big marlin and the larger sharks. There is a recent trend towards some rods being multi-rated ie 12–30lb (6–15kg) class or 20–50lb (10–24kg) class. Though this is a compromise (a rod has an optimum test curve which is its true rating) some are progressive enough to allow a wider degree of flexibility than with a precisely designated rod. If you want the minimum tackle for the widest use, then a multi-rated rod may be for you.

Rods also have a particular action, which may be different even though they are of the same line class. Thus they may be called 'fast tip', or 'fast action', where most of the flexibility is near the tip of the rod, and it becomes progressively stiffer towards the butt section. Fast-tip rods give a nice feel when fish are being played, and are ideal for species such as black bream that may require quick, firm striking.

The other common term used is 'soft' or 'through-action'; this sort of rod is more 'forgiving' than the fast tip, giving extra cushioning (in addition to any reel clutch setting) from sudden surges by the quarry. It is particularly sensible to use a soft-action rod when fishing with non-stretch lines such as wire or Dacron.

The old greenheart and split cane rods of the past have long given way to more advanced materials, first to solid fibreglass, then to tubular fibreglass, and more recently to tubular carbon-fibre (sometimes called graphite) mixtures. Other

● *Two 18lb pollack taken by the author on successive drops over a Plymouth wreck. They fell to a long mackerel strip and ragworm bait combination (see page 115)*

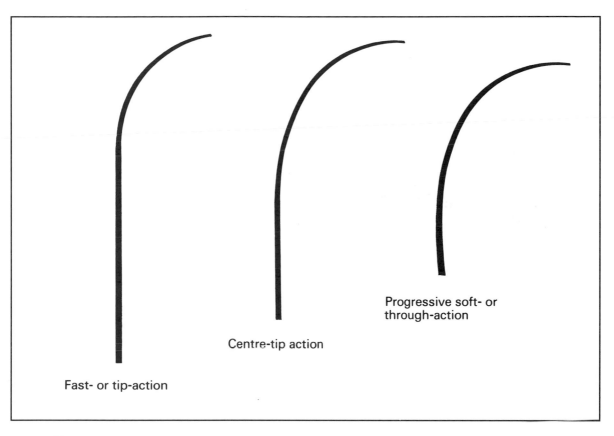

Fast- or tip-action

Centre-tip action

Progressive soft- or through-action

materials such as Kevlar and boron are being incorporated into manufacturing processes as the rod-makers seek to make rods lighter, stronger and better actioned. Nevertheless, the latest and sometimes most expensive materials do not necessarily produce the best products: during the 1990 'Bass' Plymouth International I saw four carbon-fibre rods, from three different makers, shatter during a day's wreck-fishing. These rods – three 50lb (24kg) class and one 30lb (15kg) – should have been virtually unbreakable in the anglers' hands. The manufacturers do now seem to have solved the problems associated with building carbon-fibre rods, but no doubt the next wonder material will throw up its own quirks.

Rod butts

Butts may be made of hardwood, solid fibreglass, hollow glass or glass carbon mix, hollow alloy tube, or solid aluminium. The rod may be married to the butt via a glass-to-glass spigot or joint; a spigotted graphite winch-fitting; a ferruled chromed brass

● *With a haul of double-figure cod like this, Bisley angler Tony Hudson is entitled to look tired*

winch-fitting (less common now on new rods); or in some less expensive rods, the blank may go through the handle. Though conversely in some of the highest quality rods a one-piece, through-the-handle blank is sometimes considered a positive asset: this is when the rod is intended for large game fish, or for heavy trolling where the butt may be subjected to sudden heavy leverage when set in a rod-holder, and where strength is absolutely vital.

Rod rings

The development of rings lined with really hard but smooth materials like silicon carbide, ceramic and high-grade aluminium oxide was a major step forward. As a result, line life and reliability have been greatly improved, as the damage caused by the rings' grooving has been virtually eliminated. The leading manufacturer of rod rings is Fuji, who also make other rod-building equipment such as reel seats, grips and gimbals. Seymo also make excellent rings, though their range is not as extensive. Many rod-makers make their own rings, or have them made up specifically; they normally state the type of lining in their catalogues. Anglers planning to use wire line should at the very least have a roller tip ring, and most serious wire-line anglers have rods ringed with rollers throughout; though it is possible to use intermediate rings of aluminium oxide which is tough enough to withstand grooving by wire. A rod with rollers should be kept lubricated to work correctly. The best rollers are made in the USA by AFTCO; they manufacture a full range, though unfortunately the genuine articles are quite expensive.

Uptide rods

There is a large range of rods now being marketed for this popular method of sea angling. Uptiding, or boatcasting really took hold in the UK during the mid-seventies, and owes a great deal to the enthusiasm of Bradwell (Essex) charter skippers and tackle manufacturers, John Rawle and Bob Cox. Before there were specifically built uptide rods, boatcasting anglers used beachcasters, sometimes cut down; however, these could be awkward in the confines of a boat. Now, rods are designed to allow an angler's end tackle and bait to be cast well away from the boat – yet they are not too unwieldy when playing or boating a fish.

A whole new rod-building market has developed out of the uptiding technique over the last fifteen years, and there is now an extensive range of rods available. Daiwa tackle manufacturers produce a fine selection of constantly upgraded uptide rods able to cope with variously casting weights from 2–10oz (60–300g). They are available at different price levels according to materials and standard of trim, and can satisfy every pocket.

Basic rod buying

When buying a rod, the type and frequency of fishing that you are likely to do should first be considered. Local inshore fishing in East Anglia, for example, may only require an uptider in the 4–8oz (120–240g) range. Daiwa has its excellent range of uptide rods, and another brand, Silstar, has improved its product range enormously in recent years too – the 'Traverse X' and 'X-Citer' uptiders are very good value rods at reasonable prices. Shakespear Tackle's 15lb (7kg) class 'Ugly Stik' is a bit out-dated now, but is still useful; it is also an absolutely superb pollack rod for conventional fishing, in situations where no more than 6–7oz (180–210g) of lead is needed, and is ideal for all sorts of estuary fishing. Shakespeare also has a range of purpose-built uptiders. Other major tackle manufacturers – ABU, DAM, Ryobi and Shimano among them – all market rods specifically aimed at the uptide market.

Alternatively, you might prefer a custom-built uptider. These are available through tackle shops, specialist rod-builders, or sometimes direct from the blank manufacturers. You are likely to pay a premium for a custom-built rod, but it does mean you can have the rod whipped in your own chosen colours, and have rod length, reel seat, handle grips and so on tailored to suit your own requirements. Though if you want a rod built a certain way, you do have to be quite specific about your needs; rod-builders are not psychic.

If you intend venturing further offshore – the North Sea, or mid-Channel wrecking perhaps – a good uptider may double up as a conventional rod for pollack, coalfish and less heavyweight ling; however, for big conger, cod and the lunker ling you will need to step up to at least a 30lb (15kg) class boat-rod, and a newcomer might do better to opt for a 50lb (24kg) class outfit, but not one with a stiff action. In fact if you can find a rod built on a 50lb (24kg) conoflex hollow glass blank, with a roller tip and roller or aluminium oxide intermediate rings,

---

● (Right) *The ladies obviously enjoy their fishing, as this pair of beauties demonstrates*

you will have the perfect tool for deep-water, fast-tide, wire-line fishing, as well as an excellent, heavy wrecking rod.

All the manufacturers mentioned previously have good lines in conventional boat-rods; again, Daiwa tackle seems to have the most extensive, including multi-rated rods and an innovative range I particularly like, called their 'Super Kenzaki' line. The custom option is again available, to get precisely what you want.

Though your uptider can be used for conventional downtiding, over reefs or when boatcasting is unnecessary, you may wish to invest in a 12lb (6kg) and/or 20lb (10kg) class boat-rod, ideal for species such as whiting, black bream, wrasse and plaice. There is a good range of 12lb (6kg) and 20lb (10kg) class rods available from the sources already mentioned. Finally, never rush into too many purchases until you have gained a little experience: what feels right, is a very personal thing. Try to borrow and use as much different tackle as possible before making your purchasing decisions.

Sea tackle is much stronger than its freshwater counterparts. In general it has to be, because of the conditions it must cope with: strength of tide, depth of water, weed, heavy leads and abrasion from other anglers' lines and from the boat's side. Though the tidal respite at high or low water does give a brief period when light tackle could be employed, this is also the time, with the boat turning, when tangles are most likely to occur. However, there is no doubt that in clear water situations, fine tackle does improve the hook-up rate – but you still have to boat 'em!

Reels

Multipliers

British boat anglers favour the multiplier far more than any other type of reel. This is probably because most of our fishing is done at anchor for bottom-dwelling fish, and we have to hold our bait on the bottom with a weight. These reels cope well with hauling lead and fish up from the depths.

The multiplier gets its name from the gearing

system which increases the number of times the spool revolves, compared with the number of times the handle is turned. Ratios vary from one model to another. High ratios allow you to recover line quickly between strokes when pumping a fish. However, this means higher gearing which can make hard work of winding under load, so to counteract this there are reels available that can change ratios at the push of a button.

Reels come in different sizes and line capacities and it is to your advantage to choose your reels so they match the rods on which they are mounted; the rod should be balanced as regards line strength, capacity and reel weight. Multipliers are sometimes referred to by a size scale. This starts at 1/0 which would be suitable for 12lb (6kg) class tackle; 2/0 is for 20lb (10kg) class; 3/0 for 30lb (15kg) class; and 4/0 and 6/0 for 30–50lb (15–24kg) class; bigger capacity 9/0, 12/0, 14/0 and 16/0 sizes are also available for lines up to 130lb (60kg) bs. The 1/0 and 2/0 references are not used very often in reel promotion literature, but the scale is still valid. You occasionally come across half sizes.

A reel may also be categorised by a number relating to the manufacturer's idea of the most suitable breaking strain line, for example a 12, 20 or 30 to match the reel. In fact most can be used quite adequately with line a notch up or down the scale; the numbering is, however, a good guide.

Reels are almost universally fitted with a drag, sometimes referred to as the clutch. On multipliers this may be a star drag, a star-shaped adjuster which is wound clockwise to increase, or anti-clockwise to decrease the setting, with a lever or push button to take the spool out of gear. On the push-button types the spool automatically re-engages on turning the handle. Or it may be a lever drag, where the lever is pushed forward or back to increase or decrease the adjustment; bringing the lever back as far as it will go, takes the spool out of gear.

Popular star-drag reels are made by Daiwa, ABU and Penn. Penn is a long-established reel manufacturer, and its Senator range of star-drag multipliers is very hardwearing. On the whole, however, although star-drag reels are perfectly reliable, lever-drag reels have always been preferred, mainly because you can see precisely where the drag is set by the position of the lever and this allows smooth and more precise adjustment while playing a fish.

For decades lever drags were usually only seen on expensive big game hardware – Penn Internationals, Everols and Finn Nors – and cheaper models made in South Africa by Polikansky. It was

the Japanese firm Shimano who really brought about the revolution, in producing reduced cost, lightweight but strong lever-drag reels – this innovation has put such a reel in almost every sea-angler's tackle box. Shimano's TLD range covers five models, between them capable of dealing with just about any type of boat angling around the British Isles. And if these are not powerful enough for you, their Beastmaster and Triton ranges have models to deal with every conceivable type of fish.

Fixed spool reels

Some anglers maintain that fixed spool reels are a positive asset for uptiding; they believe they get a quicker drop to the bottom with their grapnel leads without the spool resistance of a multiplier, and that the high-speed retrieve of a big 'coffee grinder' takes up slack line and gets them in contact with a fish quicker. On the Continent virtually all boatcasting is done using fixed spools, and they are certainly a little easier to cast with from a heaving deck on a rough day, or in a restricted situation. Personally I still feel you have better control over any fish with a multiplier, especially when you run into a lunker; though in the US large fish are taken regularly on fixed spool reels. However, these are generally pelagic species, taken near the surface, and although this shows that fixed spools can deal with powerful fish, it is a different matter when you have to fish hard on the bottom with a hefty lead.

Line

There are three types of line commonly used by sea anglers: monofilament, braided material, and wire.

Monofilament line

Commonly called mono or nylon, monofilament line is the most widely used line in sea angling. There are in fact many different types of mono line, with many different characteristics of varying desirability: low stretch, limpness, softness, springiness, fluorescent colouring, improved knot strength, and ultra-thin diameter for a given breaking strain. Lines may be of some sort of co-polymer, or nylon alloy, they may even be oval-shaped.

Improved knot strength is obviously desirable; low stretch will improve bite detection and ease of setting the hook, but it reduces the cushioning effect of line stretch. On balance I think low stretch is preferable, as it means there is less build-up of pressure when the line is wound on a spool under tension. Reels with plastic spools can distort quite easily under pressure, and for this reason are of little use to boat anglers when using monofilament.

Whether economy or premium grade, mono is best bought in bulk – the bigger the spool, the lower the cost. Provided you keep the line in a cool dark place where it is not exposed to extremes of heat or sunlight, it should last a number of years without deterioration.

For practical and mechanical reasons monofilament is the only line suitable for use with fixed spool reels. It is also the only line to use for boatcasting or uptiding, for casting shallow water plugs and lures, or for fishing baits such as live sandeels on inshore banks and reefs.

The breaking strain indicated on most of the monofilament on the market is usually the minimum – barring damage – at which the line will part. It is possible, though, to purchase IGFA-rated mono which is guaranteed to break at the stated breaking strain. Note that line of this type must comply with IGFA rules when submitting a line class record claim (IGFA stands for International Game Fish Association).

Braided material lines

These are normally made of Dacron or Terylene, both of which are made from a synthetic polyester fibre, and are resistant to rot, sunlight, mildew, water and salt. They are generally a little more expensive than monofilament lines. Braided lines are usually IGFA-rated – that is, they comply with line class rules and will break at the stated breaking strain. The useful qualities of braided line include excellent bite-detection and easier hook-setting (unlike mono there is very little stretch); thin diameter for a given breaking strain; and it holds a knot well. This makes it an excellent line for fishing deep water where the tide is not too strong. It is also ideal where the aim is to trot the bait as far astern as possible from a boat in shallow water, while still retaining direct bite detection.

Many British charter skippers hate anglers using braided lines on their vessels. This dislike is mainly founded on its apparent tendency to snag the hooks and tangle with the lines and tackle of other anglers. However, this only really seems to happen in situations where a number of anglers are fishing close together, as on a charter vessel, and the irritation is perhaps rather because braided line is a little more difficult to untangle. It is also true that novice anglers are less likely to lose a fish if they use nylon – the inbuilt stretch of monofilament has saved many a newcomer with too stiff a rod or with the reel drag set overtight from his own mistakes. But used correctly and in the right situation, braided lines *can* be an asset, so don't be put off by prejudiced skippers if you intend giving it a try.

Wire line

There are two types of wire used for fishing line: single-strand wire and multistrand. Why use wire? The main reason is in order to fish strong tides and deep water successfully. Wire has no stretch, is thinner than nylon for a given breaking strain, cuts through the water without bellying, and is superb in transmitting bites and the feel of your lead on the sea-bed. For the same reasons it makes an excellent deep water trolling line and is widely used by US anglers for this purpose.

Single-strand wire

The most widely used single-strand wire is made from nickel chrome and commonly called nicro, and makes good quality fishing wire. There are a number of proprietary brands on the market, some with slight variations in the alloys and processes used in the wire's construction. So-called 'soft-drawn' wire is the easiest single-strand to use.

Wire is usually sold in tackle shops in 100m or 200m spools, and is available connected if required. The cheapest way to buy nicro is in bulk one-kilogram (2.2lb) spools from an electrical wholesaler; ask for 24 SWG 80/20 nickel chrome. This will be about 50lb (24kg) bs; it performs well and is very durable.

Some types of single-strand wire are based on piano wire and are springy, not very reliable, and soon fall apart. A fishing wire made from Monel metal, an alloy of nickel, copper, iron and manganese, is the most durable I have come across. It is springier than nicro or multistrand and is therefore not so pleasant to use, but it is virtually rotproof.

Multistrand stainless wire

A good quality multistrand is my own first choice of wire to fish with; it is no more effective at fish catching, but is a little easier to use. All wire is somewhat unforgiving of errors and needs to be kept under tension to prevent kinks forming; braided wire is a little less prone to these problems. It is also marginally thinner than nicro for the same breaking strain. Unfortunately it is the most expensive wire to purchase.

Some anglers dislike multistrand, maintaining it frays easily and that the strands flatten and wear at that portion of line which is most in contact with the top roller (this varies according to the depth most regularly fished). However, by using braided wire of at least 50lb (24kg) bs problems with fraying should be avoided, as the strands are that much tougher in this gauge. Other important points in avoiding problems are ensuring that the roller tip and intermediate rings are, and remain, in good condition; giving the line a good rinse in fresh water after use; and treating it with a corrosion-resistant oil. If you think WD40 or marine corrosion block sprays may be off-putting to fish, try a little pilchard or vegetable oil on your line. Because of the minerals in it, pilchard oil is said to be no help against corrosion. However, I use it and reckon to get two or three seasons out of a spool of wire. It does make your fingers black, smelly and grubby, though!

A little tale to express some of my points: a fishing colleague of mine – not known for taking care of his tackle – complained to me that his multistrand wire had fallen apart the first time he used it, the year after he bought it. When I inspected his rod I found the top roller seized and my friend had also apparently slung his reel loaded with wire, unrinsed, in some dank cupboard. As it was a reel with a metal spool, some electrolysis probably took place, a common reaction between two dissimilar metals in a marine environment (alloy spools are especially at risk). This sort of damage can be minimised by putting a layer of self-amalgamating tape over the backing, beneath the wire and up the sides of the reel; this insulates the wire from the spool as much as is reasonably possible.

With care and attention, both when being used and between trips, a spool of any good quality wire should give at least a couple of seasons' use.

Wire trace material

This differs from braided wire fishing line because it is invariably covered in nylon. It is available with this coating from a variety of manufacturers, in breaking strains ranging from 15lb (7kg) up to at least 200lb (91kg). It is also possible to obtain cable-laid wire without the nylon coating in breaking strains from 90lb (41kg) to 800lb (364kg). As well as the braided variety, single-strand trace wire is available. This is not popular in Britain, but its thinner diameter makes it less conspicuous to shy

biters, and it is widely used in game fishing off the coasts of America and Africa as well as in the Mediterranean. Wire traces are used by some British anglers for conger, ling and rays; I only use wire for spurdog and tope and other bigger sharks, preferring heavy nylon traces for conger and ling.

End tackle

Booms and sliders

These are useful accessories, both in helping to avoid tangles and in presenting your bait, and there is a large and constantly growing selection of them on the market. Some of the booms are fixed, and present your bait either singly or in multiples,

● *Despite tying its tail up so that it did not rest on the ground, this conger was tantalisingly ounces short of 60lb (27kg) for its young Dorset captor*

stood out from the main line, in what is called 'paternoster style'. Others allow the line to run through the centre of the boom's arm, for use as a sliding leger or as a sliding boom.

Some of the more popular fixed or paternoster type booms are Drennan sea booms; French booms, available in stainless steel or plastic; Avis booms; Bristle booms; and KF Tackle's knotless paternoster and spreader rigs. You can also make your own paternosters by tying blood loop snoods in a length of line. They can be improved by sliding a piece of plastic tube over the snood.

Of the sliding type, Cox and Rawle's uptide and downtide booms are popular; Clements' booms are an old favourite; Ashpole's triangular sea boom is well liked, as are zip-sliders; and the innovative KF Tackle has a range which includes the knotless maxi-boom, mini-boom, KF line-slider and the KF tubi-boom, all excellent. These sliding type accessories also serve the function of carrying the weight.

The maxi, Clements, downtide and Ashpole booms lend themselves particularly to downtide fishing, especially when combating the stronger

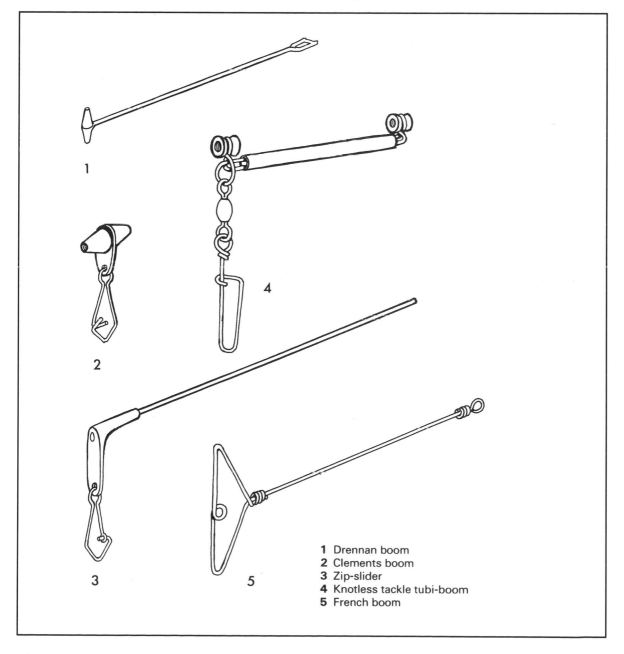

1 Drennan boom
2 Clements boom
3 Zip-slider
4 Knotless tackle tubi-boom
5 French boom

tides where heavier weights are needed. Uptide, tubi-booms, spreader-booms and paternoster-type rigs all lend themselves to uptide and boatcasting tactics. They are also useful for drift fishing and downtiding when the tide is not too strong.

Single long rigid booms, both fixed and slider type, are ideal for fishing offshore wrecks and reefs, when presenting baits or lures intended for pollack and coalfish, when a long trace is favoured. The long booms are vital to minimise the risk of tangles as the baits drop to the bottom in deep water.

The smaller mini-sliders, zip-sliders, uptide booms and tubi-booms, as well as the lightweight paternosters such as the Drennan, are all excellent for inshore fishing after species such as plaice, flounders, dabs and whiting.

Swivels and links

There is a variety of swivels and links on the market, and it is always best to use good quality ones – those that rust or corrode are unacceptable. Swivels help to reduce line twist and even breakage caused by baits and lures twisting in the tide or on the retrieve, or when reeling in some fish. The body shape of pouting, for instance, causes them to spin, and this can snap or ruin traces made even of monofilament or wire up to 50lb (24kg) bs. The conger eel is another fish that can spin like a top as it is drawn towards the boat, and many an angler has lost an eel at the surface through lack of a quality swivel. My main line almost always ends in a link swivel. Traces and paternoster rigs that I might

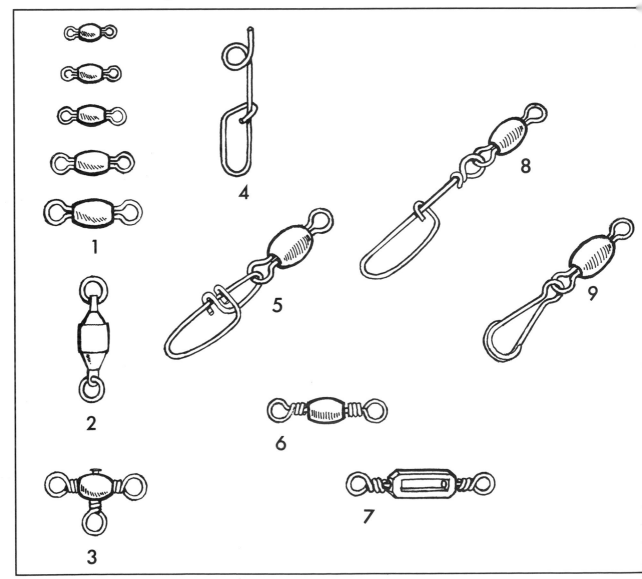

wish to attach have a swivel as well. Berkeley swivels and links are consistently reliable, and are available in predetermined breaking strains that can be matched to the tackle being used. Rigging gear in this way gives good protection against line twist; it also means the angler can change rigs or traces quickly as necessary.

The cheapest swivel is probably the *barrel swivel*. These are usually made of brass or bronzed steel, and although reasonably strong when new, they deteriorate rapidly after use. They can be purchased in a range of sizes suitable for different line strengths, and a three-way version is also available. Most swivels, including these, can be obtained with several different types of link attached: snap, scissor-snap, cross-lock, buckle and corkscrew links;

the link material may be the same as the swivel, or it may be stainless steel.

The *crane swivel* is a more reliable design than the barrel swivel, though basically similar; there are several manufacturers producing swivels of this type. I choose the Berkeley brand, because of their quality, price and availability in different breaking strains. The swivel links I use are the same company's McMahon scissor-snaps. A range of other links is available attached to crane swivels.

Diamond-eye wire swivels are made from stainless steel. They are tougher and more efficient than they appear to be, but not seen as widely in tackle shops as the crane and barrel varieties. They are a durable and reliable swivel.

Box swivels, probably because of their open construction, seem more durable than barrel swivels; they are usually made from brass, but I have come across them constructed from stainless steel when they are unlikely to fail.

Ball-bearing type swivels, such as those made by Sampo, are probably as good as can be obtained. Primarily intended for game fish, they are available in predetermined breaking strains. They are the best, but are much more expensive; nor are they widely on sale in the UK, so you might have to shop around for them.

1 Berkeley McMahon crane swivels
2 Positive poundage link, designed to part at pre-determined breaking strains
3 Crosslock link swivel
4 Coastlock link swivel
5 Berkeley McMahon snap swivels
6 Sampo link swivel
7 Diamond swivel
8 Sampo ball-bearing game swivel
9 Three-way swivel
10 Traditional barrel swivel
11 Box swivel

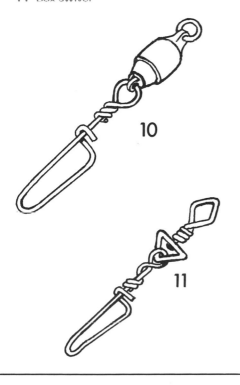

Lures

There is an infinite variety of lures available to the sea angler. New ones are constantly being introduced, and old ones that had gone out of favour or production are being resurrected. Certainly lures can be extremely productive at the right time and place, but it is probably true to say that overall, lure sales catch and are maybe intended to catch more fishermen than fish.

Any discussion on lures inevitably includes the attraction and effectiveness of different colours. Scientists may tell us that fish don't see colours as we do, that at certain depths there is insufficient light for colours to be distinguishable. What is certain is that light penetration and its effects on whatever a fish does perceive, is going to vary tremendously. The time of year, the time of day, cloud cover, the depth of water, the amount of entrained sediment, even the colour of the sea-bed and the quantity of plankton in the surrounding water – all of these are going to affect the way a fish perceives different shades and variations in colour. If they cannot in some way see colour, why have so many fish developed differing camouflage to suit their

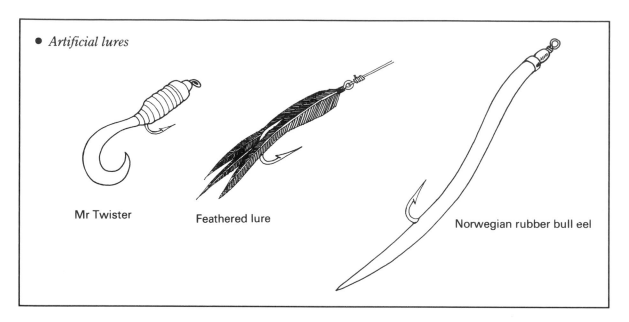

● *Artificial lures*

Mr Twister

Feathered lure

Norwegian rubber bull eel

habitat? Maybe one day we will have some sort of electronic gadget that can tell us the current best fish-catching colours!

Mackerel feathers

A set of mackerel feathers, or variations on them – slivers of insulation tube or strips of Flectotape – is the commonest lure in sea angling and one of the boat angler's prime sources of bait. Though strings may be of a dozen feathers or more and most retail sets contain six, many anglers will only use three feathers. This is primarily because according to the National Federation of Sea Anglers and the rules of most clubs, fish caught whilst angling with more than three hooks would not be recognised.

There is a knack to consistent mackerelling. Most mackerel are taken on the drop, but of course the lures don't want to be travelling too fast, so allow the weighted feathers to drop for a dozen feet or so, then stop the spool with your thumb. Lift the rod tip, and repeat until you find the fish. Work down to the sea-bed, retrieve and start again when fish are scarce. On those days when you find the fish consistently you will soon know how far to drop your lures.

Artificial eels

These are popular fish-takers and there are a number of differing eels available. Early types of eel consisted of a strip of coloured rubber or surgical tube slid over a hook, the tube sliced off with an angled tail below the gape; sometimes the hook shank would be offset and a swivel might be set in the eye. Eels of this type are still available and work well where there are still plenty of fish competing in the food chain.

The Mevagissey eel was an improvement on the earlier version, a two-piece, translucent, coloured body with a separate flexible tail that successfully enticed fish where the competition was less fierce. This inspired the Redgill, an injection-moulded artificial eel and the first of the modern generation in use today; amongst these the Delta and Eddystone eels are leading rivals. All rely for results on subtle differences in tail action. They are also quite detailed in their finish; as well as single-coloured models, there are eels whose subtle colour changes and translucence may increase the fish-catching qualities. Other offerings have also been produced in the shape of various fish, though rubber or plastic eels remain the big seller in British waters. They are available in a range of sizes and colours.

Artificial squid and muppets

These are extremely popular lures or fish-attractors and widely used in all areas of boat angling. Their bright, often fluorescent and sometimes luminous colours can be mounted above a baited hook and fished static, allowing the tentacles to wave in the tide. They can be fished sink-and-draw with bait. They can be jigged, at anchor or on the drift, with or without bait, their wafting, changing shape and vibrations all stimulating fish to snatch at the plastic.

Muppets are available in many colours – shock-

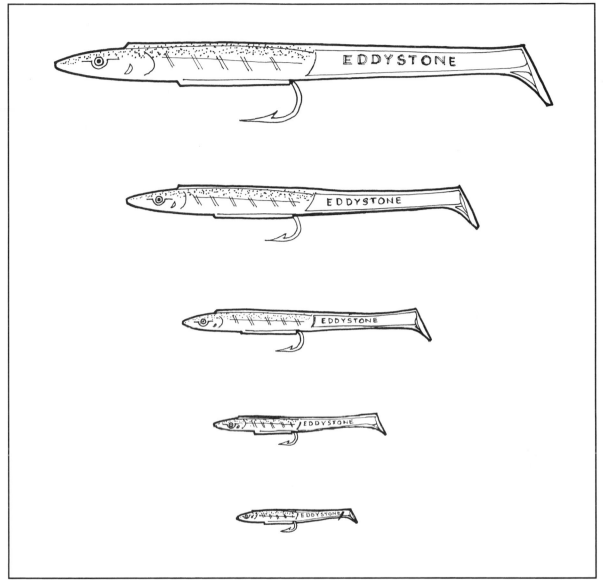

● *Artificial eels like the Eddystone variety shown here are available in various sizes*

ing pink, black, and luminous yellow/green are probably the most popular sellers. Carry a selection when using this effective lure.

Mr Twisters

Another artificial lure resembling a small grub with a curly flexible tail that twists when worked in the tide or on the retrieve. Available in basic black and white and a range of vivid or translucent hues, these can be used effectively against cod and pollack, particularly when drifting inshore ledges and kelp beds around the country.

Pirks

Some huge catches of fish have been made using a pirk, which is basically a fish-attracting weight with a hook attached. As with most lures, pirks are more effective in clear water. They can weigh over 2lb (1kg) and may be fished in combination with one or more muppets or artificial eels. Fishing a hefty pirk all day takes stamina, but is productive in the right circumstances; there is also a lot more skill to consistently successful pirking than many anglers realise. On some occasions this may be in the speed of retrieve. I recall fishing with Steve Barrett on the *Boa Pescador*, out of Plymouth; Steve was using a 50lb (24kg) class rod, a Penn Senator 114HL reel (a

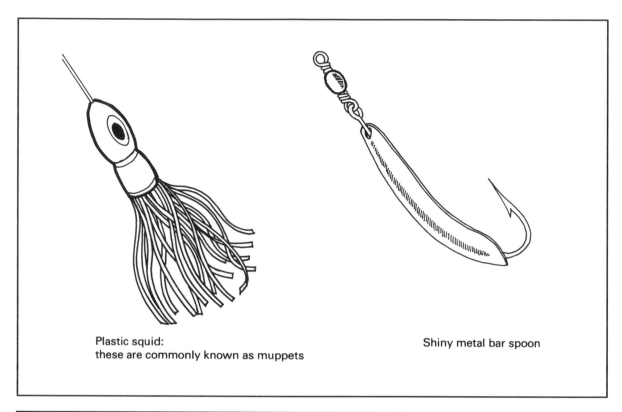

Plastic squid:
these are commonly known as muppets

Shiny metal bar spoon

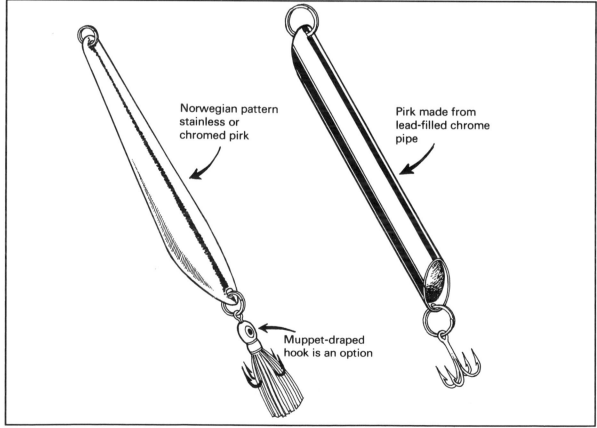

Norwegian pattern
stainless or
chromed pirk

Pirk made from
lead-filled chrome
pipe

Muppet-draped
hook is an option

• *A pair of big blonde ray. Note how the spots go right to the wingtips*

Spoons

Another favourite fish attractor; there are several types, including *bar spoons* which are primarily a casting or trolling lure. They are sometimes used in strong tides when downtide bottom fishing as an attractor on the trace above a baited hook. They are made from a flattish elongated piece of metal, usually chromed brass or stainless steel; hopefully this is shaped in such a way as to give it an action enticing to any fish that spies it being retrieved to a rod or trolled behind a boat. The Toby lure is a particularly effective bar spoon, obtainable in a number of sizes.

Wobbler spoons are often the plaice fisherman's choice. The favourite used to be ABU Tackle's rauto spoon which went out of production some years ago, but a number of similar models have taken its place. Best of these is probably Delta's sonic spoon; similar in shape and action to the rauto, it also has slots in its body to give its action added effect, and the water supposedly creates some fish-attracting sound as it passes through the slots.

Spoons that spin are usually shaped just like the business end of a conventional spoon, and revolve around a central rod or wire. There are several makes on the market, usually made from chromed brass or steel, also from white or coloured plastic. They have long been a favourite of flounder anglers and large spoons are sometimes used by cod fishermen as an attractor; these are fished on the trace, 1 to 3ft (0.3 to 0.9m) above the hook.

6/0 size, high-geared multiplier) together with an enormous pirk. This he proceeded to drop to the sea-bed surrounding the wreck we were fishing over, and once it touched bottom, his fingers would fly as he wound his reel at the most tremendous speed. He kept this up all day long, an impressive exhibition of skill and stamina. His reward was to land more fish than the experienced charter party who were aboard could catch between them.

Otherwise, subtle flicks and flutterings imparted through the rod and transmitted down the line to the pirk, make the big difference to catch ratios. The Norwegians have some anglers who are terrific exponents at giving a pirk the right action to induce fish to strike; the clear northern waters of their homeland are particularly suited to lure fishing, and give anglers the opportunity to hone inherent skills to perfection.

Pirking is not all about heavyweight lures. Pirks can weigh as little as an ounce or so and be used effectively in quite shallow inshore water. Scottish anglers have imported a technique they picked up in Denmark during the European Federation of Sea Anglers Championships where the pirk is cast down drift and worked back towards the boat sink-and-draw; catch rates have proved themselves significantly better using this method.

Lead weights

The weight is a simple but important part of an angler's armoury. Most of our fish are bottom feeders, and successfully holding a bait on the sea-bed can be the difference between catching and blanking; carrying a good selection of weights is therefore important. As an example, perhaps there is an angler catching particularly well on a boat; look at the angle of his line – check, is he fishing a bit heavier or lighter than the other anglers aboard? Switching your own leads up or down in weight may be all that is necessary to improve your own catch rate.

Boat anglers will use even more leads than the shore angler, depending on the ground and the type of fishing. An angler who expects to cover most aspects of boat angling will need at least the following selection of leads: first of all, a variety of small weights or shot to match float and line size for trotting a float astern, baited for garfish or mackerel.

Then, some drilled ball leads are useful, 1–3oz (30–90g); these can be used to make a bait roll in a semi-circle round the boat, a method that covers a lot of ground. Or you could use them on the drift, perhaps when presenting a live sandeel as bait.

A selection of bomb-shaped leads of 1–12oz (30–350g) will cover most aspects of light to medium bottom fishing. Use these when holding bottom is not a problem, or for drift fishing.

Downtiding in a strong tide calls for something less inclined to move such as pyramid- and cone-shaped leads or – another big seller – the Bopedo lead. All of these are readily available from tackle shops in sizes up to 32oz (900g).

There are some leads which are specially designed for trolling a lure or bait behind a boat; these are usually curved in a banana shape to prevent any tendency to twist, and can be extremely useful.

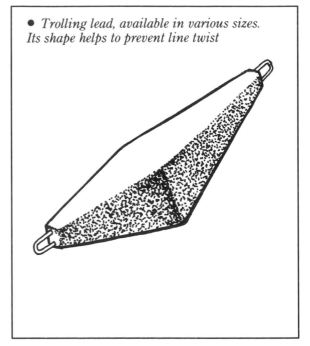

● *Trolling lead, available in various sizes. Its shape helps to prevent line twist*

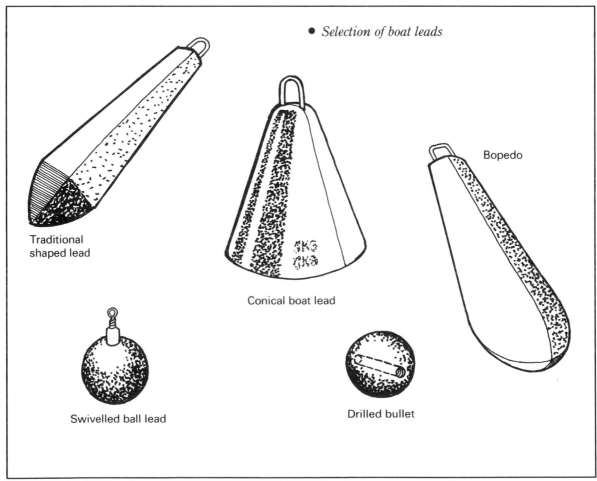

● *Selection of boat leads*

Traditional shaped lead

Conical boat lead

Bopedo

Swivelled ball lead

Drilled bullet

Making weights

Moulds can be bought to make your own weights, but if you decide to do this, be very careful. Cover all bare skin, and wear face and eye protection – a good visor is probably best. Wear thick heavy gloves, and *not* plastic. Do not work with more lead than you can comfortably handle at one time. If you have not got a crucible for melting the lead, use a blowlamp and a sturdy pot made of cast iron, one with a stout handle; use a heavy ladle to pour the lead.

Get everything really hot, including the mould: it is most important there should be no moisture about, as vaporising moisture can cause molten lead to splatter everywhere. Be particularly careful if filling lengths of chromed or galvanised pipe with molten lead (this is a quick, cheap way of making pirks or weights for wreck and drift fishing).

Properly carried out, lead-making is quite safe, and it can certainly save you a lot of money.

Grapnel leads

Sometimes called grip or anchor leads; boat anglers need them for the type of fishing known as uptide or boatcasting. Both the Breakaway and fixed variety of grapnel lead are used in boat angling, according to preference, depth of water and strength of tide. There are several patterns of grapnel in common use. Both the gauge and temper of the wire used for the grapnels, as well as the shape of the grapnel itself, influence the holding ability of the lead. Again, there is a wide variety available.

Grip leads can also be made at home. Make sure the mould is drilled for the shape of the grips required. The wire to use is 16-gauge stainless for heavier leads of 6 to 10oz (170 to 285g), and below this 18-gauge stainless wire. A stout bucket makes a good carrier for your lead selection.

Hooks

Hooks come in a range of sizes, and the most common, but not the only, size scale used by hook manufacturers is the British (Redditch) Hook Scale, in which hook sizes correspond to a number: numbers followed by a stroke then a zero get progressively larger as the number gets bigger, ie 1/0, 2/0, 3/0; numbers without the stroke zero get progressively smaller as the number gets bigger, ie 1, 2, 3, size 1 being a size smaller than size 1/0.

There are hundreds of hook patterns throughout the world, but probably four or five of the most popular patterns are all you will ever use. Many hooks today are sold with a label indicating no more than that a hook is suitable for a certain type of fishing, or bait presentation – for example 'uptide hooks' and 'crab hooks'. The points of all hooks need to be regularly inspected to ensure they are sharp both before and during use.

One pattern of hook you will undoubtedly use is the *Aberdeen*. These are made from tempered wire and are available in a variety of finishes including blued, nickel, gold and black. They are a fine, sharp hook. In the smaller sizes they are widely used in fishing for dabs, flounders, plaice and other small species; in slightly larger sizes they are popular for presenting live sandeels when drifting for bass or pollack, since the fine wire and light weight of the hook does not interfere with the sandeel's presentation. However, because of their tendency to gape and straighten out under sustained pressure, Aberdeen hooks, even in the larger sizes, are not ideally suited for large fish such as cod, conger and rays, especially at anchor when fish may have to be encouraged up from a considerable depth against a powerful tide. In this sort of situation a stouter hook is called for.

The *O'Shaughnessy* pattern is extremely strong. This is a forged hook, and is ideal for use when angling for big cod in strong tides or for hooking and holding powerful conger. However, check the points of even such strong hooks as these, as a point can soon be turned on a rock or piece of rusting metal. They are available in a cadmium-plated or brown-lacquer finish as well as stainless steel.

The *Limerick* is another pattern of hook, not as strong as the O'Shaughnessy but still tough. It has a turned-in eye. Usually sold in a brown-lacquered finish, this pattern is not as popular as it was.

A big-selling hook pattern is the *bait-holder*, though personally I think this is a poor quality fish hook. A plated hook, it does not hold a point well, nor does it penetrate that easily; moreover the metal does not seem well tempered – I have seen anglers lose decent fish through the shanks snapping where the bait-holding barbs join. However, they are cheap, and some anglers obviously like them.

Pirks, Toby lures and many other fishing lures bought from a tackle store will almost certainly come fitted with a *treble hook*: these use the same size scale as other hooks, except there are three which are welded or brazed back-to-back triangularly. They are sometimes called 'triangle hooks' and are available cadmium-plated or brown-lacquered.

There has been a move in recent years towards *barbless* hooks. These reduce damage to fish, which is particularly beneficial for those that are to be returned, and they also make for quick unhooking in competitions; though of course it is necessary to keep steady pressure on any fish being played to prevent them throwing the hook. Certainly I, for one, would like to see their use more widespread.

Hook selection is an important factor in angling. Some anglers insist on fishing with hooks far bigger and heavier than they need for the fish they are targeting, with the excuse that if they hook a lunker cod or conger they don't want to risk losing it. In fact these anglers are missing out on what they ought to catch, because it is as important to match hooks against the species sought, as it is to balance all tackle, if you wish to maximise catches. You can still use a tough hook for small fish; for example, where I usually fish for sole, I use a size 6, model perfect, carp hook – this is an entirely appropriate hook for sole, but tough enough to give me a good chance against the smooth-hound, thornback or sting ray which are likely to be encountered on the same grounds.

For boat angling around Britain you are unlikely to need any hooks smaller than size 6; the largest might be 10/0, possible 12/0 for the bigger sharks sometimes found off parts of the British coast.

Probably the largest supplier of hook patterns to the British market today is the Norwegian company Mustad. It has an enormous variety of quality hooks on offer and these are usually available in bulk boxes, with considerable savings to the angler. A number of hooks on the market now originate in Japan and the Far East, and some of these brands are excellent; notable amongst these is Kamasan.

Some years ago the Spearpoint company introduced a range of quality hooks for sea anglers; although they adopted a different pattern of sizes which some anglers found confusing, the hooks themselves were needle sharp and without the coarse barb associated with most sea-hooks. Spearpoints have the fineness of an Aberdeen style but with improved penetration, strength and holding power.

Innovative anglers, charter boat skippers and tackle manufacturers Cox & Rawle then introduced their own range of superior quality hooks, Uptide hooks, and later on the Uptide 'extra-strength hooks'. These are very popular around Britain and Europe. Mustad has therefore had to contend with increasing competition: first, from these relatively small firms, who had spotted the demand for a finer fish hook; coupled with increasing imports from the Far East; and from some of the major tackle companies who began to market such hooks under their own name (for instance Daiwa has its very popular 'Superstrike' line of hooks). All these no doubt made considerable inroads into the sales of Mustad, the major hook-maker. Mustad responded to the challenge from these competitors, not just by improving its own range of hooks, but by linking up with other companies to produce ready-built hook rigs and items of end tackle to suit the UK market.

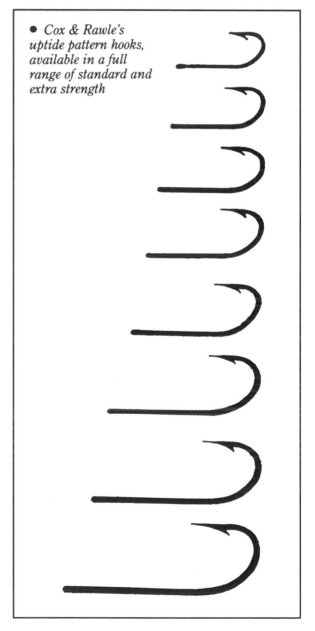

● *Cox & Rawle's uptide pattern hooks, available in a full range of standard and extra strength*

Gaffs and nets

Gaffs

Nowadays, more and more anglers and charter skippers avoid the use of a gaff whenever possible. If you intend keeping the fish, gaffing causes unnecessary weight loss, and if returning it, why injure it in the first place? However, for really large fish, particularly big conger, a gaff may be necessary, (though I have seen fish up to 60lb (27kg) successfully netted). Mustad makes a range of plated lash-on gaff heads, obtainable from good tackle dealers. A stout ash or hickory pole makes an ideal handle – any good gardening centre should provide one. As an alternative to lashing on the gaff head use marine-grade, stainless-steel jubilee clips which make a quick and secure job.

Even the most experienced anglers will sometimes make a mess of gaffing a fish. Personally I believe a good eye, a strong arm and a positive strike and lift are what is needed – but *do not* stab at your quarry.

There is also the flying gaff, not often used in north European waters, where the head detaches from the handle, usually by a snap-off line, and has an independent stout cord or rope attached to hold the fish. These might be of use against the larger sharks to be found in our waters, though to obtain such a gaff in this country, you will almost certainly have to go to a specialist in big game tackle. Alternatively it might be cheaper to have one made by a local marine welding company; or you could order from one of the US tackle retailers, such as 'Capt. Harry's Fishing Supply', 'Fisherman's Paradise' or 'Offshore Angler', all of which ship worldwide.

Nets

To net big fish you will need a tough net. There are proprietary brands available in the tackle shops that will cope with most cod, rays, smooth-hound and the like; you can also make quite a strong-framed net out of stainless tube, bent around an appropriately sized drum, fitted with a section of old trawl netting and fastened to a stout handle with stainless jubilee clips. However, for a net capable of handling anything likely to come along, you may need a braced frame fabricated in stainless steel by a marine welding firm. Again, fit it with a section of trawl netting and mount it on a stout ash or hickory pole.

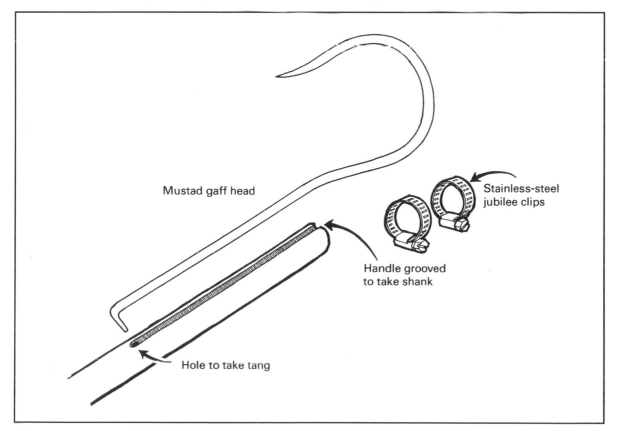

Mustad gaff head

Stainless-steel jubilee clips

Handle grooved to take shank

Hole to take tang

12 Boat-angling baits

AS A GENERAL RULE, select baits that are seasonal and that are likely to be part of the natural food chain for the area. A major exception to this might be the imported calamari squid – though we have plenty of indigenous species which are similar. Virtually all fish respond more readily to a well presented bait, so take care in the cutting and mounting of your offerings; a razor-sharp, thin-bladed filleting knife is a prime requisite – too many anglers simply impale a lump of flesh on the hook in a totally unnatural manner, so the hook point is buried, and then wonder why they don't get a bite.

A fish hunting for food will probably be swimming uptide, ready to pick up and follow any scent trails it comes across. Its excellent sense of smell enables it to home in to an area where several baits are being offered. It then has to use its mouth and swimming ability to contend with the natural wafting motion of the bait in the water.

Most fish will take a bait in one of two ways. Where there is a strong tide flow and your bait is wafting, maybe even being worked downtide, the fish will swim past it, turn and, using the tide, swoop on it 'head-first'. This results in a large number of hook-ups in the corner of the mouth. When

● *This haul of plaice was taken in a few hours off Hayling Island, Hants*

114

there is less tide running, fish – especially big fish –
will inhale bait; they do this by passing water
through their gills, sucking the bait in and swallow-
ing it in one gulp – though sometimes I am con-
vinced they repeatedly inhale and exhale a bait,
testing and tasting, before deciding whether to bolt
it down. This is difficult for them to do if your bait is
a shapeless lump lying on the bottom of the
sea-bed.

Mackerel

Mackerel, an oily fish, is widely used as bait by the
boating sea angler. Fresh, fridged or frozen, it can
make a first-class meal for a wide variety of fish,
particularly these species: black bream, conger,
ling, pollack, shark, spurdog, turbot, whiting, huss,
dab, garfish, ray and other mackerel.

Virtually all fish will prefer freshly caught mackerel, with the possible exception of dogfish who will
eat it fresh, but prefer it fridged, or previously
frozen.

Mackerel used for bait is mainly taken by anglers
on strings of feathers. It is in perfect condition
when it comes out of the sea, and it is best to keep it
that way. One of the first things you should do if you
want to keep fish fresh and wholesome, is to wash
them off in clean salt water, otherwise they get a
film of scum-like material on them. Then either

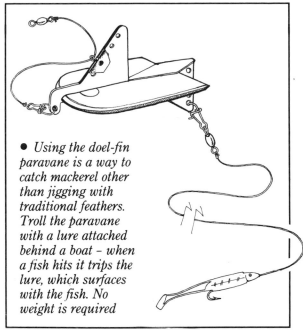

● *Using the doel-fin
paravane is a way to
catch mackerel other
than jigging with
traditional feathers.
Troll the paravane
with a lure attached
behind a boat – when
a fish hits it trips the
lure, which surfaces
with the fish. No
weight is required*

store them in an insulated box containing pre-
frozen ice-packs or cover them with a damp cloth –
anyway stow them out of the sun and keep them
cool. Some anglers get mackerel fever and take far
more fish than are required for bait, then don't look
after them. This is dreadful waste: take only what
you really need, or can sensibly refrigerate or
freeze for future use.

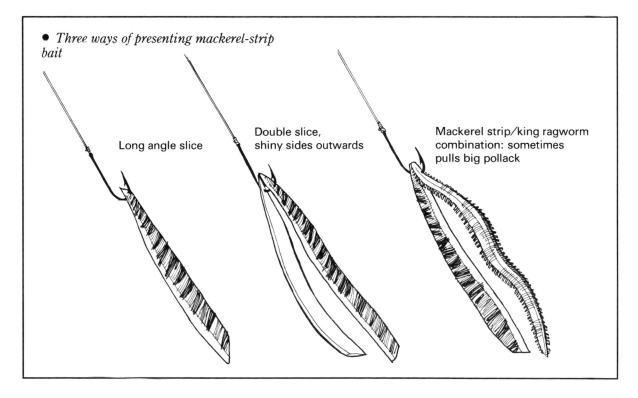

● *Three ways of presenting mackerel-strip
bait*

Long angle slice

Double slice,
shiny sides outwards

Mackerel strip/king ragworm
combination: sometimes
pulls big pollack

- (Above) *Over the years you can accumulate mountains of tackle!*

- (Below) *This small brill grabbed a live sandeel bait drifted over an offshore bank*

● *This specimen dab, the best taken during an EFSA championship, fell to Portsmouth angler Trevor Stuart*

Herring

This is another oily fish that is frequently used as bait. However, unlike mackerel it is not easily caught in most sea areas, nor is it such a good all-round bait – its flesh does not fillet as easily, nor does it cut into strips or stay on the hook as well as mackerel. Nonetheless it is still effective for example with conger, and cocktails with lug or squid can provide a heavy scent trail that fish may follow up. Herring can be a particularly effective bait for thornback ray.

Herring is usually bought from the local fishmonger, but it is sometimes possible to feather a few fresh fish yourself, if you can buy or make a set of feathers, with hooks about size 4. This is worth a try in the late autumn and early winter, when they are inshore in some regions. However, the easiest and cheapest way to obtain a supply of herring is to buy it off a local fishing vessel if you can, when it is landing its catch – ask the charter skippers.

Sprats

Again, another oily fish bait. It is too small to fillet easily, and the filleted flesh does not stay on the hook very successfully, so it is probably best used whole, the fish being hooked just once through the head. Although usually available in late autumn and winter from your fishmonger, sprats are best obtained and used when fresh-landed from a local boatman, as the flesh is then much firmer.

Squid

This is a popular bait with anglers, and can be fished whole, in strips or slices. It is tough, stays on the hook well, and some species are particularly partial to it, black bream, dabs, whiting, pollack and bass all readily taking it in strips at times. Conger, too, will sometimes show a marked preference for whole squid rather than baits. However, it is with the capture of large cod that squid, fished whole, has proved its worth as a bait over the years.

The squid most anglers use for bait and the one most readily available is known as calamari, and is largely imported from the pacific coasts of California and Mexico. These may vary in size from 4–10in (10–25cm) but are generally about 8in (20cm) long. Available deep-frozen from most tackle shops and many supermarkets, calamari comes in 5lb (2.3kg) and 1lb (0.45kg) boxes, though it is much cheaper to buy it in bulk from a local fish wholesaler, say twenty-four 5lb boxes at a time. Some clubs take a van up to Billingsgate fishmarket and buy a vanload at the start of each cod season, making even bigger savings. The squid should be a nice clean white colour – avoid buying any with an excessive pink or purple tinge.

We have our own native species of squid, too, though these are not generally available from fishmongers or tackle shops; a local fishmarket could be a source. These domestic squid – and there are several varieties – grow considerably larger than the imported calamari, and can reach lengths around 2ft (0.6m) long. They will occasionally hook themselves while attacking a bait intended for

● *Expert angler Jim Whippy, from Pevensey Bay, Sussex, travelled to a mark off the Needles, Isle of Wight, to take a close look at this 22lb (10kg) cod. An exception to the rule, this fish ignored all the conventional whole squid offerings and took a small worm-and-squid strip-bait, on a size 2 hook, intended for whiting* some other fish species. There are several spiked jigs on the market, specifically intended to catch squid. Commercial fishing supply stores and some tackle shops carry them, so stick one in your tackle box – it may be the answer to any strange plucking bites you experience.

Cuttlefish

A similar type of bait to squid, the flesh of the cuttlefish is thicker and if anything tougher; all the species that take squid will take cuttle. To be most effective, prepare bait strips carefully as these generally work best if cut very thin. The head and whole small cuttlefish can be a very good bait for conger.

Cuttlefish is sometimes available from local boatmen and from the occasional tackle shop near the coast, but if you have your own boat, it is best to gather it yourself. From May to July whole cuttle will often be seen floating on the surface of the sea – the best time to search is at slack water. Keep a lookout for one or two herring gulls or black-backed gulls (not the smaller common gulls) on the water, sometimes with their heads pecking; this will invariably indicate a dead or dying cuttlefish on or near the surface. Net it as you come alongside, and if it is still alive try and get it to eject as much of its ink in the water as possible; then put it in a bucket to avoid your decks being stained by any ink it may still contain. Cuttlefish freezes well; a few trips at the right time and you can easily lay down a year's supply.

Peeler and soft crab

This sort of crab is an excellent bait and works particularly well for inshore boat fishing. In traditional uptide areas peeler is probably the best bait you can use for cod, and bass love it too, especially in the spring, and when used in areas enjoying the first flush of peeled crab. Soft-back crab is particularly good for thornback rays, and smooth-hounds love crabs – they are one of the few fish that will readily take hardbacks. When boatcasting, peeler can usually be mounted naturally, hooked once through the carapace with the point protruding through the body; though shirring elastic may be needed to hold it on the hook.

(Further tips on the gathering and storage of these and other baits can be found in the Shore-fishing section, Chapter 9.)

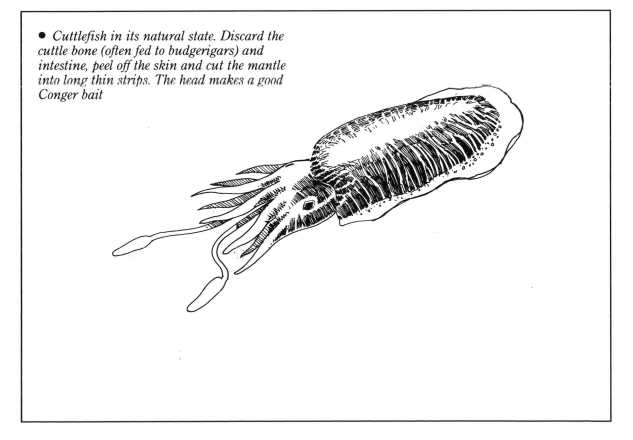

● *Cuttlefish in its natural state. Discard the cuttle bone (often fed to budgerigars) and intestine, peel off the skin and cut the mantle into long thin strips. The head makes a good Conger bait*

Hermit crab

A very worthwhile bait that you can gather yourself with a drop net. It is particularly effective in taking smooth-hound and thornback rays, and the tails are excellent for plaice, dabs, codling, whiting, bream and pout. Hermit crabs can be stored alive for some time in a tank of clean, cool, aerated sea-water; however, don't put too many together as they fight like gladiators!

- (Right) *A brace of thornbacks; hermit crabs were the downfall of these two fish that fell to Hythe, Hants angler, Archie Blandford*

- (Below) *Blackfield, Hants, angler 'Dink' (King of the Stings) Lemoignan with a superb 46lb (21kg) Solent sting ray*

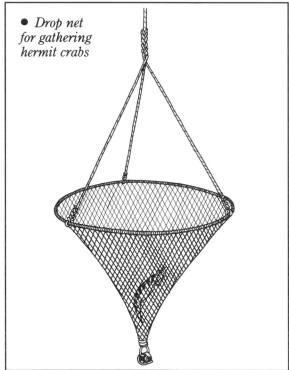

- *Drop net for gathering hermit crabs*

Ragworm

Ragworm is another major bait and can be fished in various ways: whole, threaded up the hook, bunched, threaded up the hook and line, or singly hooked through the head so it can swim naturally. Flounder, plaice, dabs, bass, cod, wrasse, sting ray and pollack are all species that respond well to

• *Charter skipper, Mike Gregory, who operates the 33ft (10m) lochin,* Leander, *out of Langstone Harbour, Portsmouth, displays a specimen male black bream*

• (Below) *These fine Solent dabs all fell to squid-strip and ragworm-cocktail baits*

ragworm; it can also be fished in cocktail combination with other baits.

(For gathering and storage, see pp83–6 of the Shore-fishing section.)

Lugworm

Lugworm vies with mackerel as the bait most often offered by sea anglers to tempt a fish. It is used extensively in eastern regions, and is a first-class bait for cod, whiting, dabs, plaice and bass. There are several types of lugworm; black, blowlug and yellowtail. It is fished by threading the worm up the hook and line singly or several at a time, depending on hook-size, the fish species sought, and the type of worm. It can be very effective in cocktail baits with squid.

(For gathering and storage see pp80–3.)

Mussel

A widely used bait in the north of the country; in the south, fresh wild mussels are not so easily obtained nowadays – though thanks to more widespread commercial mussel farming, mussels are nonetheless fairly easy and inexpensive to obtain in quantity. Southern anglers should find them particularly effective against plaice, which love to browse over underwater mussel beds; in the north, mussels are excellent bait for cod, haddock, plaice, dabs and catfish.

Mussels can be dipped in and out of hot water to make the shells open, though this may destroy some of their scent attraction. Alternatively, use a knife to sever the muscle at the point of the shell and prise apart. Mussel is difficult to keep on the hook; the easiest way is to use elastic surgical tubinet: roll a length of this over a slim tube, then slide the shelled mussels down the tube into the net, which is pulled off the tube, gradually making a long sausage of succulent mussel-bait. This can be cut up according to hook size and species being targeted; it can also be frozen. Take only enough for a day's fishing, stored in a flask or the cool box.

Clams

These are large shellfish often encountered when bait-digging. Not easy to dig in large numbers, a good supply can sometimes be purchased from the skippers of local clam-dredging vessels. A large, tough bait, clams are readily taken by bass and cod. In North America, they are considered a prime inshore bait for cod.

Razorfish

Once widespread, now prolific only in some areas: a razorfish lives in a straight, narrow, tubular burrow up to a yard deep with an opening like a keyhole; they can move quite quickly, so digging them out can be a tedious process. The easiest way is to probe a long, slender, barbed metal rod down the burrow – the razorfish clamps its shell on the rod and you gently extract it. It takes a bit of practice! Whole razorfish is excellent for bass, particularly on offshore sandbars after a blow; it will also take cod, plaice and rays.

Slipper limpet

In many areas slippers can be gathered just by picking them up at low water springs, and clusters will sometimes be pulled up when fishing offshore. They are similar to mussel but probably not as good as bait. However, pout love them, and flats and bass will eat them too, so it is worth taking the trouble to prepare them when other more effective baits are unavailable. The elastic tubi-net is a good method of bait presentation, as for mussels.

Sandeels

Sandeel is a natural food for many species of fish. It is obtainable live from only a few tackle shops, namely the ones that have a big enough market and that can be supplied by local boatmen. Live sandeel will take many species, particularly bass, pollack, coalfish, turbot and brill; dead, fresh or frozen, it is a real killer for small-eyed ray and dabs.

A number of companies market frozen sandeel, the leading supplier being Ammo Baits; these are sold by tackle shops nationwide. For live eels, besides the few tackle shops that supply them, it is sometimes quite possible to dig or scrape a few out of the sand where they have burrowed; try this on sandbars that are exposed at low water. When the tide is in, you can try netting for them with a sandeel net at similar locations.

Alternatively, go direct to the commercial netters, an obvious source; take along a suitable container filled with clean, fresh, sea-water, and an aerator to keep it fresh. Sandeels may also be kept alive wrapped in a clean cloth, dampened with sea water, and stored in an insulated box, with chemical ice-blocks to keep them cool.

Shrimps and prawns

Live prawn or shrimp is a bait for the specialist, and not one widely used by boat anglers. However, it will be eaten readily by bass, pollack, wrasse and most flatfish, as well as several other species. It is best presented as naturally as possible, either freelined or on float tackle, trotted away from the boat. Freshly dead prawn and shrimp baits are successful in taking wrasse and flatfish. Prawns can be caught in fine mesh drop nets and kept alive in the same way as sandeels.

Other baits

As well as the 'regular' baits described, there are other creatures that can be used as bait with varying degrees of success. While bait-gathering you may, at the extreme low-water mark, come across a creature called a seamouse – not a great bait, but a cod will sometimes gobble one up. Sea-slaters and sandhoppers are readily taken by wrasse and can be easily gathered at times. And all the little fish, the blennies and gunnels found under stones and in rock pools, will be snapped up by marauding bass. Do not forget, either, that live pout is a first-class bait for bass and conger; that small wrasse on inshore rock marks can be the downfall of big eels; and that in the final resort, if you run out of regular bait, the flesh of virtually any fish you have previously caught, can be used to try and tempt its brothers.

13 General techniques

IF YOU ARE GOING BOAT FISHING for the first time with a friend or club member, you should be well served for advice and assistance, both on what to take and what to do. On a charter boat, without friend or colleague to show you the ropes, a first trip can be a daunting even if exciting prospect. Where does the multiplier reel go – on top of the rod? How many hooks should be put on a trace? And where does the trace connect, is it to this link, or that snap? If this trip is to be on a charter boat, let the skipper know when you book that you are a complete novice; ask what tackle and bait to bring and once under way never be afraid to ask either him or other anglers for help.

It is always helpful, when fishing a new venue, to find out the favoured local rig and to see if the local methods include any subtle little differences. Obviously, fishing tackle and techniques will vary from one area, month and species to another – sometimes you will be advised to lower just a general fishing rig to the bottom, a sort of catch-all; but usually you will be fishing with some sort of target in mind.

Downtiding

This style of fishing, whether in deep water or shallow, is probably used more than any other. The normal tackle is fairly basic: first, a conventional boat-rod, its class depending on depth of water and tidal conditions – usually a 20lb (10kg) or 30lb (15kg) class rod will suffice, fitted with a multiplier, or centre pin reel and loaded with line to match the rod. Fixed spool reels are not suitable for downtide fishing. Suitable end tackle would consist of a sliding boom on the main line, bead, and link swivel connected to a swivelled, 4ft (1.2m)-plus monofilament trace with one, two, or maybe three hooks, hook sizes commensurate with likely catches for the area. The lead weight clips onto the sliding boom. Longer traces, 10ft (3m) or so, with a single

hook and a natural, well-cut, flowing bait are sometimes very successful.

Some anglers like to fish a smaller hook from a trace attached to a boom above the weight, commonly called a flyer, in an attempt to cover all fish-catching possibilities. This does, however, lead to a greater risk of tangles, and a flyer should certainly not be used when fishing for large, lively species such as tope or conger. It is unfair to expect a

● *A happy angler with a ling of 24lb (11kg), taken off open ground from Chris Savage's Lymington-based boat,* Private Venture

● *English anglers find the cod during a practice day prior to an EFSA European Championship in Holland. The main event was more difficult*

● *A brace of black bream, safely netted*

● *Anglers enjoy some fine weather over the Eddystone reef aboard the Plymouth charter vessel* Marco

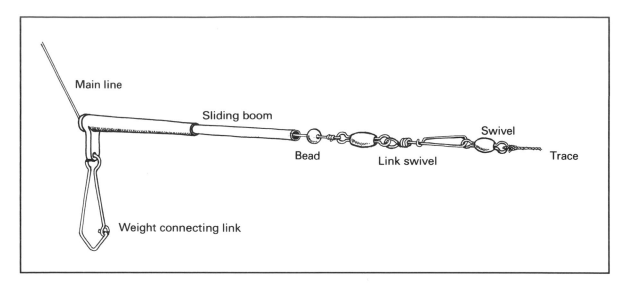

Main line

Sliding boom

Swivel

Bead

Link swivel

Trace

Weight connecting link

● *The basis of a running leger rig, used for most downtide fishing. The use of a link swivel allows quick trace changes*

skipper to net, tail or gaff your fish whilst risking a hook in his finger as he does so.

The technique of downtiding is fairly simple; lower your weighted and baited tackle to the sea-bed, using enough weight to maintain contact with it, and then try to entice a fish to inhale your bait. Unless you want the bait to remain static (after conger, perhaps, fishing on a snaggy wreck) use as light a lead as possible, and use the tide's flow to work your bait steadily downtide. Not all in a rush, but pausing, giving a fish a chance to grab the bait, allowing time for the tide's pressure to bow the line and lifting your tackle off the bottom. Then lift into your lead and drop it back again, repeating the process until you can no longer feel contact with your end gear.

At this stage you might just reel in and rebait and then repeat the process; or you might increase your lead by a few ounces before doing so. This method covers a great deal of ground and seeks out fish-holding gullies downtide – often bites will keep occurring at the same stage in the sequence of lifting and dropping back, as your bait keeps finding the same shoal of fish; the movement of the bait is sometimes the final inducement for it to bite. Successful downtiding depends on the angler being able to feel his tackle in contact with the bottom, close to which most European sea fish spend most of their time.

One point to consider: whilst inexperienced anglers are bound to be cautious, be aware that heavier breaking strain lines are thicker and thus

the tide acts on them to a greater degree. Therefore use line appropriate to the type of fish you are likely to encounter: don't use 50lb (24kg) bs line when 25lb (12kg) would be quite sufficient, or 15lb (7kg) when 10lb (4.5kg) would be ample.

Another thing to bear in mind: on charter boats the usual practice is to draw for fishing positions, and your position on the boat will influence how you fish. Near the stern you can fish with a lighter weight, so use the opportunity to trot well astern of the boat, away from the other anglers' tackle. Drawn to fish by the cabin you will need to fish with a heavier lead so as to reduce the chance of tangles with your neighbours towards the stern. Anglers between the forward positions and the stern should adjust their weights progressively downwards. However, the odd snarl-up of tackle is inevitable, so just try and keep a sense of proportion. Allocating precise weights to each position, as is done in some boats, is a nonsense and no more successful in preventing entanglements.

In downtiding, all the fishing lines generally available are used: monofilament, braided Dacron and of course wire. When using monofilament line, because of its inherent stretch you may experience a loss of contact with your weight earlier than you would when using the same diameter line made from braided Dacron, which has very little stretch. However, braided line absorbs water to some extent and can be carried more readily downtide; and *because of* its non-stretch quality it retains good bite detection. You can sometimes use these char-acteristics to advantage, by trotting a bait well downtide and away from a boat in shallow water (noise from charter boats in shallow water is believed to set up scare patterns).

Using paternoster rigs

A multi-hook paternoster is not the most productive rig to fish from an anchored boat in a strong tidal flow. But at slack water, and especially during the periods either side when there is a gentle current trickling astern, it can be used successfully in conjunction with a downtiding session; there are times when, fished from a 20lb (10kg) – at most a 30lb (15kg) – class outfit, it can score heavily. Why?

When the tide is running hard, a paternoster with its booms, hooks and baits above the weight, is more easily swept up and off the bottom by the tide and away from any fish, than is a legered rig. Also, during those times of gentler tide flows, many of the smaller fish, such as dabs, whiting, bream, pout and gurnards become active, emerging from the rocks and gullies where they have been sheltering, and starting to look around for food. At these times they will often rise up off the bottom, giving the angler who is fishing a three-hook paternoster rig, a chance for multiple hook-ups. Competition anglers can win or lose an event around this time by anticipating – or not – a hot half-hour of action.

Some sea-angling areas, usually the inshore regions of large bays, never experience much in the way of strong tidal flows; in these parts it is possible to use a paternoster and take fish throughout the tide.

Using wire line

Wire line allows you to beat the tide; also, because it is non-stretch it gives superb bite detection and positive hook-ups.

One of the first things to consider is whether the rod is suitable. As the main reason for using wire is so you can fish strong tide flows, it has to be able to carry heavy leads at times. This means at least a 30lb (15kg) class rod, but more realistically a 50lb (24kg). Ideally the rod needs to have a soft or forgiving action, as wire has none of the elasticity of nylon – a soft-actioned rod helps cushion over-enthusiastic strikes or the sudden lunges of a heavy fish. The rod must have a good quality roller ring at the tip; the intermediate rings may be of Carbuloy or aluminium oxide, but can be rollers as well. A stout reel is important – Penn 4/0s and 6/0s are ideal – or alternatively one of Shimano's TLD 20s or 25s, loaded with at least 150 yards (138m) of single or multistrand wire; over some sort of backing, normal nylon line is adequate. One advantage of a reel like the TLD 25 is that whilst strong, it is relatively light, and this helps compensate for the weight of the wire itself.

The end tackle is similar to a standard leger rig,

● *Elements of wire-line fishing for cod: roller rings, vibro-type spoons, pennel-rigged whole squid bait*

- *Joining monofilament to single strand wire via a haywire twist and Allbright knot. The completed knot can be whipped or superglued, or both for added security*

Haywire twist

Allbright knot

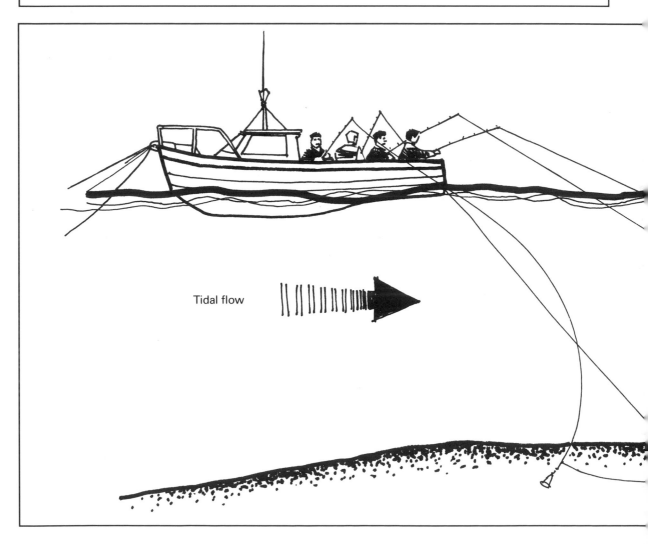

Tidal flow

with a trace appropriate for the species sought; the difference is that the sliding boom is mounted on a separate leader of heavy nylon. This leader is then connected to the wire via a swivel and figure-eight knot, a haywire twist, or straight to the wire by an allbright knot. Some anglers dispense with the leader altogether, allowing their weight-carrying boom to slide directly on the wire. It can work, but the wire needs constant monitoring for wear.

Common mistakes are that anglers don't use enough lead, and/or they try to use or carry on using their wire outfits when there is little or no tide. It is most important that wire line is kept under tension; all wire has a tendency to form coils when allowed to flop loosely, with the consequent risk of forming kinks.

Check regularly that your roller rings are ungrooved and rotate smoothly; also intermediate rings for signs of grooving. Regularly inspect your wire, and discard any length that appears worn or damaged. Rinse it thoroughly in fresh water after use; if it is not going to be used again soon, it should be removed from your reel and stored on a large plastic or wooden spool – not as much trouble as it sounds, and with the cost of wire, well worth the effort.

With the tide running hard you can use a wire-line outfit to trot a bait away, following the basic principles of downtiding.

Uptiding and boatcasting

This style of fishing has grown tremendously in popularity over the last twenty years, and for certain areas and types of ground it is considered far and away the most productive method of boat angling. It is probably most effective in areas where the tide sweeps over relatively shallow banks and gullies. A rod of 8ft 6in–10ft (2.6–3m) in length, suitable for casting the various grapnel leads away

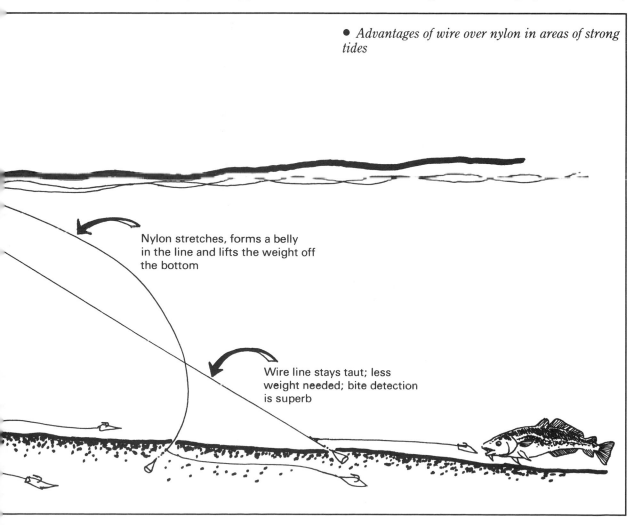

● *Advantages of wire over nylon in areas of strong tides*

Nylon stretches, forms a belly in the line and lifts the weight off the bottom

Wire line stays taut; less weight needed; bite detection is superb

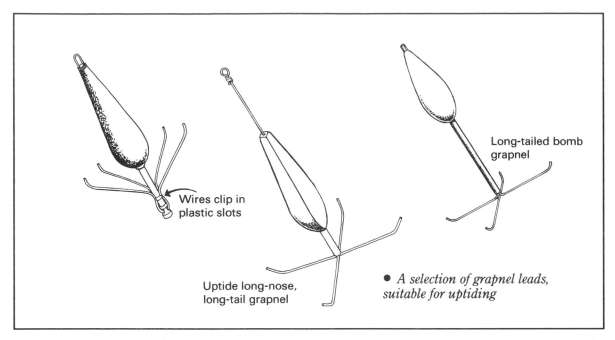

Wires clip in
plastic slots

Long-tailed bomb
grapnel

Uptide long-nose,
long-tail grapnel

● *A selection of grapnel leads,
suitable for uptiding*

from the boat, is required. Generally speaking a rod capable of casting 4–8oz (120–240g) will cover most requirements around Britain.

You will also need a multiplier or fixed spool reel loaded with 15lb (7kg) bs line, which must be fitted with a leader of at least 35lb (16kg) bs – and if your

casting technique is either long-distance or plain unreliable, use a 50lb (24kg) leader.

Favoured end tackle is a running leger consisting of an uptide sliding boom, bead, link swivel and swivelled nylon trace around 3ft (0.9m) long. Some anglers believe they benefit by using a longer trace length when the tide flow increases, and a shorter length as the tide slackens. As an alternative to the sliding boom, a one or more hook paternoster may be used. Hooks should be sized for the anticipated quarry.

The tackle should be cast uptide or outward from the boat with respect to your relative position (see diagram). It is most important that the tackle is allowed to drop unhindered to the sea-bed after casting, and that once it has touched bottom you allow a large belly of line to run off your reel. It is the pressure of the tide on the bow in your line that pulls the grapnels on your lead into the sea-bed, pinning that bait hard to the bottom where the fish are; if you haven't allowed sufficient line, your baits are likely to be off the bottom and out of the catching zone.

After you have cast out, set the rod in a holder; there are portable ones that clip to the rail, though most charter boats have rod-holders around the gunwales.

Now, your line should be running a little astern,

● *These small-eyed ray, taken by Hants angler Ann Kitcher, fell to slivers of mackerel presented on uptide tackle*

the tip of your rod pulled down slightly by the pressure of the tide on the line. A good uptide rod will have a soft tip that flexes with the boat's natural motion, and a decent bite is usually indicated by a slight dip, followed by the rod tip springing back as the fish pulls the grapnel wires from the sea-bed. At this stage the angler should pick up his rod and wind quickly to get the belly out of the line, establishing contact with the fish before it has time to get any distance downtide.

Boatcasting is successful, especially for large parties in charter boats, as it ensures there is a wide spread of baits over a large area of sea-bed. It also ensures those baits are anchored tight to the bottom, where hopefully the fish are busily searching for food. Moreover it puts anglers' baits well away from the potential scare area around the vessel that could result from turbulence on the hull, tide-strum on the anchor rope, or just the clatter of boots thumping around on deck.

Pirking and lure fishing

Most pirk and lure fishing is carried out on the drift, and is most successful in regions of clear water. Tackle needs to be balanced: if fishing a very heavy pirk, then a 50lb (24kg) class rod will be needed, whilst lighter pirks allow lighter tackle. As a general rule, use the thinnest line possible when pirking as this reduces drag on the line; the best catches usually come when the lure is straight up and down. Pirks are very often fished in conjunction with one or two other lures; the rig most widely used is two muppets, rubber eels, Mr Twisters or similar, fished off snoods above a pirk. This rig is then worked just off the bottom, jigged up and down to try and induce a fish to grab the pirk or one of the lures. The size of pirks and lures can vary according to depth of water, strength of tide and anticipated catch. Over a deep-water wreck the pirk may weigh 2lb (0.9kg) or more and the muppets may be 4–5in (10–13cm) long, necessitating rods in the 50lb (24kg) class. Inshore, pirks or jigs may be much lighter, with smaller muppets or redgills, and a 20lb (10kg) class rod may be quite sufficient.

Techniques are still being developed for pirking, using uptide rods, and when fishing on the side of the boat facing the direction of drift. The pirk, or pirk and lures, is cast in the direction of the drift with a boatcaster and then fished sink-and-draw back to vessel. This system covers a lot of ground, and in fact is producing significantly better catches than conventional pirking.

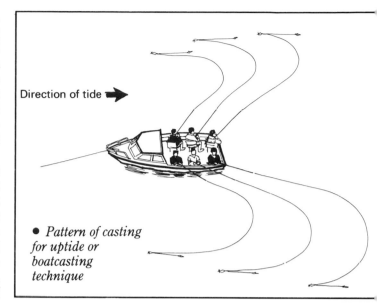

Direction of tide ➡

● *Pattern of casting for uptide or boatcasting technique*

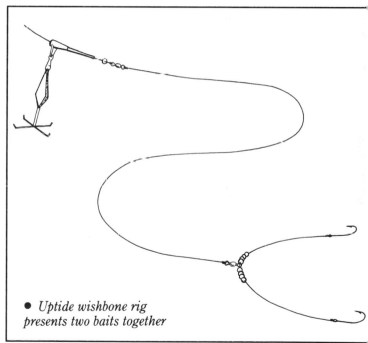

● *Uptide wishbone rig presents two baits together*

Fishing a pirk and two lures is particularly effective for species such as cod, coalfish and pollack and can take huge catches in the right circumstances. However, multiple lures can also be successfully fished on the drift for these species, without a pirk. Three hook traces of muppets or Mr Twisters are great fish-catchers, and baiting the lures improves the hook-up rate when the fish are a bit shy.

Lures can also be fished singly; for best results fish them off longer traces rather than short snoods. The trace is attached to a long metal or

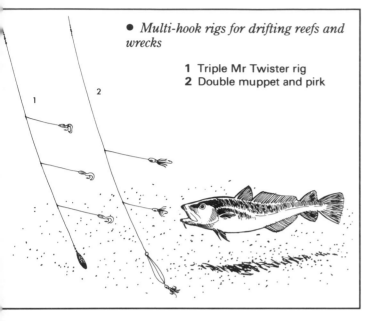

● *Multi-hook rigs for drifting reefs and wrecks*

1 Triple Mr Twister rig
2 Double muppet and pirk

plastic boom that helps prevent it tangling. This method can be particularly successful with some of the artificial eels.

Wobbler spoons and bar spoons can be very good at attracting the attention of other species, wobbler spoons baited and fished on the drift particularly so with flounder and plaice. Three or four fluorescent beads above the hook are an added inducement. Bar spoons such as the Toby lure are excellent casting lures, and can also be trolled from a boat. Either way they can be equally good at enticing fish such as bass and pollack.

Fishing artificials requires different skills to those needed for bait-fishing, and there is a host of different lures and techniqes for using them. The ability to impart that subtle action to a pirk, muppet, spoon or some other lure that will make fish grab it while ignoring others, is a skill all its own.

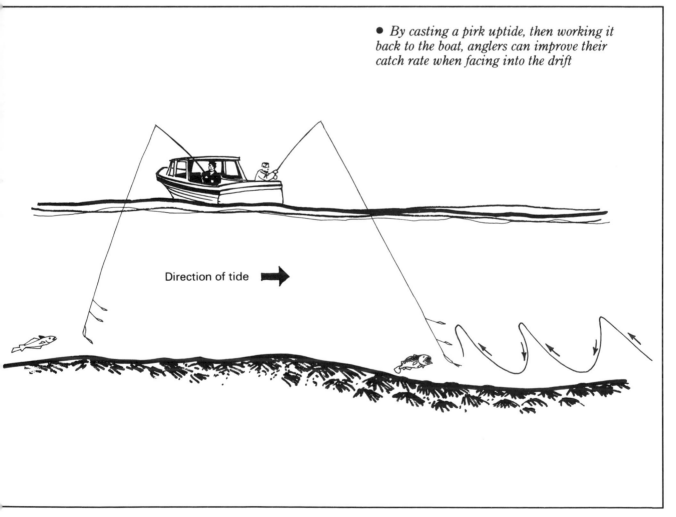

● *By casting a pirk uptide, then working it back to the boat, anglers can improve their catch rate when facing into the drift*

Direction of tide ➡

14 Species and catching methods

Bass

(*Dicentrachus labrax*)

THE BASS IS CONSIDERED by many sea anglers to be the finest fish in British waters both to catch and eat. It is certainly one of the most sporting. The boat-caught British record is held by a fish of 19lb 2oz (8.876kg) but any bass in double figures is considered a good fish. It is greeny-grey on its back, with silver sides and a silver-white belly. It has two dorsal fins, the first of which has eight or nine spines; there are also some sharp spines on the gills, so handle carefully.

Bass is found throughout the English Channel, the Irish Sea as far as Cumbria, and the North Sea as far as the Wash; it becomes less common north of these points. Commercially it commands a high price and is much sought-after, but it is a slow-growing fish and susceptible to fishing pressure. Nursery areas have been set up around the coast in recent years, which may help the species' long-term future.

Many of the bass caught by anglers each year are taken by chance, but they do follow certain habits and these can be exploited when targeting them. They like to roam and they also like to eat sandeels, so find an offshore sandbank and bass will probably visit it; you can then catch them from a drifting boat with a live sandeel as bait.

Tackle can be fairly light by sea-angling standards; Shakespeare's 15lb (7kg) class Ugly Stik is ideal, but a medium spinning rod or 12lb (6kg) class boat rod will do fine. A small fixed spool reel or multiplier loaded with 10lb (4.5kg) line makes a fine outfit.

End tackle is best kept simple: a drilled bullet of 2–3oz (60–90g) with the main line running through its centre, then through a small bead and tied to a link swivel which is connected to a swivelled nylon trace of around 10lb (4.5kg) bs; the trace length needs to be 6–10ft (1.8–3m) long, culminating in a

● *This 6lb 6oz (3kg) bass took a small strip of mackerel offered on uptide tackle by Hampshire fisherman Mike Hannam*

fine wire Aberdeen hook size 1/0 to 4/0, depending on the size of the sandeels.

Charter skippers will normally supply the sandeels. These can also be bought from a few tackle shops with special storage tanks, and from commercial sandeel fishermen who will supply anglers direct. The live sandeel is mounted on the hook by passing the point through the bottom of the mouth and lightly nicking the eel's belly. The rig is

133

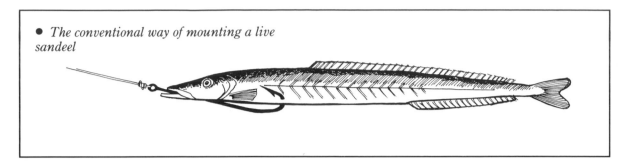

● *The conventional way of mounting a live sandeel*

then lowered or cast away from the boat to the sea-bed.

Depending on the speed of drift you may need to adjust your weight to keep your bait near the bottom. Instead of the drilled bullet, a single light metal or sliding tubi-boom may be used with a light weight connected. Bites are usually quite positive, so set your drag correctly before you start fishing and once hooked, don't point your rod at the fish. Make sure the rod is held so it can cushion any sudden runs. There is also a very good chance of picking up other species; pollack, turbot, brill, plaice and dabs are all partial to sandeel.

Another method of taking bass is to troll or cast an artificial lure through or into a likely feeding area, for example around a headland where there is a strong tidal flow and turbulent water. Redgills, Delta eels and Eddystone eels are all favoured lures. A word of caution, however: do not venture into areas of tide races or overfalls unless you are with an experienced skipper in a well-found craft.

The presence of bass is often revealed by sea-birds diving into the sea. Sometimes the attraction is mackerel but a Toby lure or plug tied direct to the main line and cast across the action from a medium spinning rod and fixed spool reel, then wound back below the surface, will reveal what the shoal is – maybe bass, or bass working beneath mackerel. At other times, sea-birds sitting in a group on the water may indicate the presence of bass below; then the fish may be hard on the sea-bed, so a set of feathers, a deep-worked rubber eel or even a pirk may then be required. Forays at dawn are most likely to find these feeding bass shoals, but if you have your own boat, keep a set of gear made up ready for action, should you run across a pack of bass at any time.

Bass like to prowl inshore banks, rocky gullies and obstructions such as small wrecks; these may often be in areas that dry out at low water, so particular care in navigation may be required. Moreover, other baits may be more productive in these circumstances – cuttlefish, squid, peeler crab, live pout and other small live fish. Spring tides invariably stir bass into feeding more readily; the young flood tide on low water springs can often be the best time to start fishing. Anchor uptide of a rocky gully, a wreck in a sandbar, or some other feature that the tide floods over or around; time this with the onset of darkness and your chances of success improve substantially.

The method is standard downtiding with a basic leger rig, and if you are fishing any sort of solid structure tackle strength needs to be 20lb (10kg) class, substantial enough to turn and hold a fish heading around an obstruction. On clean sandbars and gullies lighter gear may be used. Whatever bait you offer, use a flowing trace 6–8ft (1.8–2.4m) long of 17lb (8kg) monofilament; and bass will take enormous baits so you can choose a big hook, a 6/0 or 7/0 Cox & Rawle uptide or similar-sized Aberdeen.

Cuttlefish is one of my favourite baits for bass; it sometimes fishes particularly well in May and June when the spawning female fish appear along the south coast and are a natural food for bass. Remove the skin and cut off slices about 7 or 8in (18 to 20cm) long, nice and thin. Hook the bait once at the tip so it

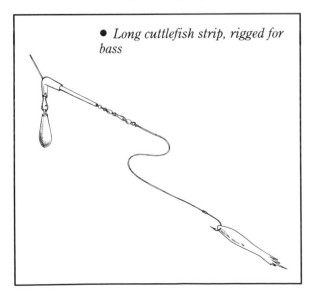

● *Long cuttlefish strip, rigged for bass*

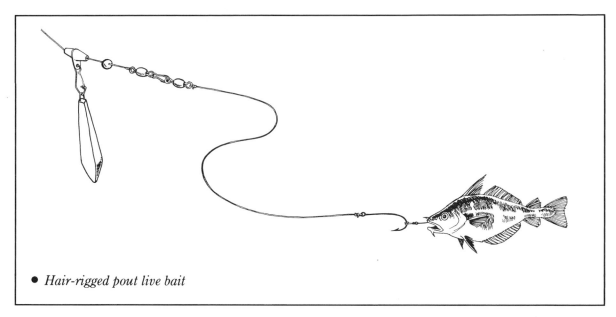

● *Hair-rigged pout live bait*

wafts naturally in the tide, then cast or work the bait downtide towards your chosen feature. In shallow water it should be possible to use just enough lead to hold your bait in the desired position. Whole calamari squid can be presented in the same way, hooking the bait just once through the tip. Double-hook pennel rigs, favoured for cod-fishing, will catch bass, but the single hook presentation is probably more productive.

When fishing around rock formations, particularly in late spring, peeler crab is a very good bait. Again, don't be afraid to use a large whole crab, presented on a 5/0 or 6/0 hook. And in the autumn a live pout can be deadly; just lip-hook your pout, either on a large hook as already recommended, or even better on a hair rig, with the pout lip-hooked on a small hook trailing from a large hook (tie it to the gape of the large one by a short piece of light line).

Occasionally you may find the bass in suicidal mood. If you do, enjoy your sport. Take a fish or two to eat by all means but return the majority. It is your future fishing.

Black bream

(*Spondyliosoma cantharus*)

Anglers are most likely to encounter black bream in the English Channel and parts of the Irish Sea. Bream are migratory, but with predictable habits, returning to certain patches of offshore reef to spawn each year. They are grey on the back with metallic silver sides, and reach a maximum weight of around 7lb (3.1kg). Males in breeding colours have distinct iridescent blue markings around the head, though these fade quickly after capture if the fish are not returned to the sea.

Black bream are extremely sporting to catch; there are several well-known marks off various locations along the south coast where they are regularly encountered, Weymouth, Lulworth, Swanage and Littlehampton among them. All have reefs where shoals of black bream can be expected to appear in late spring, and where they stay for a few weeks before dispersing more generally over reefs and wrecks throughout the Channel. In the late autumn they may sometimes be found shoaled up again, and this is when the best specimens are often taken, just before they disappear for the winter.

Bream may still be caught on any south coast wreck or reef mark from April to late October, though your best chance will probably be in May and June. Tackle need only be heavy enough to cope with whatever weight is required to keep contact with the bottom. A fast-action 12lb (6kg) class boat rod, small multiplier and line to match, is normally sufficient. Favourite end tackle consists of a single hook, size 1 or 2, fished from a 6ft (1.8m) long, 10lb (4.5kg) bs nylon trace, attached to a metal or plastic boom and fished above the weight. Trot the tackle downtide and always be ready to strike as bream are adept at ripping the bait off a hook. With bream, a bag of rubby dubby, regularly replenished, probably influences the overall catch more than with any other species, except perhaps for garfish. To bring the bream in the area onto the feed, fill an onion sack or diver's bag with chopped or minced mackerel and tie it to a cord, weight it heavily and lower it to the bottom beneath the bow of the boat. Successful baits are ragworm, lugworm and small strips of squid and mackerel.

When the tide is running hard, keep the boom close to the weight as the fish will be near the sea-bed sheltering; as it eases, move the boom further up the line, because then bream have a habit of swimming some way off the bottom.

Black bream should also be taken only sparingly; moreover many charter boat skippers expect all hen fish to be returned.

Brill

(*Scophthalmus rhombus*)

The brill is a delicious-tasting flatfish that reaches a maximum weight of about 16lb (7.25kg). It is a speckled sandy colour on top and creamy-white beneath. Found all around the British coast throughout the year, it is at its extreme northern range in British waters.

Brill are occasionally caught when drifting for bass with live sandeels on offshore sandbanks, and they like this type of fishing ground and bait. They will also take fresh mackerel – mount a long slender strip of about 7in (17.5cm) on a 2/0 or 3/0 fine wire hook, from an 8ft (2.4m) flowing trace of 20lb

(10kg) monofilament, ledgered and trotted away downtide. Alternatively use uptide methods and fish the mackerel on a size 1 or 2 hook (a Cox & Rawle extra-strength is perfect) on a shorter trace, about 4ft (1.2m) of 15lb (7kg) bs nylon.

Brill are most likely to be caught by anglers during the late spring and summer.

Bull huss

(*Scyliorhinus stellaris*)

Similar in appearance to the lesser spotted or common dogfish, the bull huss grows considerably larger; the maximum recorded weight is 22lb 4oz (10.09kg). It prefers rocky areas with patches of sand between; and although it is found all around Britain, it is most common off the coast of Wales and throughout the English Channel.

The hardest part to catching a bull huss is probably getting the boat anchored over the type of ground it likes to inhabit. The fish itself will eat a variety of baits, including mackerel, herring, squid, peeler crab and hermit crab; and once it has found the bait it will persevere in trying to eat it. Whole mackerel flapper baits, intended for conger and with large strong hooks, will often be attacked by bull huss, who will happily chew away at the bait. Often an apparently hooked bull huss will just open its mouth as it breaks the water, letting the bait go

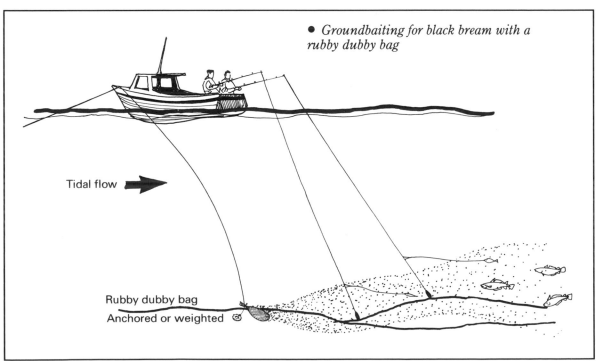

● *Groundbaiting for black bream with a rubby dubby bag*

Tidal flow

Rubby dubby bag
Anchored or weighted

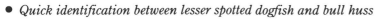

• *Quick identification between lesser spotted dogfish and bull huss*

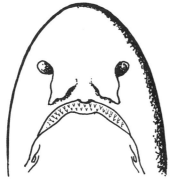

Bull huss:
nasal flaps do not
reach the mouth

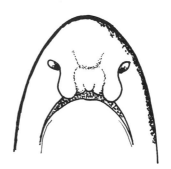

Lesser spotted dogfish:
the nasal flap reaches the
front lip

and sinking back to the depths. They are not good fighting fish, but make reasonable eating.

Use smaller baits of fish fillets with sharp hooks to ensure hooking the fish. A 30lb (15kg) class rod will still give you some sport and a chance of coping with any conger you might run into. End tackle needs to be a basic running leger with a 4ft (1.2m), 50lb (24kg) bs nylon trace; a 4/0 or 5/0 uptide extra-strength hook should complete the rig – these are sharp, strong and penetrate well.

Coalfish

(*Pollachius virens*)

The coalfish is found all around the British Isles, though it is far more numerous in northern waters. Perversely the largest specimens generally come from wrecks in the south-west part of the English Channel. The fish is dark grey-green on its back, fading to silvery sides and belly; the lateral line is straight and pale-coloured. It can attain weights in excess of 40lb (18kg).

Coalfish are mainly mid-water feeders and are usually caught on artificial lures. However, they will take worm and fish baits readily enough – anglers fishing for other species sometimes find they are unable to get their baited tackle to the bottom because of dense shoals of coalfish in mid-water, which seize the bait before it can reach the intended target area. Huge hauls of coalfish can then be made by using a three-hook trace of feathers, or rubber eels. More sporting enjoyment might be gained using a 12lb (6kg) or 20lb (10kg) class rod,

a matched multiplier and line, fished with a single Redgill on a flowing trace, off a boom attached above the weight. The fish in these large shoals are generally about the same size, not much bigger than 5–7lb (2–3kg). Sometimes you will get two distinct shoals and sizes of fish, one above the other at different depths, with the smaller fish invariably on top.

As coalfish get larger they are less likely to be found in shoals of any size. Double-figure coalfish fight really well, and the biggest specimens are taken off wrecks or reefs such as the Eddystone in the South West. A good skipper can often identify a small pod of coalfish over, say, a wreck from the echo-sounder readings before an angler has wet a line. Unlike most other species, coalies can withstand pressure changes perfectly well when hooked and brought up from the deep, and will fight all the way to the surface.

To tackle these big Westcountry coalfish you need a 20lb (10kg) or 30lb (15kg) class rod; some anglers prefer to use an uptide rod. A medium-sized multiplier, for example an ABU 7000, is ideal, and line to match the rod. End tackle should consist of a long flowing trace – up to 20ft (6m) for some anglers, of 30lb (15kg) bs nylon. Coalfish are tough fighters, and in a prolonged skirmish on the reefs may saw through lighter trace material with their jaw; however, 8ft (2.4m) is usually sufficient when fishing a wreck. The trace is attached to a long boom, below which is a weight. The business end of the trace usually carries a large rubber eel (Eddystone, Redgill, or Delta) and hook size is commensurate with the eel, perhaps as large as an 8/0.

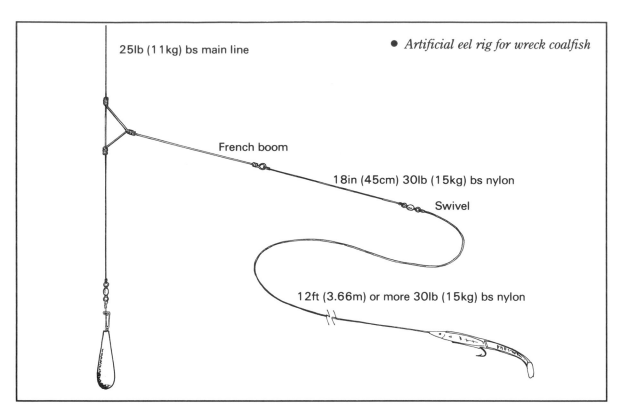

• Artificial eel rig for wreck coalfish

25lb (11kg) bs main line

French boom

18in (45cm) 30lb (15kg) bs nylon

Swivel

12ft (3.66m) or more 30lb (15kg) bs nylon

The same end rig but with a smaller hook, 3/0 or 4/0, will be suitable in fishing a natural bait for large coalfish. This could be a live launce, or a long strip off the belly of a mackerel – if you remove the flesh from this leaving mainly the skin, it is much more effective.

The tackle should be lowered to the sea-bed, the long boom helping to prevent the trace from tangling around the main line. On touching the bottom begin winding – with an artificial eel you should wind fast. If you think you are getting some sort of bite, don't stop or strike: keep winding at the same pace until the fish turns and dives with the lure (you will find out then if your drag is set correctly). If you don't get a fish, wind all the way to the surface and count the number of turns on your reel; this will give a rough scale of depth. If you then continue to count the turns on subsequent drops, you will know approximately where your bait or lure is in relation to the depth, and can stop halfway or three-quarters of the way to the surface, then drop back again if you wish. Remember, coalfish are likely to be above any pollack that may be on the same mark.

Exactly the same principles apply if using a natural bait, except you can wind a good deal slower. Do still keep winding at the same rate if you think you are getting a bite, until the fish dives and starts stripping line against the clutch.

Cod

(*Gadus morhua*)

A fat-bodied fish, with a pronounced barbel under the chin; generally olive-green with mottled brown speckles and a grey/white belly, though sometimes copper- and golden-hued when living amongst areas of heavy kelp. Cod have been caught off New-foundland weighing over 100lb (46kg), but the British record stands at 53lb (24.03kg). They eat a wide variety of food and are a quick-growing species.

Cod is almost certainly the fish most widely sought by North European boat anglers. It is caught in British waters throughout the year. In late winter many of the larger fish move offshore to oversummer on wrecks in the English Channel, and the Irish and North Seas. They can still be caught, but if fishing privately you will need a sound craft, suitable navigation equipment and some knowledge of where to look.

Alternatively you can book a specialist wrecking boat. Wreck-fishing for cod usually involves a heavy chrome pirk suspended under a brace of muppets or rubber eels, on short snoods of heavy nylon. Fished from a 50lb (24kg) class rod and a large multiplier loaded with matching line, the rig is jigged along close to the bottom as you drift down

● *This perfectly conditioned cod, its speckled markings very distinct, grabbed a whole calamari squid in the Solent*

the wreck. This can be a very efficient way of catching cod and filling your freezer; it can also be expensive on tackle and line, as when you are not catching cod you are often catching the wreck. A

single eel or muppet fished from a 4ft (1.2m) trace off a boom, still close to the bottom, means you can use a 30lb (15kg) class outfit – and fewer hooks inevitably reduces snags.

Uptiding for cod

A lot of cod are caught using the uptide style of fishing, widely used from the Solent to the Wash as well as in other parts of the country where depth and conditions suit. In some of these areas it is practised alongside downtide methods.

Most uptiding is concentrated in the autumn and winter when a run of smaller cod moves inshore; the South East usually has a run of spring cod as well. Most of these fish will be in the 3–6lb (1.4–2.7kg) range, though a few much bigger ones will fall to uptide rods every year. Tackle is standard 4–8oz (120–240g) uptide rod, multiplier or fixed spool reel and 15lb (7kg) line. Hooks are sized from 2/0 to 4/0, maybe bigger, sometimes rigged tandem fashion in a pennel rig, with traces 2–4ft (60–120cm) long of 20lb (10kg) bs nylon, fished from a boom or sliding leger. Favoured baits vary, but peeler crab, various lugworms, ragworm, squid, and cocktails of squid with any of the previous baits are all successful, lugworm baits being the most widely used of all. Uptide cod bites are usually quite positive, the rod

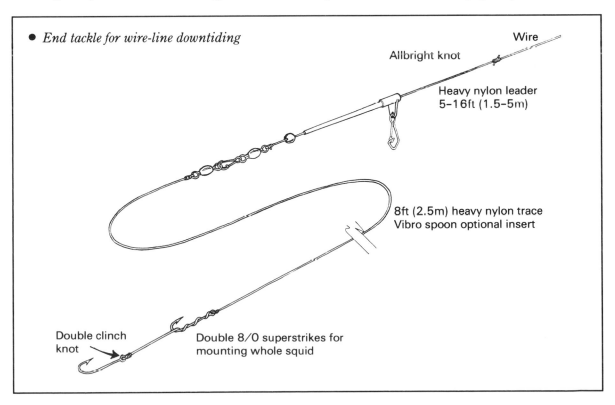

● *End tackle for wire-line downtiding*

Wire

Allbright knot

Heavy nylon leader
5–16ft (1.5–5m)

8ft (2.5m) heavy nylon trace
Vibro spoon optional insert

Double clinch
knot

Double 8/0 superstrikes for
mounting whole squid

● *This cod opened his mouth once too often to take a whole squid bait, fished downtide from wire line, and ended up in the arms of Winchester angler Andy Barret*

tip first dipping, then springing back, allowing the angler to pick up the rod and wind into the fish. If you miss bites, and believe these are cod biting shy, try dropping down to a small strong hook, about a size 1 extra strength, so the cod can swallow the bait right down. It sometimes makes all the difference!

Downtiding for cod

Big cod like big baits, and when downtiding you can provide these – and the premier bait for big cod must be a whole calamari squid or two. Cod love it,

it's tough, it will stand up to the attacks of dogfish and whiting for a while, and compared to the cost and effort of obtaining lugworm, it is relatively cheap. It will also attract large fish of other species.

The usual method of presenting whole calamari is on a pennel rig (see diagram) consisting of two strong hooks – at least 5/0s, but up to 8/0s for really deep water where a fish may have to be retrieved from some way astern against the tide. The nylon trace should be 6–10ft (1.8–3.0m) long and needs to be fairly strong, at least 40lb (18.4kg) bs. Use a heavier trace where strong tides and deep water necessitate wire line to hold bottom.

As well as whole calamari, lugworm still works well when downtiding, as does ragworm and cocktails with squid. Frozen black lugworm are considered a prime bait by some leading anglers; several of these when added to a whole squid lay down an excellent scent trail. Peeler crab is of course a proven cod killer, especially in the South East for the spring run of cod. Mackerel and hermit crab baits take cod, but these are not particularly effective.

Some anglers like to fish with a large spoon in the trace, about 2ft (0.6m) above the hooks. There is a variety of spoons about; some, like the fluttering white plastic types, rely mainly on visual attraction, others such as the rotating metal spoons have visual and vibratory effects. Many of the latter are homemade, and based on Normark's now discontinued Vibro Lure.

Drifting reefs for cod

In much of the north of England and in Scotland cod fishing is very often done on the drift, invariably in clear water, but also over reefs and broken ground where tackle losses can be heavy. A pirk fished below two muppets, Mr Twisters or artificial eels is a favoured rig; although the pirk may need to be heavy at times, it is often possible to fish with lighter ones of just a few ounces.

In areas where these lighter pirks are practical, Scottish anglers have been experimenting with ideas gained in Denmark to improve catches. When they are on the side of the boat facing into the drift they have taken to casting their pirk, with an uptide rod, in the direction of the drift, then working the pirk back towards the boat. Anglers on the other side of the boat, away from the direction of drift, carry on pirking in the usual fashion. It does mean switching between two sets of gear, if the boat continues to alternate sides for each drift, as is normal. Long casters tend to score well. Results have been

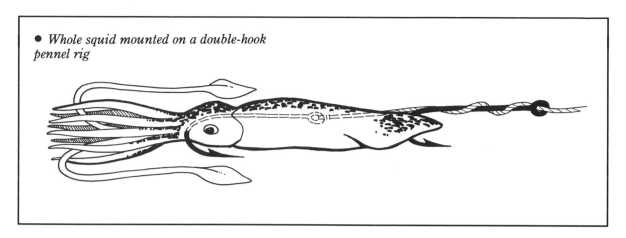

● *Whole squid mounted on a double-hook pennel rig*

encouraging, but it is a new technique and still developing.

Conventional pirking is an art in itself. The Scandinavians are masters at this, and have a knack of being able to impart a fluttering action through the rod to the lure. Drift fishing the inshore reefs, where lighter pirks can be used, is an opportunity to develop this skill.

Baited and unbaited muppets, Mr Twisters and other lures work well on the drift for northern cod. Preferred baits are lugworm, ragworm, white rag, mussel and peeler crab, and at times the colour of the lure seems to be particularly significant.

Conger

(*Conger conger*)

A large eel, grey-brown on top, creamy-white underneath. The upper jaw is longer than the lower. It is reputed to reach weights of 200lb (91kg), and some extremely large fish have been caught in trawls. The British rod-caught record is over 109lb (49kg). The conger can be one of the hardest-fighting fish in British waters. It is very popular with sea anglers, and the British Conger Club is one of the most successful angling clubs in the country.

Conger are occasionally caught off open ground when fishing for other species; however, any serious attempt to catch them involves anchoring over and fishing a wreck or reef, or some other craggy obstruction in which conger might make their lair.

Tackle for conger eels needs to be strong, since their first instinct on being hooked is to head back to some rock crevice. This, and the abrasion on your line that can result from fishing into rock and wreck, demands tough tackle: a 50lb (24kg) class rod, a 4/0 or 6/0 reel loaded with 50lb (24kg) bs monofilament line is suitable. End tackle should

● *Vibro-type spoon, a popular lure with some south-coast anglers who fish it a short way above the hook when using whole squid baits for cod*

consist of a running ledger, bead, link swivel and a swivelled 3–5ft (90–150cm) monofilament trace of at least 100lb (46kg) bs. Some anglers still prefer to use wire traces, but heavy mono is superior for conger; it can be tied to the hook and swivel using a double-clinch knot, or it can be crimped.

Popular baits for conger are: whole calamari squid; whole small-to-medium cuttlefish; large cuttlefish heads; herring; mackerel fillets; and probably the most-used conger bait, a flapper mackerel where the tail and backbone are removed but the head, entrails and side fillets are left intact. Conger will also take a live bait, a lively wrasse or pout being very effective at times. My own favourite is a flapper pout (backbone and tail removed, as for mackerel).

For such a large fish, conger can give exceedingly shy and gentle bites, which should be given a little time to develop – it's a matter of judging when the fish has eaten the bait, and when it is returning

● *Trying to hoist 86lb (41kg) of conger eel is not easy, even with Graham Hannaford, skipper of the Plymouth charter boat* Tiburon, *giving a hand*

to its lair – though occasionally conger will go into a feeding frenzy, bolting baits down as soon as they hit the bottom and trying to pull your rod over the side and you with it!

A final tip: on some particular wrecks or reefs it is worth presenting the bait about 1ft (30cm) off the bottom, instead of on the sea-bed as normal; perhaps this is some peculiarity of weed growth or an awkward bottom structure, but at times it does make a substantial difference in the bite ratio. Do this by using a length of nylon to connect your lead to your boom; you could also use a rotten bottom (a weaker length of line) to attach the lead, which can save tackle and fish if it snags.

Dab

(*Limanda limanda*)

A small flatfish, a mildly flecked, mid- to sandy brown on top, and white underneath. These can be semi-translucent in their more juvenile sizes. They grow to a maximum of around 3lb (1.2kg) in weight.

Dabs are a regular catch for inshore anglers all around Britain – they take no great skill to catch and are not renowned for their fighting qualities. However, they are quite tasty eating.

Tackle for dabs need only be light, though you may feel there is a limit as to how much you scale down, because of the larger fish likely to pick up the bait. A three-hook paternoster, or three-hook flowing trace can be used if numbers are needed. Kamasan Aberdeens size 4 are ideal, but a size or two larger will probably not affect your dab catch significantly and may hold a larger fish a little better. Small strips of squid and mackerel, ragworm, lugworm, peeler crab segments and hermit crab tails, are all excellent baits for dabs. Bites can sometimes be difficult to detect, but generally have a slight fluttery sensation to them.

● *Double clinch knot: use for tying heavy monofilament to hook and swivel*

● *Two ways of mounting a flappered mackerel*

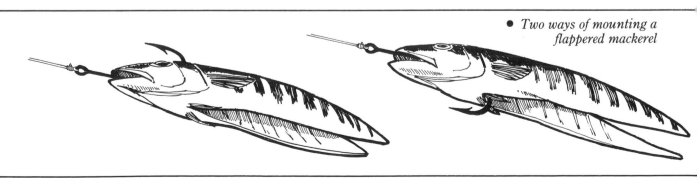

Dogfish

(*Scyliorhinus canicula*)

Also called the lesser spotted dogfish. A small shark, colour-mottled, sometimes banded brown on top with creamy undersides; maximum weight about 4lb (1.8kg).

Anglers spend a lot of their time feeding dogfish with bait intended for other species. However, this is no reason to abuse them when they are brought into the boat; if you don't want them to eat, unhook them carefully and return them to the water.

Take care that you don't let any dogfish rub its skin backwards against wrist or hand as its rough skin can cause a nasty wound. To minimise this risk, hold the fish's tail and head firmly together in a loop in one hand whilst unhooking it with the other; barbless hooks will obviously greatly facilitate hook removal.

Dogfish will eat virtually any bait, but unlike most fish, I believe they prefer frozen mackerel, or some that has been stored in the fridge for at least a day or so. To catch dogfish in any numbers try a two-hook flowing trace with sharp 1/0 Kamasan or uptide model hooks, using small strips of mackerel from the fridge for bait. Fish this running leger style, from a 20lb (10kg) class rod. And if you really want to get the dogfish going, lower a rubby dubby bag of ground mackerel over the side and anchor it to the bottom.

Flounder

(*Platichthys flesus*)

A popular flatfish with anglers, in colour a dull mottled green/brown, occasionally with indistinct orange spots on top, grey-white underneath sometimes with partial mottling as well. Boat fishing for flounders in British waters is usually best in creeks and estuaries, and there are several methods which bring success.

For good sport, a 12lb (6kg) class boat rod or a medium spinning rod coupled with a small multiplier or fixed spool reel and loaded with line to match is ideal. Freshwater tackle could be used if preferred. End tackle when bottom fishing can be a two- or three-hook paternoster or a multi-hook flowing trace. My own favourite is a running leger with a two-hook flowing trace. Top baits are ragworm and peeler crab, though lugworm, white rag, cockle, mussel and razorfish all produce well at times. When bottom fishing, baits are generally

kept static. But flounders are inquisitive, and a turn on the reel handle to give the bait a little movement, or to send up a puff of mud from the weight, will sometimes attract their interest. Some of the biggest hauls and heaviest fish are taken near the mouths of estuaries in January and February, when shoals group up for a final feed before moving offshore to spawn.

A baited spoon can be a very efficient way of catching flounder, though during the winter it seems less effective, perhaps because at that time of year a bait needs to be kept tight to the bottom for best results. However, during the late spring and summer flounder will rise off the bottom to chase a baited spoon. There is an old saying that when you turned a piece of seaweed over on the beach and found sandhoppers underneath, then the flounders would rise to a spoon; this is not far wrong, even today. They will take both spinning and wobbling type spoons in a variety of sizes up to 5in (13cm) in length; Delta Tackle's sonic spoon is a popular choice today.

A medium spinning rod and fixed spool reel loaded with 8lb (3.3kg) bs line completes the outfit for spooning. The spoon can be tied direct to the main line, or you could tie it to a 3ft (0.9m) trace of marginally lighter monofilament, which is then attached to the main line with a swivel. Some anglers may also find it easier to cast the spoon, depending on its size and weight, if a small barrel lead is placed immediately above the spoon, or above the swivel trace connection.

Another method is to pay out the spoon to the sea-bed from the back of a rowing boat and row along just fast enough to keep the spoon moving.

Garfish

(*Belone belone*)

Garfish are plentiful from late spring to summer, and are great sport on appropriate gear. They can be found all around the British Isles from late April/May until November. Though sometimes caught on the bottom, they are extensively a midwater and surface feeding fish, and very inquisitive and playful. They have a long slender body, and an elongated beaky mouth with a number of small sharp teeth. In colour, the top and sides are a greenish-blue becoming silver on the belly. Maximum weight is about 3lb (1.4kg).

Only light tackle is required to catch this fish. A light, 6ft (1.8m) baitcaster from the USA is ideal, but any light spinning rod would be satisfactory. A

garfish they must be encouraged to shoal up behind the boat. Anchor near the end of some promontory or headland where there should be plenty about, then hang a rubby dubby bag of ground mackerel over the side, just dipping in the water – that should bring the gars astern and in a feeding mood. Give it a shake every now and again, and replenish it regularly.

Grey mullet

There are three distinct varieties of grey mullet that can be caught in British waters: the thick-lipped grey mullet (*Chelon labrosus*); the thin-lipped grey mullet (*Liza ramada*); and the golden grey mullet (*Liza aurata*).

All three are migratory and have similar colouring – grey-blue on top, grey-striped silver flanks, and a silver-white belly. Each has a small dorsal fin with four sharp spines.

The distinguishing marks between the three are as follows: the *thick-lipped grey mullet* has a deep, broad upper lip, the bottom part of which is very coarse. It is the largest of the mullet, reaching weights in excess of 10lb (4.5kg). The *thin-lipped grey mullet*, as its name suggests, has a thinner top lip without the roughness of the thick-lipped mullet. It has a black spot at the base of the pectoral fin, and reaches a maximum weight of about 6lb (2.8kg). The *golden grey mullet* has a distinctive golden mark on the cheek and gill cover, and grows to around 3lb (1.3kg).

Boat angling for mullet is not widely practised, yet there is some excellent sport to be had in estuaries and harbours with this hard-fighting 'grey ghost' as it is frequently called. There are times when mullet will feed readily at the warm water outfalls of power stations; and sometimes they have a 'mad' period, when they throw off their reputation for shy feeding and freely take larger hooks and baits intended for other fish. In Southampton Water this period is usually for a week or so in late September.

For consistent success a range of freshwater tackle will be required. A 12ft (3.6m) carp rod with a 1–2lb (0.5–1.0kg) test curve is a suitable rod; couple it with a small, good quality fixed spool reel loaded with 5lb (2.2kg) monofilament. Hook sizes will need to be varied to suit conditions and the shyness of the fish – from 4 to 10 should suffice. Baits may be presented below a float and trotted downtide. Floats need to be freshwater standard, in keeping

● *Freshwater reef, off the Isle of Wight, produces lots of species. This garfish grabbed a strip of mackerel as it dropped to the seabed after casting*

fixed spool reel is preferred, but a small multiplier would also be suitable. Line need only be 3–4lb (1.3–1.8kg) bs, though if you are fishing with a boat-load of anglers you might prefer to go slightly heavier. For hook size, use a 4 or a 6.

You can fish in two ways: either, take a small sliver of mackerel (more skin than mackerel is best) and nick it on the hook; this is set 2ft (0.6m) beneath a sliding float, appropriately weighted, and then allowed to trot downtide. Or, bait the hook with a sliver of mackerel and just freeline it downtide. When a garfish hits the bait, the first you will probably know about it is when he catapults out of the water, probably turning a cartwheel at the same time.

To have some really spectacular sport with

with the other tackle; for example, a large quill, an Avon, or a waggler float in the 5 SSG range.

When the fish are shy biting, try fishing a freelined bait astern; and if the line won't float, treat it with special flotant. To hook fish feeding deep, lower a lightly weighted nylon paternoster over the stern and fish it straight from the rod tip. And a technique that works for mullet in some areas is to spin for them with a small fly spoon or Mepps lure, tipped with a little harbour ragworm.

Mullet can be tempted with maggot, bread-paste, breadflake, the tips of harbour ragworm and catfood. Groundbaiting, and rubby dubby bags hung over the side of the boat just below the surface, will help to get the fish feeding.

Pre-baiting over a week or more can persuade mullet to eat what you want. I know one local angler who used to hang a fly-blown joint of meat in a tree that overhung the estuary near his boat mooring. As the maggots hatched they fell off the meat into the water, where the mullet soon learned to wait for them. The fish were then quite ready to feed on maggots when the angler anchored his boat uptide and freelined a maggot under the tree for them.

Haddock

(*Melanogrammus aeglefinus*)

This delicious-tasting fish has been under intense commercial pressure for some years, and overall numbers have declined dramatically. Haddock are most common in waters to the north of England and Scotland, though a small haddock fishery that has produced some of the best specimens in the past, still exists in the south-west English Channel. The fish are dark grey-brown on the back with silver-grey sides, and the belly is white. There is a conspicuous black spot behind and above the pectoral fin. Weights can exceed 13lb (6kg), but the average is about 2lb (1kg).

The haddock is primarily a bottom- or near-bottom-feeding shoal fish, usually encountered over mud or sand. When a shoal is found, a good catch often depends on how well the skipper can keep in touch with the fish. Note also that haddock have soft mouths, and though not heavy, they can tear themselves off the hook altogether if put under too much pressure; it is steady continued winding which brings them to the boat. Swivelled rubber shock absorbers about 2ft (0.6m) long, really for use by long liners, are favoured by some anglers

because they act as a cushion to prevent fish tearing themselves off the hook.

Tackle for haddock need not be heavy. A 20lb (10kg) class boat rod with a medium-size multiplier such as an ABU 7000 or Shimano TLD 15 is ideal; load with matching line. Also a single or multiple paternoster end rig with fairly short snoods about 1ft (0.3m) long, with needle-sharp size 2/0 hooks.

Bait can be lugworm, mackerel or squid strip, but mussel is most productive, although it can be difficult to retain on the hook. To overcome this, use surgical elastic tubi-gauze. Slide a length of the gauze over a plastic tube about 1in (25mm) in diameter, and feed the mussel into the gauze via the tube. The elastic gauze is self-sealing at the ends, and you can make sausage lengths of mussel-filled gauze, ready to cut into bait sizes.

Haddock will also take lures; most effective are slim spoons of the combined type, where the shiny spoon is mounted direct to the shank of the hook.

A tip when bait-fishing: a small fly spoon, sequin or fluttering lure inserted in the trace length above the hook can often improve the catch rate.

Halibut

(*Hippoglossus hippoglossus*)

These fish grow to enormous size, and halibut over 700lb (320kg) have been recorded. They are greeny-brown on top, white underneath, and have substantial teeth. They resemble a very large flounder.

In the UK, the best chance of finding these mighty flatfish is from the northern parts of Scotland, the Orkneys, Shetlands or the Western Isles. However, the main problem is to find enough anglers keen to travel to the areas likely to produce a fish to keep the charter-boat skippers in business. It is sometimes possible to hire a commercial fishing vessel for a day's fishing in ports from which a halibut might be encountered.

The Pentland Firth is a noted mark for Halibut, and charter vessels operate from the harbour at Scrabster. For those prepared not to be sidetracked by the excellent possibilities for other species, the chance of a halibut is still there.

Tackle for halibut will need to be strong – at least 50lb (24kg) class, and 80lb (37kg) would not be excessive. Halibut normally spend their time in very deep water, offshore. During the summer and autumn, a few will sometimes move to deep inshore marks (relatively shallow for them) and this is where any angling effort should be concentrated. I would choose a Penn 6/0 reel loaded with Dacron line appropriate for the rod; the Dacron line would help bite-detection in the deep water to be fished.

Halibut will take a baited pirk fished on the drift, but heaving 2lb (1kg) of chrome up and down for hours on end is hard work, though a few large cod and ling might come along to brighten the pirker's day. The alternative is to fish at anchor and use a running leger rig. The trace needs to be at least 100lb (45kg) bs commercial nylon, hook size a 10/0 or 12/0 – a Mustad O'Shaughnessy or Sea Demon should be adequate.

Bait could be a whole pollack or coalfish, about 2lb (1kg) in weight; I would remove the tail and backbone, leaving the guts intact to improve the scent trail. Whole fillets from the side of a coalie or pollack would also be suitable.

● *This skinny summer ling weighed 21lb (10kg). In the winter, when full of roe, it would probably have topped 30lb (14kg)*

Ling
(*Molva molva*)

A long-bodied fish, browny-green on the back and upper sides becoming white on the belly, with occasional black spots along the sides; it has a number of small, needle-sharp teeth. Ling reach weights exceeding 50lb (24kg) and on deep-water wrecks, double-figure fish are quite common.

Ling can be found all around the British Isles, though mainly in deep water; it is frequently caught by anglers fishing over wrecks. It will take a lure, but bait is more effective. Being considerably affected by pressure changes in water depth, it is not the strongest of fighting fish for its size.

Tackle for ling need be no more than 30lb (15kg) class, with a medium-size multiplier and line to match, and a 5ft (1.5m) trace of 100lb (45kg) monofilament ending in a size 6/0 Mustad O'Shaughnessy, or Cox & Rawle uptide extra-strength hook. A lighter trace of 40lb (18kg) nylon with a short wire hook-length is an alternative to

the heavy mono. Ling will be taken both on the drift and at anchor.

Anglers who anticipate hooking large conger as well as ling when wrecking, may feel uncomfortable with 30lb (15kg) class gear, and prefer to step up a class.

Ling may be easy to catch on some deep-water wrecks, where large shoals mean that competition for food is fierce. However, it can be a finicky biting fish, and at these times a switch to a longer trace, about 8ft (2.4m), and a smaller hook size, 3/0, might be advisable; use a slender fillet of fresh mackerel as bait. A slow, gentle wind for ten or fifteen turns off the bottom can then entice the fish to bite. Ling can also be found on and along the deep-water edges of reefs, where drifting a mackerel fillet bait on a similarly long trace can work quite well.

Mackerel

(*Scomber scombrus*)

This slender-bodied fish is a mainstay of British angling. It provides a large proportion of the bait used by sea anglers, and is obviously a very important link in the marine food chain.

A mackerel is a brilliant blue-green with wavy black bands on its back and the top of its flanks; its lower sides and belly are silver. Maximum weight is about 6lb (2.8kg). They feed and can be found at all depths, from the surface to the bottom. Most mackerel are caught on shop-bought mackerel feathers; there are several kinds of these about, from the traditional feathered variety, to those made from strips of Mylar and other glittery material. A 20lb (10kg) class rod with matching reel and line is ideal for feathering. The set of lures is connected to the main line via a link swivel and weighted at the bottom; a bomb weight of about 5oz (150g) is normally sufficient.

When using feathers from a drifting boat, work them to the sea-bed and back again; mackerel will very often take them as they drop. Use your thumb to control the reel spool so that the feathers drop down a little at a time, lift the lures, then drop again. If you reach the sea-bed without hooking any mackerel, then reverse the pattern – wind up a few turns, then lift the rod. When you find the fish, you should have some idea where they are in relation to the surface, so you can drop back into them straight away. Mackerel can also be caught by trolling a set of feathers behind a slowly moving boat.

A more sporting method of catching mackerel is to take them singly on any small shiny lure, or on one of the smaller Redgills or Delta-type plastic eels; use a light spinning rod and work the lure at different depths. Try a small bead mounted just in front of the hook, then trolled behind a boat or cast, and retrieved from a spinning rod: the bead creates a vortex of bubbles around the hook as it moves through the water, which attracts the fish. Mackerel are also extremely cannibalistic, and a strip of mackerel flesh nicked on the tip of a size 1 hook then lowered and wound up through the depths, will catch as well as anything.

Large mackerel, or 'jumbos', can be really good sport on light tackle. Small shoals of these larger fish often appear inshore late in the year, around October; this is a good time to try for specimen mackerel.

Plaice

(*Pleuronectes plattessa*)

This brightly marked flatfish is found all around the UK coastline. It is widely sought by anglers as it

● *Fine plaice like these beauties can be caught in the spring*

provides good sport on light tackle, and it makes delicious eating. It is brown on top with bright-red or orange spots, and there is a row of small bony nodules behind the eyes and before the gill slit. It grows to weights exceeding 10lb (4.5kg).

Spring produces the biggest catches, as this is when the fish first move back inshore after their spawning migrations. At this time they are grouped together and feeding well, often in traditional areas, before scattering to the grounds where they will oversummer. They can still be a regular feature in summer catches, but big hauls are unlikely. In about October plaice may briefly congregate again, before moving off to spawn once more. The fish are in better condition than in the spring – they are tastier, and provide better sport.

Tackle for plaice need be no more than a medium spinning rod and matching fixed spool reel, or a 12lb (6kg) class boat rod and small multiplier reel, with 10lb (4.5kg) bs line for either outfit. End tackle can be a single or a multi-hook flowing trace. If fishing on the drift, or if there is a nice run of tide to work the lure at anchor, use a long trace with a spinning or wobbling spoon. A popular compromise is to fish a spoon on a flowing trace, with a second hook off a dropper above the spoon. Some plaice fishermen like to add several small, fluorescent col-

● *A 14lb (6.5kg) pollack for one of Kent's top boat anglers, Alan Crampton. The fish tried to eat a black Eddystone eel*

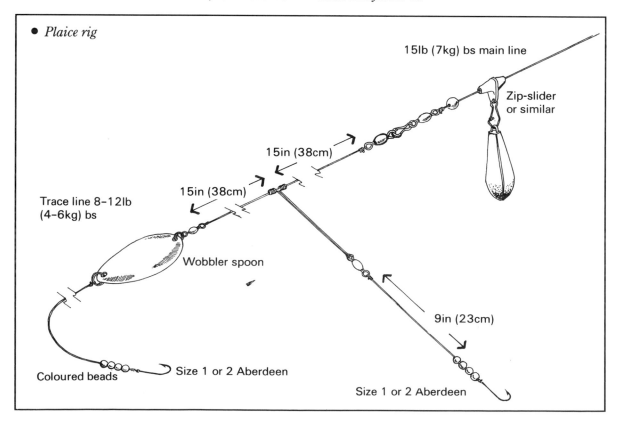

● *Plaice rig*

15lb (7kg) bs main line

Zip-slider or similar

15in (38cm)

15in (38cm)

Trace line 8–12lb (4–6kg) bs

Wobbler spoon

9in (23cm)

Coloured beads

Size 1 or 2 Aberdeen

Size 1 or 2 Aberdeen

oured beads, slid on the trace above the hooks; it certainly does no harm.

When fishing at anchor it pays to keep working the bait downtide, when there is enough flow to take the tackle away, as plaice respond to a moving bait. If fishing on the drift with a baited spoon, the bites are generally positive; but if you should miss a take, be ready to drop the lure back to give the fish another chance. When fishing bait on the drift, especially a substantial one such as a peeler/squid cocktail, it is essential to feed the fish a bit of line and give it time to take the bait when you feel one of those typical, plucking plaice bites. Not always easy to detect in forty feet of water on a windy day!

Plaice will take a variety of baits; among them are mackerel strip, hermit crab tails, squid, peeler crab, lugworm, ragworm, mussel, slipper limpet, razorfish and live sandeel: all will work well at times, but some are much better in some areas than others. For example, the peeler crab/squid strip cocktail is a bait favoured by Dartmouth skippers to take the big skerries plaice.

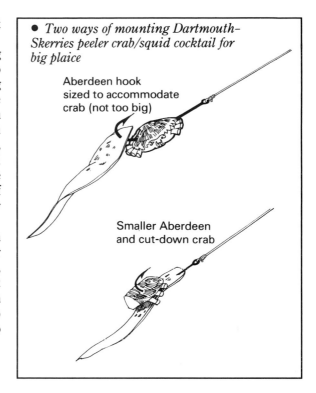

● *Two ways of mounting Dartmouth-Skerries peeler crab/squid cocktail for big plaice*

Aberdeen hook sized to accommodate crab (not too big)

Smaller Aberdeen and cut-down crab

Pollack

(*Pollachius pollachius*)

A fast-growing fish found all round the British coast, the pollack is most common off rocky areas of coastline. Dark brownish-green on its back, often with a scattering of fine black speckles fading to golden-yellow on the sides, and white underneath; and in certain areas of kelp, pollack will take on a distinct copper hue. They grow to a weight of almost 29lb (14kg). They feed at all depths but, like coalfish, probably spend most of their time in areas of mid-water.

These golden-olive fighters of reefs and wrecks are an angler's delight. They can be fished for with light tackle, yet the angler can expect to boat double-figure specimens over wrecks – provided, of course, he has remembered to set the drag on his reel correctly.

Pollack, especially small ones, will happily give themselves up to a set of mackerel feathers. Other specimens, sometimes exceptional ones, will occasionally take a large bait being fished on the bottom and intended for cod or conger. But the best pollack fishing lies in persuading a fish from the shoals in mid-water to grab an offering.

Tackle for pollack need not be heavy, and 20lb (10kg) class should be ample; many anglers today use a 4–8oz (125–250g) uptide rod for pollacking. They find the extra length of rod makes it a little

easier to present and control the ultra-long traces favoured by some pollack fishermen. End tackle consists of a swivelled flowing trace at least 8ft (2.4m) in length but up to 20ft (6m), connected to a stainless fine wire boom; the boom is attached to the main line with the weight linked underneath. A rotten bottom of nylon, weaker than the main line, may be used to attach the weight to the boom – though a freezer-bag tie can also be used.

Hook sizes will depend on fishing location and the type of bait or size of lure to be used. An inshore reef with ragworm as bait, where the average fish size may be only 3lb (1.4kg), would call for perhaps a 2/0 Aberdeen or some other fine wire hook. Over an offshore wreck or on deep-water reefs where the pollack run larger, hooks of 4/0 or 5/0 will be more appropriate.

The technique for catching pollack is similar to that for catching coalfish, and can be carried out on the drift or at anchor. For best results at anchor, precise positioning of the boat is required. The bait is lowered to the sea-bed, the long boom helping to prevent the trace tangling on the way down. On touching bottom a retrieve is begun immediately, and continued for sixty or seventy turns off the bottom; if no take occurs, the tackle is dropped down to bottom again and the procedure repeated. Pollack like a moving bait, but its speed can affect your catch rate. When drifting wrecks and using

149

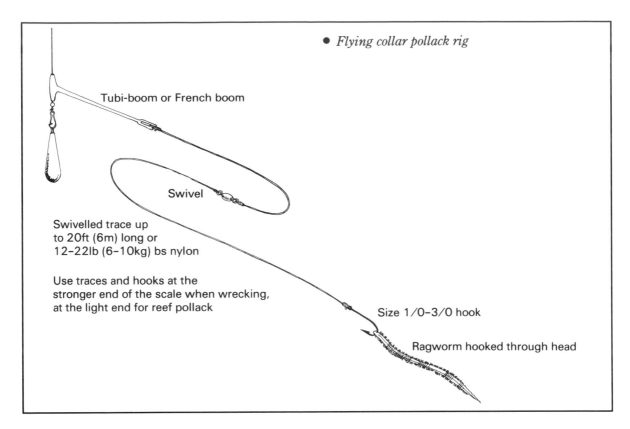

● *Flying collar pollack rig*

Tubi-boom or French boom

Swivel

Swivelled trace up
to 20ft (6m) long or
12–22lb (6–10kg) bs nylon

Use traces and hooks at the
stronger end of the scale when wrecking,
at the light end for reef pollack

Size 1/0–3/0 hook

Ragworm hooked through head

artificial eels, a fast retrieve is usually necessary; but live baits, king ragworm or sandeels do not need to be worked so fast – nor does a long flowing slice of mackerel, a good bait for pulling in the big fish. Over reefs, and when using ragworm or live sandeel, often only a very slow wind of the reel is required; again, however, wind quicker when using artificials.

If takes are not forthcoming, try varying the speed of retrieve. If the fish are finicky, and not taking a moving bait readily, use a ragworm bait – but stop at intervals on the retrieve, say at twenty, thirty and forty turns off the bottom. Pollack may ignore a bait momentarily going past, but they can't usually resist a live ragworm, wriggling under their nose for thirty seconds or so, if you can put one there.

A most important aspect of pollack fishing is *not* to strike at any takes; in a typical pollack take, you will feel the tip of your rod beginning to drag down as you wind your bait or lure upwards – at this point, stifle any other urges you may have and continue to wind at the same pace, until the fish turns and dives with the bait. Any reasonable pollack will make at least three deep diving runs – recover line in between if you can, but give the fish his head when he wants it. In deep water, pollack are

affected by water pressure changes as they are brought to the surface; otherwise they would probably equal coalfish in fighting ability.

Pouting
(*Trisopterus luscus*)

Also called 'pout', 'bib'; a moderate-sized member of the cod family, and found all around the coastline of Britain; it reaches a maximum weight of about 5lb (2.4kg). It is rather deep-bodied, with coppery-brown back and upper sides, becoming white beneath. Depending on the type of sea-bed that the pout is inhabiting, it may have four or five dark cross-bands on its flanks. It has a single barbel under the chin.

There is very little skill involved in catching pout, and they offer scant resistance when hooked, even on light tackle. Because of this, many sea angling competitions have put some sort of restriction on the numbers of pout – if any – that may be weighed in. No special technique is required to catch them, though a three-hook paternoster is probably the most efficient way of taking them in numbers. They do make useful baits for a variety of other fish, notably conger and bass.

Rays

Blonde ray

(*Raja bachura*)

This large ray has been caught in increasing numbers during recent years. It is at its northern limit in British waters and is mostly caught in the English Channel, Bristol Channel and southern parts of the Irish Sea. Its maximum recorded weight is 37lb 7oz (just over 17kg). As to colour, the back of the fish is light brown, with a few creamy blotches and a dense scattering of spots that extend to the wingtips; the belly is white.

Blonde rays are mainly found offshore, usually at depths of over 100ft (30m), but they can be taken quite close to land, near major promontories such as Start Point, Portland Bill and St Catherine's Point; they tend to lurk around the edges of deep banks. Because blonde rays are mainly found in deep water, wire line is often an asset in presenting a bait successfully, though braided Dacron, nylon line, even an uptide outfit can be used when the tide is not running strongly.

A soft-action, 50lb (24kg) class rod is the best one to use in conjunction with wire line, together with a powerful reel such as a Penn 4/0 or Shimano TLD 20. Use a running leger rig with a nylon leader and adjust weights to suit tidal conditions.

Squid baits are most effective – for example, two whole calamari mounted on a pennel hook rig of two 8/0 Daiwa Superstrikes or Mustad O'Shaughnessy hooks. An equally useful bait is a flappered fresh mackerel, or a mackerel fillet presented on a single hook. These rays are mainly caught in summer and autumn, but this may be because more effort is concentrated on likely areas then.

In some regions further west, off west Devon and Cornwall where the tide run is not as strong but the water is clearer, considerable success has been achieved with lighter, 12lb (5.4kg) tackle, and using both uptide and downtide methods. The local skippers insist on the light traces needed, though this does inevitably mean the loss of some fish. Fresh mackerel fillet is the most effective bait.

There has been a good deal of speculation as to why blonde ray catches have increased in recent years. My own view is that the upsurge is largely due to the greatly extended ranges now fished by both private and charter boats.

● *A 22lb (10kg) blonde ray that fell to a whole calamari squid bait*

Common skate

(*Raja batis*)

Skate also belong to the ray family Rajidae. The common skate is one of several skates with elongated snouts that live mostly in deep water. It is found offshore all round the British Isles, but is only taken regularly in a few locations: the southwest and west of Ireland; and off the west of Scotland. It is here that most of the British anglers interested in catching a large skate gravitate, particularly to the Isle of Mull and the harbour at Tobermory. Also of interest is the Glasgow Museum of Natural History, which in the early 1990s ran a tagging programme to improve our knowledge and understanding of the skate's lifestyle.

You can catch a modest or even large skate on 30lb (15kg) class gear if the tide and conditions are right; however, a 50lb (24kg) class rod gives a much better lever to lift the sheer weight of a big fish. A 4/0 or 6/0 sized reel, loaded with 50lb (24kg) bs line, makes up the outfit. As you will probably be fishing in deep water, braided line will give better bite detection. End gear is a basic running leger consisting of sliding boom, bead and link swivel, connected to a swivelled trace of heavy monofilament at least 125lb (57kg) bs about 6ft (1.8m) long. Hooks need to be strong; Mustad's O'Shaughnessy or Sea Demon in the 8/0–10/0 size range are ideal. A whole flapper or side of mackerel is the favourite bait, though herring or a split coalfish or pollack is acceptable; the bait is lowered to the sea-bed, and the wait is then on.

Do not strike at any initial bites you may think you can feel. The skate is a large fish, and it has to move over the bait before eating it, so it may well brush your main line with its wingtips as it does so. Give it time to take the bait and begin to move off with it; then, as it drags down the rod tip, lift and wind to set the hook, and keep winding to try and get the fish's head up. Once you have the skate coming in the right direction it is a matter of keeping the pressure on and wearing it down; and if it wants to go back to the bottom – and almost certainly it will when it sees daylight – you will have to let it go. You then face the struggle to haul it back from the depths again.

One conservation-minded skipper at Tobermory will weigh any fish caught at the side of the boat with the equipment he has rigged aboard, then tag it and return it to the sea. Long may his example last!

Small-eyed ray

(*Raja microocellata*)

A short-snouted ray reaching a maximum weight approaching 17lb (8kg). Its range extends well into the English Channel and southern parts of the Irish Sea. In colour it is sandy-brown on top with pale wavy streaks, and underneath it is white. The eyes, as the name suggests, are small.

This ray is popular with anglers along the south coast, where it moves inshore in late spring to deposit its eggs in areas of mixed sand and rock. Rays continue to be caught into December, at which time they seem to move offshore to overwinter before returning again in spring. They are caught on and around sandy banks and gullies, sometimes in quite shallow water. Though downtide techniques can be used quite successfully, these rays often respond best to uptide tactics.

Tackle should consist of a 4–8oz (125–250g) uptide rod and medium-size multiplier loaded with 15lb (7kg) line – don't forget your leader. Trace length needs to be about 5ft (1.5m). The use of small strong hooks often gives the most rewarding results. During the spring and summer months the best baits are small strips of fresh mackerel about 2in (5cm) long, and small fresh or blast-frozen sandeel – small-eyed rays love sandeel. In the autumn they readily take squid baits.

Strangely, for a fish quite prolific all around the Isle of Wight, they seldom venture inside the Solent itself.

● *A small-eyed ray, displayed here by Weymouth, Dorset angler Ivan Wellington. This fish fell to frozen sandeel bait, presented using uptide methods on the Freshwater reef area, off the Isle of Wight*

Spotted ray

(*Raja montagui*)

Also called 'homelyn ray': found throughout the English Channel and the western side of the British Isles to the north of Scotland, but rarely in the North Sea. The spotted ray is a honey-brown colour on its back with black spots which occasionally form an ocellus; the spots do not reach to the wingtips. It grows to weights in excess of 8lb (3.7kg).

Anglers would be hard pressed to fish specifically for these rays, but if you do catch one and are able to note the mark, you will probably catch more of the species if you continue to fish the same spot over the years, as they seem to have some preference to certain patches of ground.

Spotted ray move inshore from spring to late summer to lay their eggs, though even during this period they seem to prefer to keep well under water – by at least 30ft (9m) – and are seldom caught among the shallow banks and gullies where the thornback ray is often found. Tackle as for thornbacks will be quite adequate.

In the Solent area the spotted ray seem to have a preference for ragworm, though squid also catches its fair share – and both baits are superior to mackerel.

Thornback ray

(*Raja clavata*)

Also called 'roker': the commonest ray around the British Isles, and the most widely caught by anglers. It can reach weights in excess of 35lb (16kg), but the average size taken is about 7lb (3.4kg). It is found over all types of sea-bed, though is less common in rocky areas. The back is very variable, from purple shades to medium-brown to light grey, with yellow-white blotches, scatterings of black spots and occasional faint ocellus; the belly is light grey-white. Both male and female have 'thorns', though the adult female is generally more heavily covered.

Thornback rays will give a reasonable account of themselves when taken on uptide or 20lb (10kg) class tackle. Their wide range of depth and habitat means they are often taken when fishing for other species. Certain areas enjoy a run of thornbacks from mid-spring to early summer; for example, marks in the Bristol Channel, in Cardigan and Liverpool Bays, and on the offshore banks of Essex and Suffolk traditionally feature thornback rays amongst catches from the boats.

On the shallower marks, uptide tackle is probably the most productive style of fishing; use a running leger rig and a 25lb (12kg) bs trace 4ft (1.2m) long. Hook size is not critical, but hooks do need to be fairly strong: 2/0–4/0 uptide or uptide extras would be fine. Rays have grinders rather than teeth, but even so they can still do your fingers a bit of mischief so take care when unhooking them. Similarly, watch out for the spines; if lifting the ray by its tail to move or return it, use a cloth.

If downtiding for thornbacks in deeper water, you may have to step up to a 30lb (15kg) class outfit, particularly if there is any strength in the tide. It is also advisable to beef up the trace strength to 40lb (18kg) bs monofilament, and to use a strong hook – a 4/0 extra-strength or Mustad O'Shaughnessy – since bringing in a large ray against the tide can put substantial pressure on the hook and cause considerable abrasion to the trace.

Thornbacks will take any of the sea-angling baits, but along the south coast and in the Irish Sea they prefer fresh mackerel, and on the east coast herring are productive; these rays also like peeler crab, especially the spring run of fish. Squid, ragworm, lugworm and sandeel are all effective, and I have taken scores of thornback rays on hermit crab, while smooth-hound fishing.

Undulate ray

(*Raja undulata*)

Not a common ray, but possibly the most beautifully marked. In the British Isles it is only likely to be taken by anglers in the English and Bristol Channels and to the south and south-west of Ireland. It can reach a weight of 21lb (9.6kg). In colour it is variable yellow to mid-brown on top, with distinct, long wavy dark bands edged with light spots. The underneath is white. Tackle and tactics are as for blonde rays.

Sharks

Blue shark

(*Prionace glauca*)

This shark is at the extreme limits of its range off the western shores of Britain, and only appears there during the summer months and early autumn. Realistic angling chances are in the South West of England and along the west coast of Ireland.

The blue shark is long and slender, its back a beautiful deep blue colour, fading to a lighter blue on the sides and becoming white on the belly. It can reach weights exceeding 400lb (182kg), though the largest caught in British waters was 218lb (99kg). It was fairly common in the South West until a few years ago, but the killing of too many fish by anglers both in this country and abroad, as well as commercial pressure by overseas fisheries, has led to a decline in its numbers. Charter skippers and anglers are more enlightened now, and nearly all blue shark taken by anglers are returned.

For a number of reasons, the tackle needed to fish for blue shark doesn't have to be heavy. First, you will not be fishing on the bottom, so you have not got the problem of large amounts of lead; second, you will most likely be fishing on the drift, so you won't have to bring a fish in against the tide; and finally, the blue shark is a free-running fish – it isn't going to head behind the nearest patch of rock,

● *Sharks are big, powerful creatures. Plan how you intend to deal with them before they are alongside the boat*

it will fight you in the open sea. All of which means a 30lb (15kg) class rod and a good quality reel loaded with at least 300yd (275m) of 30lb (15kg) bs line; the Shimano TLD 20 with its lever drag control is ideal, and as long as its clutch is in first-class condition, it should be quite adequate for any blue shark you are likely to encounter in UK seas.

A butt pad may be useful, though I have seen a great many fish lost through an angler's haste to put the rod into the butt seat, before the fish was hooked properly. So use only when required, and when a secure hookhold has been ascertained.

The technique for blue shark fishing is carried out from a drifting boat, and normally some way offshore. It requires a good supply of fresh mackerel, some for bait but most for two rubby dubby bags. The mackerel should be mashed or minced, and the filled bags hung either side of the boat so they dip just below the surface of the water as the boat rolls. Add some bran and pilchard oil to the mix to extend its life and enhance its effectiveness. The idea is to set up a scent trail that a shark will follow up until it arrives at the boat and finds the bait presented. This is usually a single whole dead mackerel mounted on a 10/0 hook, but a live mackerel can also be used; live baits should be presented on a

smaller, short-shanked hook – Mustad's model 9175 in a 6/0 size would be perfect.

The hooks, which should be checked and honed to needle sharpness, are attached to a 6ft (2m) long wire trace; in Britain this is traditionally cable-laid wire of at least 100lb (45kg) bs. The bite ratio might be increased by using a stainless single strand wire trace; though less supple, it would be a good deal thinner than multistrand wire for the same breaking strain and thus less visible, and will still stand up to a shark's teeth. The wire trace is connected via a swivel to a rubbing leader of 100lb (45kg) bs nylon about 15ft (4.6m) long. If this is connected to the main line by a knot rather than a swivel, you will be able to reel in the leader if necessary when bringing a fish alongside for capture or release. The leader and baited wire trace is suspended from a float astern of the boat – the float need be no more than a balloon or plastic bottle.

Several baits are usually fished at different depths, with about 20ft (6m) between them. The rods are then put in free spool on the ratchet. Sometimes a bite is indicated when all at once the float dives and a zipping run occurs; more often, however, it is the float bobbing around which indicates the first enquiries by a shark. Some anglers and skippers assert you should wait for the first run to stop and for a second run to begin, before putting the reel in gear and setting the hook. That is fair enough, but sometimes the fish will drop the bait and no second run occurs, and you are left regretting that you didn't strike the first time!

Whether using a lever or a star drag reel, it should be pre-set to allow the strike when it is put in gear. This should be set at one-third of the line's breaking strain, no more, and can be done ashore with a spring balance.

Once a fish is hooked, other lines should be wound in. Then it is a matter of letting the fish have its head when it wants it, but keeping the pressure on until it is alongside the boat. There is no need to use a gaff, though having a couple handy for any unexpected circumstance is not a bad idea. If the fish is not to be freed straight away, it can be tailed using a 20ft (6m) length of ½in (13mm) rope, with a stout snap-shackle spliced to one end and a loop at the other. This can be used to form an instant loop that can be passed around the angler's line and over the shark's head like a lasso, then pulled up to tighten on the wrist of the shark's tail.

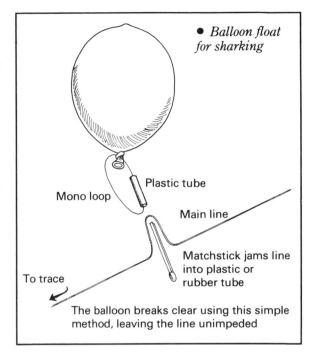

• *Balloon float for sharking*

Plastic tube

Mono loop

Main line

Matchstick jams line into plastic or rubber tube

To trace

The balloon breaks clear using this simple method, leaving the line unimpeded

Mako
(*Isurus oxyrinchus*)

The mako shark is recognised worldwide as a game fish, and specimens have been caught in British waters up to 500lb (226kg). It is deep blue or blue-grey in colour, with a white lower half. However, very few have been caught in UK waters in the past, and it is unrealistic for anglers to fish specifically for makos. There is evidence to suggest that they may be encountered near underwater pinnacle rock. Odd fish taken by commercial long-liners indicate there is a chance of taking a mako anywhere off the south-west of England, the west of Ireland or north-west Scotland. Some lucky angler will no doubt one day spot one finning on the surface. If he has the right gear with him – tackle at least as substantial as that required for porbeagles – he may persuade it to take a bait, and with luck will boat it.

Porbeagle
(*Lamna nasus*)

A large, deep-bodied shark, its range extends all round the British Isles, though it is not often encountered in the lower North Sea. This could be said to be the British shark, as all the significant catches of the species, including the world all-tackle record of 465lb (211kg), have been made in UK waters. Padstow, in north Cornwall, has become the porbeagle angler's Mecca. The shark is blue-grey on its back, becoming light cream underneath. Commercial long-line fishing for porbeagles takes place off the west coast of Ireland and the north of Scotland.

The largest porbeagle seem to be confined to the seas either side of the south-west of England, the west of Ireland and the north-west of Scotland; smaller porbeagle are frequently encountered throughout the English Channel and Irish Sea. These smaller porbeagles – up to 100lb (46kg) – are often found lurking over wrecks, and will frequently take fish that have been caught and are being reeled in, biting them off angler's lines and causing tangles in the process. These smaller porbeagles can be taken on the tackle described for blue shark; a live bait is frequently better than a dead one.

For tackling the larger porbeagle it is advisable to step up a gear to at least 50lb (24kg) class tackle, and the quality multiplier – preferably a lever drag – needs to hold at least 450yd (410m) of low stretch mono. The rubbing leader should increase as well, to at least 200lb (91kg) bs and the wire trace to 300lb (135kg) bs. Set up a rubby dubby scent trail as for blue shark; dead mackerel baits will take the porbeagle, but live baits of mackerel can also be very successful, or better still cod, pollack or coalfish in the 2lb (1kg) range.

With any shark fishing, anglers must be ready to move around the vessel as the fish charges off in different directions, and to keep the line away from the keel and rudder if the fish dives under the boat. The larger the shark, the more powerful it is, and potentially more damaging to your boat. I would suggest that anyone contemplating sharking makes his first trips with an experienced sharking skipper. How to deal with a shark once it is caught and alongside involves careful consideration. The rope lasso is one option, but both the lasso and fish gaffs (of forged steel) if you are going to use them, need to be well made, with a good gape of at least 5in (13cm) and about 9in (23cm) or so in the throat. A pair of bolt croppers is also necessary for quick release of the wire – your average sidecutters might struggle with 400lb (182kg) cable-laid wire, especially if you have a big porbeagle thrashing about on the other end.

Thresher
(*Alopias vulpinus*)

A summer visitor but only occasionally sighted, and this could be anywhere around the British Isles. It is most likely to be encountered around the Isle of

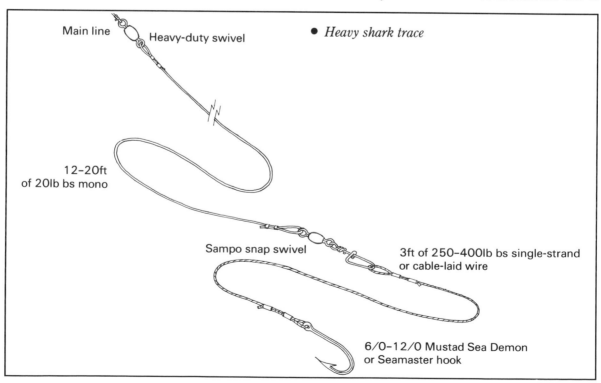

Main line

Heavy-duty swivel

● *Heavy shark trace*

12–20ft of 20lb bs mono

Sampo snap swivel

3ft of 250–400lb bs single-strand or cable-laid wire

6/0–12/0 Mustad Sea Demon or Seamaster hook

Wight and the south-west English Channel, but it is never common. The chances of catching a thresher are therefore limited, particularly as an angler wishing to catch one has only a brief period to do so, from maybe sometime in June until the end of August.

There is no mistaking the thresher: it has a long, sickle-shaped tail and a short snout, and is grey-blue to near black in colour, with white on the belly. It is said to use the tail to herd fish together before attacking them.

Tackle for threshers needs to be of the same standard as for large porbeagles – a 50lb (24kg) class rod with a quality multiplier, containing at least 450 yards (410m) of 50lb (24kg) bs low stretch monofilament or braided Dacron. Threshers are likely to run further than porbeagles – 300yd (275m) runs in one hit are not uncommon. Fishing methods and ways of coping with the fish once alongside should follow the same lines as for large porbeagle.

● *A double-figure summer smooth-hound. This is the unspotted variety* (mustellus mustellus)

Smooth-hound and Starry smooth-hound

(*Mustellus mustellus* and *Mustellus asterias*)

For both species of smooth-hound, tackle, bait and fishing technique are the same, and so are the areas they are likely to be found. The fish is a slender-bodied shark which grows to weights of 28lb (12.7kg), possibly more. The mouth and teeth are very similar to a skate's, and in some parts of the world it is known as the skate-toothed shark.

Mustellus mustellus has plain grey back and sides, and occasionally a few black spots or blotches; there are no noticeable white spots. Its underside is creamy-white. It is viviparous, and more than a dozen young can be born at a time.

Mustellus asterias is the more common of the two species; it is grey on its top and sides with a scattering of white spots, occasionally quite dense. The nasal flaps are somewhat narrower than the plain smooth-hound. The starry smooth-hound is ovoviviparous, and up to a dozen young may be born at one time.

Smooth-hound are mainly taken by anglers from April through to September, the mid-summer months usually seeing the best catches. Although they may turn up anywhere around the British Isles, there are particular areas where they always

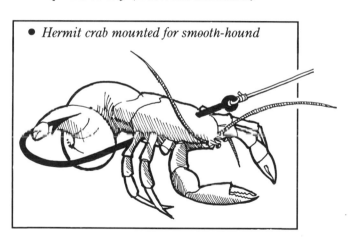

● *Hermit crab mounted for smooth-hound*

feature strongly; these are around the Anglesey region of Wales, the estuaries and offshore banks of Essex, and around the Isle of Wight, the Solent and Nab Tower grounds.

Crab-bait is the key to catching smooth-hounds, and they are not too fussy whether it is peeler, hard-back or hermit (note that with hard-back, however, you are unlikely to take fish other than smooth-hound). The next most successful offering after crab is a multi-worm bait of king ragworm.

Most smooth-hound fishing is done using uptide or 20lb (10kg) class rods and medium-size multipliers loaded with 15–20lb (7–10kg) bs line. This tackle allows smooth-hounds to show off their speed and sporting prowess, especially in shallow water; though for this sort of fishing, clutches need to be checked and hounds given their head when they want to run. When fishing relatively deep marks where the fish feed through the tide, 50lb (24kg) class rods and wire line are necessary.

End tackle will be similar in either case: a simple running leger rig of zip slider, bead, link swivel and swivelled 5ft (1.5m) trace of 35lb (16kg) bs nylon, culminating in a sharp hook – a Cox & Rawles uptide, or a Mustad Vikings model 79515 in about size 3/0 would be fine. When deep water and strong tides necessitate wire line, it is advisable to step up to a 50lb (24kg) bs nylon trace and an extra-strength hook. The skin of the smooth-hound is quite abrasive, and in a lengthy tussle it could well abrade the line; a 50lb (24kg) mono trace reduces this risk.

Though competition anglers may want to use more than one hook, this can be risky as large smooth-hounds are powerful fish and spare hooks flying about at netting or tailing time are not a good idea.

The smooth-hound has a twelve-month gestation period, and with only seven to fifteen pups a litter, they are very susceptible to overfishing. Therefore return as many as possible to the sea after capture, doing them as little harm as possible in the process.

Sole

(*Solea solea*)

A slender-bodied flatfish, distributed all around the British Isles. It has a peculiar, small curved mouth. In colour the top is a medium- to dark-brown, sometimes almost black in large specimens. Sole can reach weights in excess of 6lb (2.8kg). During the summer when water temperatures rise, they move inshore; August is usually the best month to seek them. As the coastal water cools they move offshore again, and are seldom caught on rod and line after November. Sole are not widely sought by boat anglers, and in fact you have a better chance of catching one from the shore. They travel, and are taken by trawlers offshore, but when they can be persuaded to take a bait, it is usually within 50yd (46m) of the shore-line, if not closer, during the hours of darkness. The boat angler wishing to catch sole should bear this in mind.

At one time I briefly held the boat-caught sole record: when I caught that fish it was 2am, and I was anchored 50yd (46m) off a private beach, the fish being hooked almost in the slight surf.

A 12lb (6kg) class rod would cope with any sole, but there is always a chance of running into other, larger fish. In the Solent, sting ray and smooth-hound both move into the same margins that sole can be expected in and at the same times of year. My own choice when specifically targeting sole, is a 20lb (10kg) class outfit, with end tackle a basic running leger concluding in a 5ft (1.5m) trace of 18lb (8.3kg) bs nylon, with a size 6 model perfect hook at the business end. This is a small but strong hook suitable for sole, that will still give a chance of success if the bait is taken by some larger, more powerful fish.

Solent sole like ragworm and plenty of them, three or four threaded on the shank of the hook and up the line. Elsewhere, smaller baits are more successful, sometimes just little pieces of lugworm or ragworm. Sole seem to feed best during the high- or low-water period, over the turn of the tide.

Spurdog

(*Squalus acanthias*)

The spurdog is a small sharp-toothed shark that can reach a size of 20lb (9.6kg); it is distributed all around the British Isles. In front of each dorsal fin is a sharp spine which can cause a nasty puncture wound if the fish is handled carelessly. The back is grey-coloured, with a scattering of white spots on most fish. The spurdog is ovoviviparous and bears only 3–11 young at a time. The gestation period is 18–22 months, and females are not sexually mature until they are about 30in (75cm) long. This fish is therefore very susceptible to overfishing.

Though spurdog move closer to shore to give birth, they prefer to stay in water deeper than 100ft (30m). A 30lb (15kg) class rod and medium multiplier reel loaded with matching line is appropriate for spurdog on most occasions, though in areas of strong tide a 50lb (24kg) wire line outfit may be required.

End tackle should be a conventional running leger, with a 5ft (1.5m) nylon trace to which is attached a 1ft (30cm) length of 50lb (24kg) bs wire; this is connected to a strong size 3/0–5/0 hook. The wire is necessary to defeat the spurdog's sharp teeth – heavy nylon 100lb (45kg) bs plus will stand up to a certain amount of chomping, but a large spur is still liable to bite through it.

Spurdog are not too fussy about what they eat, and any squid or fish bait fillet will be wolfed down. Spurdog will often appear when anglers are winter cod-fishing on offshore marks, slashing into double squid 8/0 hook pennel-rigged baits. The angler wishing to catch them will switch to smaller hook and bait size, plus a wire hook-length; some consider a muppet above the hook an additional spurdog attractor.

Sting ray
(*Dasyatis pastinaca*)

The sting ray is similar in shape to most other rays, though the bulk of its weight is concentrated in the middle of its body, giving large fish a sinister hump-backed appearance. In coloration the upper part of the fish is variously brown or olive, the underside being creamy-white fading to grey near the wingtips.

Sting ray are taken at times all around the British Isles, and on these occasions fall to a variety of baits including fish and squid. However, there are only two regions where an angler can fish for sting ray with any realistic intention: the confluence of the rivers Blackwater, Colne and Crouch in Essex; and the western Solent, between the Isle of Wight and

the mainland. The huge majority of large sting ray caught by British anglers are taken from these two areas. And here, there are only two baits worth considering: peeler crab and ragworm.

Sting ray can be taken on conventional 20lb (10kg) class boat tackle, but any sort of tide flow makes this a hard task. A powerful uptider could cope, especially on shallow marks. But to be certain of success, a 30lb (15kg) outfit is preferable. In shallow water the tackle can still be cast from the boat, and it will probably cope better with heavyweight sting ray.

A simple running leger end rig, with a 5ft (1.5m) trace of 40lb (18kg) bs nylon, culminating in a strong forged 3/0 hook, completes the tackle. If ragworm is the chosen bait be prepared to use plenty, six or seven worms at least; slide them around the shank of the hook and up the trace. Peeler crab is considered the premier bait for the Essex area, ragworm being preferred in the Solent.

Tope
(*Galeorhinus galeus*)

The tope is a slender-bodied shark, reaching weights in excess of 80lb (36kg). It is found throughout the coastal waters of Britain. In colour it is grey or grey-brown on the back and sides, becoming white underneath. It is ovoviviparous and bears up to forty young at a time; gestation period is about ten months.

Except for a few areas of strong tide where it may be necessary to use a wire line outfit, a 30lb (15kg) class boat rod, medium multiplier and matching line is powerful enough to deal with any tope. The multiplier should be set with about 10lb (4.8kg) of drag. On shallower marks, around offshore banks and shoals, 6–10oz (120–300g) uptide tackle is perfectly adequate. Whether uptiding or downtiding, the end tackle needs to be a running leger. Uptide gear, which should already have a substantial leader to permit casting, requires a 6ft (1.8m) trace of 60lb (27kg) bs monofilament with a swivelled 1ft (30cm) hook-length of 60lb (27kg) bs braided wire and a forged 7/0 hook. Downtide tackle may favour a slightly longer trace, 8ft (2.4m) or so of 60lb (27kg) bs nylon with a 1ft (30cm) length of the same wire joining the 7/0 hook and trace.

The number one bait for tope is now recognised as segments of silver eel: a number of charter skippers at Bradwell, Essex, experimented and proved

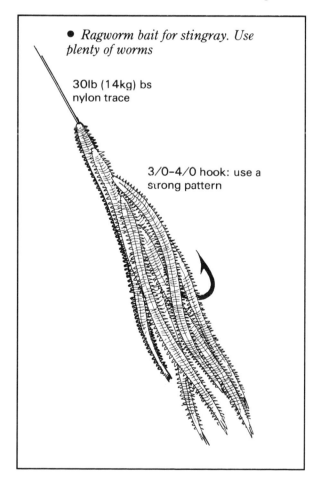

- *Ragworm bait for stingray. Use plenty of worms*

30lb (14kg) bs nylon trace

3/0-4/0 hook: use a strong pattern

- *This out-of-season tope of about 34lb (15.5kg), photographed prior to its return, took a squid bait intended for cod, south of the Isle of Wight in January*

squid bait and I suspect they would also feed on whole baby cuttlefish.

One theory of how to deal with a tope bite, is that the angler should allow the fish to run unchecked, wait for it to stop, and then to start running again, before finally setting the hook. The idea is that the tope then has time to turn the bait in his mouth and swallow it. Personally, I prefer to set the hook as soon as the tope has built up some speed after picking up the bait. I may miss the odd specimen, but it reduces the chance of gut-hooking the fish. A big tope on the tackle described will put up a good fight, but the angler should always be sufficiently equipped so he can put on the pressure when necessary in order to beat the fish. Balanced, sporting tackle is best and not overlight gear; for the well-being of the fish, the quicker it is beaten the better, as long fights cause a build-up of lactic acid in the muscles, and this reduces its chances of recovery.

its worth with some magnificent tope catches, and the bait has since been proved to work in other areas. Off Selsey Bill in Sussex some good catches have been made, and also off St Catherine's Point on the Isle of Wight. If mackerel were not so easy to obtain, more anglers might make the effort to acquire eels. Tope will also readily take a large

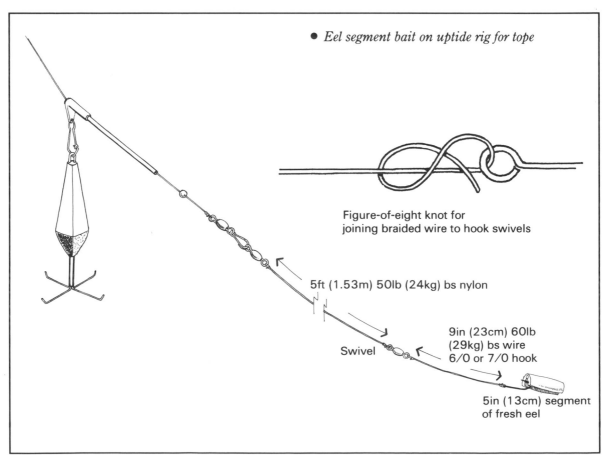

- *Eel segment bait on uptide rig for tope*

Figure-of-eight knot for joining braided wire to hook swivels

5ft (1.53m) 50lb (24kg) bs nylon

Swivel

9in (23cm) 60lb (29kg) bs wire
6/0 or 7/0 hook

5in (13cm) segment of fresh eel

● *Staines, Middlesex, angler Andrew Flintham, took this beautiful meagre off Biarritz, France (see pp184–5)*

Turbot

(*Scopthalmus maximus*)

Though it is caught all around the British Isles, the turbot is towards the limit of its range here, and becomes less common in the north of the country. A broad-bodied flatfish, its coloration is varied to match the bed of the sea, usually mid-sandy brown with irregular darker spots and blotches and white speckles. It grows to weights of 33lb (15.3kg), and commercially it is highly valuable and sought-after. Sea anglers probably prize the turbot above all flatfish.

Certain well-known offshore banks are traditional angling areas for turbot: the Varne, Shambles and Skerries are three well-known marks in the English Channel, but any offshore sandbank is a potential turbot mark, including the scours and sandbanks that occur around some wrecks. It is here that the very biggest turbot are sometimes found.

Both uptide and downtide running leger methods can be employed to catch turbot; though uptiding success depends on the depth of water and strength of tide over the bank. Downtiding means that really long traces of 25lb (12kg) bs nylon can be used, up to 12ft (3.7m) in length; and on the tip of 3/0 forged hooks the angler can impale slender, inch-wide mackerel strip baits, up to 1ft (30cm) long, that waft enticingly in the tide and can be trotted away to seek out the turbot.

Downtide tackle should require nothing heavier than a 30lb (15kg) class outfit, even for wrecking. On some banks at extreme states of the tide, wire may be needed for a few hours, though a 30lb (15kg) rod should still be sufficient.

The banks and shoals that produce turbot to anglers fishing from boats at anchor, can sometimes be more successfully fished using live sandeel fished on the drift. This method allows lighter tackle to be employed, as only enough lead to feel bottom is required: for example a 20lb (10kg) class rod, a 10ft (3m) monofilament trace of 25lb (12kg) bs, and a 3/0 or 4/0 fine wire hook, fished off a wire boom or a sliding tubi-boom. The live sandeel is mounted in the traditional way, the hook slipped through the mouth and nicked in the belly, and the bait kept close to the bottom on the drift. Turbot give a fluttering sensation as they take the bait, like a giant dab bite; they do not put up a great struggle once hooked, but more than make up for that with their superb flavour.

Whiting

(*Merlangus merlangus*)

A member of the cod-fish family, the whiting is a slender-bodied fish, reaching a maximum size of about 7lb (3kg). It is very common throughout British waters, and in some areas is caught regularly all year round. It is most prolific in the autumn, when the shoals move close inshore. In coloration the body of the juvenile fish is sandy-copper on top; as it matures this becomes olive, fading into silver-mottled sides with gold flecks. The belly is white, and there is a dark spot at the base of the pectoral fin.

Whiting can be taken on virtually any tackle, and generally speaking are an eager fish to feed. On shallow banks, anglers using conventional uptide gear may take them singly or in quantity, depending on the number of hooks and the bait sizes they are using. The fish will feed right through the sweep of the tide, but may go 'off the bite' at peak flow on springs. The whiting is a predatory fish. Off the banks, in deeper areas, there are times when they will rise to feed in mid-water; this generally coincides with high or low tide, or the hours either side when the tide is flowing gently. Any good echo-sounder should be able to pick out the fish as they hover clear of the bottom.

Whiting can be taken on the simplest of rigs – a set of baited mackerel feathers is a very efficient way of catching them in numbers. A more sporting outfit would be a fast-action, 12lb (6kg) class rod, lightweight multiplier and matching line. Fish either a single trace about 5ft (1.5m) long, with a size 1 Kamasan Aberdeen or uptide hook, off a wire or plastic boom; use just enough lead weight to touch bottom comfortably.

Bait with ragworm or lugworm, a sliver of mackerel, squid or herring, and just wind gently off the sea-bed until you feel the whiting attacking the bait. A quick strike or a faster wind usually ensures the fish is on.

Larger whiting of 2–4lb (1–2kg) provide excellent sport. Use a two-hook, two-boom rig to improve the catch rate, the booms about 2ft (60cm) apart, with traces 20in (50cm) long and size 1 hooks; drop this rig to the bottom and retrieve it in the same way as the single hook rig. The addition of some corrugated silver paper, slid up the trace above the hook, will sometimes improve the catch-rate even further.

● *Always welcome in any fisherman's bag, this turbot is one of the tastiest fish in the sea*

Wrasse (ballan)

(*Labrus bergylta*)

The largest of a number of wrasse to be found in European waters. Its coloration depends on age, habitat and reproductive condition, and ranges from greeny-brown to bright speckled red; the belly and fins are spotted with white, and the scale edges are dark. The fish reaches weights of 9lb 6oz (4.25kg). Wrasse are rock- and reef-dwelling fish found in relatively shallow water; they are of no culinary distinction and have no significant commercial value in Britain. They are mainly dormant during the deep winter months and are vulnerable to severe winters, when they may die in large numbers. For the rest of the year they can usually be relied on to provide sport for the angler.

Wrasse belong in the rocks, and they know it – they will head straight for the nearest crevice as soon as they take a bait. This means you are bound to lose some tackle! For ballans, a fast-action 12lb (6kg) or 20lb (10kg) class rod is needed, a lightweight multiplier, and matching line. Keep end gear as simple as is practicable; to reduce tackle losses, keep zip sliders, beads, swivels and so on, to the minimum.

A good simple end rig for wrasse is a trace tied direct to a blood loop off the main line – though not too light a trace as wrasse have sharp teeth; you can use a swivel to connect it to the blood loop if you like. Attach your weight using a rotten bottom via a Mustad split link. I depend on Aberdeen hooks to avoid most tackle losses; a 1/0 or 2/0 will hold pretty well any wrasse, but when these hooks snag a rock, steady pressure will generally spring them out. The disadvantage is, that if you should hook some other large powerful fish, the same steady pressure might cost you a hookhold! You can improve your chances of staying in contact with a really large fish by buoying your grapnel and rigging a quick release to your warp (a good general practice for all anchoring).

The wrasse is another fish that loves crabs, and like smooth-hound will happily eat small hardbacks, ones about 1in (2.5cm) across the carapace; peeler crabs are even better. They will also devour ragworm and lugworm and are partial to prawns; they are one of the few fish that will eat rock lim-

pets. Their large front teeth look as though they could scrunch small limpets straight off the rocks.

Ballans are inquisitive fish and always attracted by movement, so lifting the bait regularly often induces a bite. Another gimmick that sometimes speeds up the action is to use a white or coloured plastic spoon above your bait as an attractor.

163

15 Getting afloat

MANY ANGLERS GET THEIR FIRST taste of boat fishing on holiday, perhaps on a summer mackerel trip. However, those excursions where you tow a great heavy lead and a set of feathers attached to a hand-line are surely just as likely to put someone off angling. Some skippers are more enlightened and supply very basic rod and reel outfits; they may also give you the chance to try more general fishing. Even so, there are ways to get afloat and start fishing which are better value.

Probably the best and easiest way to begin boat angling is to join a club that runs regular charter trips. There are many sea-angling clubs around the country, and newcomers will undoubtedly benefit from the advice and experience that is within such a group. Some of these are quite informal, based perhaps at a local pub; many companies have sea-

angling sections within their social clubs; and others are old-established sea-angling clubs that cover all aspects of the sport. Newly formed clubs sometimes advertise for new members in sea-angling magazines. If you find a convenient club, you might make the following sort of enquiry: the frequency of trips, the venues, the availability of spaces, the deposit or payments required, and what travel arrangements, if any, there are for members.

Some clubs have their own boat or boats; these may range from small dinghies up to craft suitable for professional chartering. The skipper should always be an experienced, competent person. Most clubs have a boat commodore and some sort of system to check the ability of those wishing to skipper their boats. If they haven't, they should.

If you cannot find a club that suits your taste or

● (Above) *Roger Bayzand, skipper of the Lymington-based* Sundance II, *gaffs a large ling from a mid-Channel wreck*

● (Right) *A hefty Solent smooth-hound that fell to hermit-crab bait*

needs, you may wish to book an individual trip on a charter boat. Many skippers have days mid-week when they will take individuals, to make up a crew for a trip they would otherwise lose; there are sometimes advertisements to this effect, in the charter boat columns of the angling press. Perhaps you would like a trip with a specific skipper, but cannot raise a full party yourself: contact him, and ask if he can fit you in on one of his charters. He may be able to find a place for you either on an individual basis, or with one of his regular parties.

Should you know other potential anglers of like mind, you could arrange a charter yourselves. If you don't know which boat and skipper to choose, you will find that a number of charter boat skippers advertise in the angling press. These will usually indicate the equipment the boat is fitted with: the navigation aid system, such as Decca or GPS; the type of echo sounder; radio and safety gear. Also how fast it is, which could mean more fishing time and more options – though if you are booking just an inshore trip, a faster and therefore usually more expensive boat may not be necessary. It is preferable if the skipper is a member of the NFCS (National Federation of Charter Skippers) as this dictates a certain code of conduct, and also provides

adequate insurance cover; many skippers do not specify their membership in their adverts, however.

Once you have decided on a port and skipper, make the booking, and enquire about the type of fishing, how much choice there is, and the tackle required. Indicate to the skipper the extent of your experience and ask what types and quantity of baits you need, whether he can supply bait and if so, at what cost. Agree the full charter price, the deposit required, the embarkation point and the date and time of departure. Ask about parking if it is a strange venue. Send your deposit and an s.a.e. for a receipt and confirmation of all the relevant details, also a contact time and telephone number so you can ring up before the trip to confirm there is no cancellation due to weather or breakdowns.

If you know, or know of, an experienced angler with his own boat, ask if he would be prepared to take you out; and if he agrees, ask what tackle and bait to bring and if he would like help digging or gathering bait. This sort of thing would all be to your own benefit. You will probably be asked to assist around the boat before the trip is done, and don't hesitate to offer – skippers like their crew to show willing, even if they then prefer to do the job themselves. Offer something towards the fuel

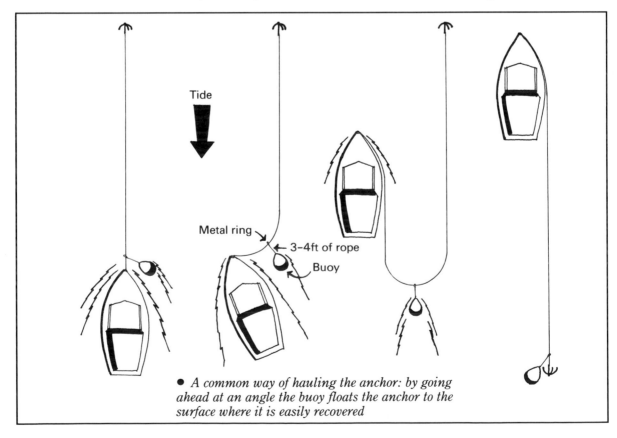

● *A common way of hauling the anchor: by going ahead at an angle the buoy floats the anchor to the surface where it is easily recovered*

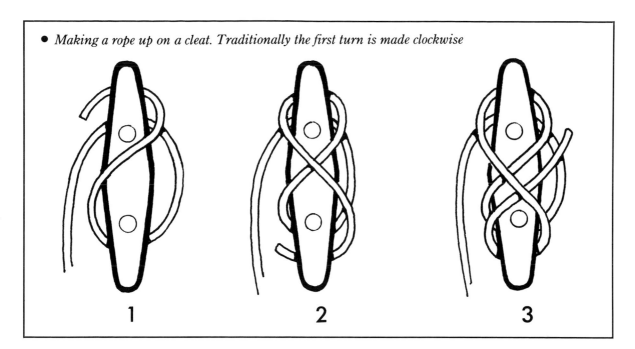

● *Making a rope up on a cleat. Traditionally the first turn is made clockwise*

1   **2**   **3**

costs, and when the trip is over, help secure the boat on its moorings or winch it on its trailer. This is all part of the learning programme.

An angler once asked me for a trip to fish a club dinghy competition – he duly came, but on return, he leapt ashore with his gear, jumped into his car and shot off to the weigh in; he didn't help unload the boat, let alone secure it. *He* didn't get any more trips!

Clothing

Before you go afloat, make sure you have sensible and adequate clothing; it is usually an overcoat colder at sea, and in cold weather it may be a good idea to wear a set of thermal underwear. One of the finest things a boat angler can buy is a top quality flotation suit, which will keep you warm, dry and – if you fall in the oggin – afloat. The leading brand is Mullion. Don't confuse flotation suits with lifejackets: a lifejacket by definition will turn and float an unconscious person face upwards; flotation suits and personal buoyancy aids will just assist in keeping you afloat. It is good practice to wear some sort of flotation device, if not a full lifejacket at all times afloat. Be sure that any vessel you go to sea in carries sufficient lifejackets for *everyone* aboard.

You will need a good set of wet weather gear, for this you need look no further than Guy Cotton oilskins. Tough, practical, reasonably priced and, moreover, widely used by commercial fishermen,

the hooded jacket and bib-and-brace trousers are ideal for angling.

Footwear should be designed for marine use and have a nonslip sole. Traditional wellingtons are impractical; they are stiff, cold and clumsy, and make dirty black marks all over the deck. Yachting boots are much more sensible, and consider buying them a half-size larger than necessary so you can wear extra socks in cold weather. On boats that you know are dry-decked, you may prefer to wear yachting shoes, when conditions permit.

Tides

A boat angler should always carry a good set of up-to-date tide tables, though remember these are normally expressed in GMT, so you may have to add on an hour when on BST.

For any fishing trip, the tide is a prime consideration: not just the time of high and low water, but the size of the tide, too – is it a neap or a spring tide? is it backing, or making? Tides have an enormous effect on fish and their feeding behaviour. They also influence sea conditions, and the direction and speed of water flow and currents, and these in turn will affect travelling time to and from fishing marks.

Spring tides coincide with the full and new moons, when the gravitational pull of the sun and moon are in line and at their greatest. These are the tides that give the largest rise and fall of water level and therefore the strongest flow of tide. Neap tides give the lowest rise and fall, and occur when the

● (Left) *This competitor from Gibraltar was pleased with his 7lb (3.3kg) reef pollack. The fish fell to ragworm bait*

● (Below) *38lb (17.5kg) of writhing conger effortlessly swung aboard* Sundance II *by skipper Roger Bayzand*

sun and moon are at 90° to each other in relation to the earth. The tidal cycle takes place over a period of approximately twenty-eight days, going from springs to neaps every seven days. All these factors influence the fishing options available, and should be considered by skipper and angler alike when planning a trip.

Once you have experienced a few sessions, and have become more familiar with dinghy and charter boat fishing, you will probably start to be more discriminating, and begin to favour certain aspects of boat angling more than others. Alternatively you may be so enthralled by it all, that any time afloat is a pleasure!

How the position of the moon affects the tides

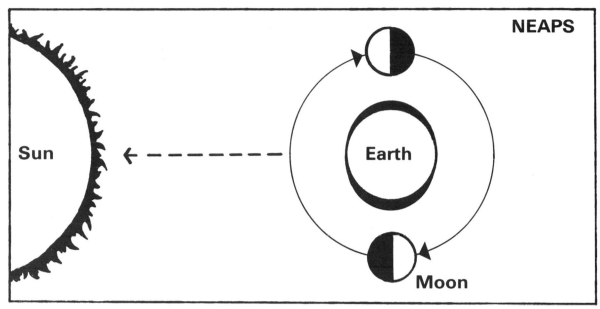

Moon at right angles to earth and sun creates neap tides

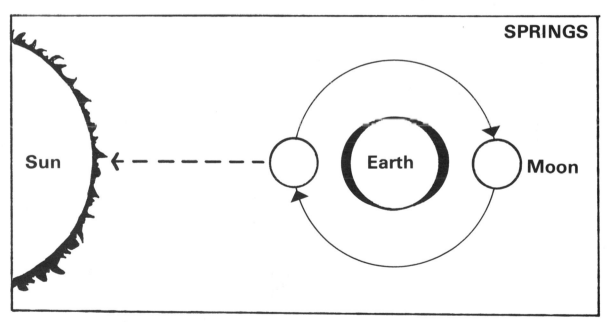

Earth, sun and moon in line creates spring tides

ICELAND

Sea areas

South-east Iceland

Faroes

Viking

Bailey

Fair Isle

Hebrides

Forties

Cromarty

Forth

Fisher

Rockall

Malin

Dogger

Tyne

German Bight

Irish Sea

Humber

Shannon

Fastnet

Lundy

Thames

Dover

Wight

Plymouth

Sole

Portland

Always check the weather forecast for your area before putting to sea

Finisterre

Biscay

Trafalgar

16 Competition boat fishing

BOAT ANGLING COMPETITIONS TWENTY-FIVE or thirty years ago were mainly confined to annual events at the big seaside resorts, generally sponsored by the local authorities. Today, clubs up and down the country run regular in-house competitions for their members; these decide who the club champion will be, and give him the chance to compete at bigger events such as the TVS Championship and NFSA Champion of Champions.

The major angling organisations are the National Federation of Sea Anglers, the British Conger Club, the European Federation of Sea Anglers, and the NFSA Divisions, and all of these hold annual championships open to their members. In addition, with the growth of small boat fishing, a number of regular, well-supported 'dinghy festivals' now take place around the country. While these competitions in no way match the opportunities available to the shore angler for competitive angling, it is nevertheless a growing trend.

Local knowledge is a big asset when fishing in these events, and the more you can acquire, the better. That does not mean you have to move home. Search through the pages of the sea angling magazines, particularly the previous year's issues from around the corresponding time. You may find a local who will divulge some relevant information. Do all this, but ideally visit any venue where you intend to fish an event and have a practice session, making it as close as possible to the competition date, and on a similar tide.

Find out all you can about local bait preferences, the tidal periods when fish are likely to feed, what species might be encountered and where. If you are to fish from charter craft, check up on the quality of boats and which skippers are considered the best. Find out if you might go wreck or reef fishing, if

there are lots of small fish to be caught; there are competitions out of some ports that could be won with a huge haul of dabs and whiting taken inshore one day, while the next is cleaned up by a crew fishing a wreck.

Make sure you thoroughly understand the rules, and that you have the tackle to deal with all eventualities: your selection of rods should allow you to fish the right tackle, in a sensitive manner, wherever and whatever the skipper takes you to. Your end tackle should also cover all possible aspects; have plenty of rigs and traces made up and stowed in a clear tackle wallet, where they can be quickly seen and assessed and easily extracted. Make them up in the styles you think appropriate,

● *This competitor was surprised yet pleased to take this 9lb 8oz John Dory, an exceptional and unusual specimen, off Portsmouth during an army angling championship*

but don't be too elaborate – the simple, straight-forward rigs usually win the day.

Have a good supply of hooks covering all possible sizes, and carry a hook honing stone to touch up any point that gets turned; discard any hook you are not entirely happy with. Service your reels and check that all the drags are set to a sensible level; if in doubt, one-third of the breaking strain of the reel line is ample. You can use a spring balance to set them up.

Check your line to ensure there are no nicks or abraded weak points that could cost you a match-winning fish, and look over your rod rings for grooves – pay particular attention to roller tip rings, especially if you intend using wire line. Make sure you have a good range of lead weights, and try not to leave them behind, as I have on occasion.

Finally the important task of bait. Don't rely on picking up fresh mackerel on the way to the fishing grounds. An adequate supply of all the favoured baits should be stowed so they keep in good condition – in a cool box is best. Inside you can have ice cream cartons with ragworm, lugworm, peeler crab, shellfish, even some sandeels or hermits; fish baits can also be stored in the cool. Use chemical ice packs to keep the temperature down.

Do all this groundwork, and it may help your chances of success; and luck does play a part, too!

● (Above) *Two hands make it a little easier for John McPherson to display his 86lb (41kg) conger, one of the largest fish taken during any Bass sponsored international at Plymouth*

● (Above) *Long-time supporter of the European Federation of Sea anglers, Peter Peck, with a large ballan wrasse taken in Plymouth Sound. The fish was part of the catch that earned Peter a gold pin in the 1991 EFSA English section championships*

● (Left) *A helping hand from skipper or crew to remove the fish, while feathering for mackerel, makes for slicker and quicker bait catching*

17 Boat fishing around Britain

Plymouth
(South Devon)

THE PREMIER BOAT ANGLING PORT in the south of England, and many would consider in the whole country, though skippers in Whitby might take exception to that.

With an angling centre, a Boatmen's Federation, a large fleet of charter boats and the numerous wrecks littering the south-western approaches, not to mention the Eddystone, Hands Deep and other reefs, plus all the inshore fishing opportunities, Plymouth is totally geared up for boat angling. Offshore, Plymouth charter boats regularly take specimen pollack, coalfish, conger, whiting and ling, and

a number of British records have been caught out of the port. Nor is the small boat angler left out of things, as there are several sheltered slipways with access to Plymouth Sound, where bass, wrasse, pollack, conger, dabs, flounder and rays are regularly taken.

Looe
(South Cornwall)

Once a major shark-angling port, there is less heard of Looe today in angling circles, and the number of boats available for hire has declined, probably because new skippers tend to set up operations from Plymouth, which is closer to population centres. It *is* still possible to hire a vessel though and the fishing and opportunities are virtually the same as for Plymouth itself. The Shark Angling Club of Great Britain still has its HQ at Looe. There are limited launching facilities for small craft.

Mevagissey
(South Cornwall)

This port has a number of charter boats available for hire, with wreck, reef and shark fishing on offer. Ling, pollack, coalfish, whiting, and conger will all be represented in catches. Small craft launching facilities are very limited in the area.

Falmouth
(South Cornwall)

There is some excellent fishing to be had from this port. It gives fairly quick access to the Manacles

● (Left) *Barry Hoskins, skipper of Plymouth charter boat* Crafty K, *gaffs a large conger*

reef, where some superb bass fishing can be enjoyed if conditions are right; however, this should only be attempted with experienced skippers. Wrecking opportunities for conger, pollack, coalfish and ling are numerous, and the area offers one of the few viable chances in the south of England to catch a large haddock. Being in the extreme South West, it also offers a better chance for the stray exotic tropical species that appear from time to time. There are several launch sites, though some are in private boat yards and require prior arrangement.

Padstow
(North Cornwall)

The port to visit if you wish to catch a porbeagle, though the numbers of boats available are limited. Other likely species are pollack, conger and rays. Smooth-hound can be caught in the area at times. Small boats can gain access to the estuary of the River Camel off a ramp, but dues are payable to the harbourmaster.

Lynmouth
(North Devon)

There is a small charter fleet operating out of Lynmouth with various fishing opportunities. These include wreck-fishing where conger, pollack and ling will be encountered, open ground fishing for rays and huss, and in winter cod and whiting. There is limited access for small craft from a ramp on the west side of the harbour.

Minehead and Watchet
(Somerset)

These two anchorages straddle Blue Anchor Bay in Somerset, and both have a number of charter boats operating over the same ground.

A variety of fishing techniques can be practised from these ports, and a wide selection of species caught. Uptiding on sandbanks can produce rays, bass, whiting and cod; mid-channel gullies can offer tope, conger, rays, spurdog and huss; wreck-fishing more conger, ling, pollack and cod; and on the reefs around Lundy there is some fine, light-tackle pollack fishing to be had. There is a ramp at Minehead where small boats may launch, with dues payable to the harbourmaster.

Cardiff
(South Glamorgan)

A substantial charter fleet operates out of Cardiff. In the winter, cod and whiting dominate angling catches, small-eyed ray are taken through the summer and into the early winter, as are spotted ray and thornbacks; the Nash Sands feature in many of the ray catches. Spurdog, bull huss and conger can be taken over the rough ground. There are a number of launch sites in the area.

Swansea
(West Glamorgan)

A substantial charter-fishing fleet operates out of Swansea. Fishing can be very productive, with opportunities for wreck, reef and shark fishing. Species to be caught include porbeagle, tope, bass, turbot, rays, cod, pollack, conger, monkfish and black bream. Flounders can be taken in the estuaries. There are several launching sites in the area, and at some you may be required to show safety equipment; also parking and launching fees may be required.

Tenby
(Dyfed)

Once renowned for its tope fishing, the quality of this has declined in recent years; however, a number of boats are available for charter in the area, and there are prospects of some good catches for other species – notably pollack, rays, turbot in summer, and cod and whiting in the winter. There is a slipway in the harbour; contact the harbourmaster.

Milford Haven
(Dyfed)

There are only a few charter boats in this area. The sheltered haven offers some interesting fishing, with pollack and bass around the reefs, and flounders further up the estuary. On the banks outside the sound, rays and turbot can be taken, while on rough ground marks huss, conger and black bream can be expected. Small craft may be launched from a ramp across hard sand at Gelliswick Bay. There are other potential launch sites at nearby Dale.

Aberystwyth

(Dyfed)

A fleet of well-equipped charter craft can be booked from this port. Tope fishing can be excellent, though a lot of the fish are pack tope and on the inner marks can be on the small side. Porbeagles usually show during the summer so there is an opportunity for some sharking. The occasional turbot is taken, and some huge ray and bull huss catches can be made. On the reefs of St Patrick's and Patches, black bream show in late spring and through the summer. There are two ramps at the southern end of the sea front where small boats can be launched.

Barmouth

(Gwynedd)

The occasional charter boat operates out of here, and fishing prospects are similar to Aberystwyth, with tope, rays, huss, turbot and black bream all a possibility. There is a ramp into the harbour suitable for small vessels, though contact the harbourmaster before launching.

Caernarvon

(Gwynedd)

This port, south of the island of Anglesey, gives anglers the chance to sample the fishing in Caernarvon Bay. Ray, huss, tope, dabs, pollack and bass can all be expected to appear in catches. There are several charter boats available.

Anglesey

(Gwynedd)
Amlwch, Holyhead, Beaumaris

A number of charter boats operate out of these three ports on the island of Anglesey, and they have built a substantial reputation for providing good catches. Sailing from this location saves a considerable amount of steaming time when the many wrecks that litter the approaches to Liverpool Bay are the objective; this, coupled with the many reefs in the area around the island and the good open-ground fishing, also means that anglers are spoiled for choice. Species to be expected are tope, cod, pollack, conger, rays, bass, huss and ling. There are

limited launching facilities at Beaumaris; and at Holyhead, launching may be arranged with the Holyhead boatyard or via the yacht club.

Colwyn Bay

(Clwyd)

A number of charter boats operate out of Colwyn, and catches include bass, pollack, dabs, whiting, huss, ray and conger. If the ramp alongside the pier at Colwyn is no longer available, there is a public slipway at nearby Rhos-on-Sea.

Rhyl

(Clwyd)

There are plenty of charter boats available here. Whiting, dabs and cod will figure in catches during the autumn; blue shark fishing is conducted out of the port during summer; and other species to be expected are rays, huss and conger. There are several slips suitable for small boat launching.

Isle of Man

Some excellent boat fishing can be enjoyed from here, though the charter boats tend to be geared to the seasonal holiday trade. Douglas, Castletown, Port St Mary, Peel and Ramsey all have ramps that give access to the sea, with varying degrees of ease. All those contemplating trailing should ensure their boats are not limited by height clearance on the ferry. Once afloat, prospects are good for pollack, coalfish, dabs, plaice, tope, conger and huss; and in the winter, cod and whiting catches increase.

Fleetwood

(Lancashire)

There is a large fleet of vessels available for charter from here. In late spring and summer, plaice fishing can be excellent over the mussel beds. Offshore, rough ground and wrecking trips produce tope, conger and huss, and some large catches of thornback ray. Small boats do quite well for bass at times. There are quite a few ramps providing access to the beach for small boats, though they will then have to be launched across the sand.

• *A Florida tarpon, alongside the skiff, ready for release*

Barrow-in Furness
(Cumbria)

Several charter craft are available from Barrow, and the angler might expect to catch plaice, dabs, thornback ray, tope and huss. I understand there is a ramp opposite the Ferry Inn, supervised by Barrow Sea Sports Association.

Maryport
(Cumbria)

A few charter craft are available at this port, and there are plaice, dabs, rays, tope, cod and bass if you know when and where to look. There are two launch sites available giving access to the harbour and Solway Firth.

Kirkcudbright
(Dumfries & Galloway)

A few charter boats are available from this sheltered little port, which is not too far from Luce Bay. Species to be caught include tope, plaice, cod, huss, dabs, coalfish and flounders. There is a ramp suitable for launching small craft, on the harbour approach.

Isle of Whithorn
(Dumfries & Galloway)

This is the name of the town: it is not an island. It is one of the most convenient ports from which to fish Luce Bay, and catches should include tope, cod, ray, conger and coalfish. There is a gentle ramp into the harbour where boats may be launched.

Stranraer
(Dumfries & Galloway)

Situated in the sheltered waters of Loch Ryan, there are several charter boats for hire. Expect to catch cod, pollack, whiting, plaice, dogfish, spurdog, tope and ling.

Tobermory
(Isle of Mull, Strathclyde)

Brian Swinbanks operates his famous charter boat *Laurenca* out of Tobermory on the Isle of Mull. You will almost certainly need to book well in advance. Opportunities here for giant skate, ling, cod, conger, pollack, coalfish, occasional haddock, and maybe a turbot or brill.

Oban
(Strathclyde)

This fishing port gives access to Loch Lorn and some fine fishing. Vessels are available for charter. Species to be expected are cod, pollack, ling, huss, coalfish and spurdog, and there is a chance of contacting a big common skate. There are several slipways in and around Oban that can be used to launch small boats.

Stornoway
(Isle of Lewis, Western Isles)

This seaport in the Outer Hebrides boasts one of the largest sea-angling clubs in Scotland; its members will be able to direct you to boatmen available for charter. Some fantastic fishing can be had from here: coalfish, pollack, haddock, spurdog, tope, cod, ling and common skate are all likely, and there is even the chance of a porbeagle, if you take the tackle and can arrange a boat. Winter fishing is less easy to arrange, as most boats will be laid up. There is a ramp in the harbour that can be used if you trail your boat over on the ferry. Only experienced hands should be launching in these waters.

Ullapool
(Highland)

It should be possible to charter a boat here. There is superb fishing to be had if you can, with the chance of giant skate, haddock, cod, coalfish, ling, pollack, catfish and dabs. Small boats can be launched over the foreshore at several points, where the road skirts the north-west shore of Loch Broom. There may also be opportunities to launch from the pier, though you must contact the harbourmaster.

Scrabster
(Highland)

This port gives access to Pentland Firth and some of the finest boat-fishing north of the border. There are some charter boats available or a crabbing vessel can sometimes be hired if the regular boats are booked. Species to be caught include pollack, cod, ling, coalfish, haddock, dabs and conger. Several catches of large porbeagle have been made by well-prepared anglers in the area and there is always the possibility of a halibut. There is a ramp that gives access to a hard sand beach at Thurso, immediately adjacent to Scrabster, where small boats can be launched.

Orkney

The fishing can be as good here as from Scrabster, and you can fish the same waters. All the same species are available, plus you have the opportunity to catch sea trout, if you work a dinghy in the right area. Boat hire to take out anglers can be arranged. Anglers should be advised that the weather in all these northern areas can be very restrictive.

Shetland

More superb fishing to be had around here, and local fishing boats can be hired to take out anglers. Species to be caught include pollack, ling, cod, dabs, coalfish and haddock; and porbeagles can be caught in the area, too, though arranging suitable boats may be a problem.

Peterhead
(Grampian)

There is at least one charter boat available in Peterhead, the *Sea Hunter*. Catches to be expected from this major commercial fishing port are haddock, cod, pollack, coalfish, plaice, ling and conger. There is a slipway in the harbour suitable for all states of the tide, though you must contact the harbourmaster in advance.

Arbroath
(Tayside)

Several charter boats operate out of this port. The main quarry will be cod, but pollack, haddock, catfish, dabs, coalfish and ling can also be expected. There is limited launching in the outer harbour.

Pittenweem
(Fife)

There are a few boats available for charter here. Cod are the mainstay of catches, supplemented by ling, pollack, coalfish and catfish.

Eyemouth
(Borders)

This little port has a number of charter vessels available. April usually sees the influx of summer codling, ling and catfish, and a few coalies will make up your catch. There is limited access to the sea via a ramp and a hard sand beach.

Berwick-on-Tweed
(Northumberland)

Several charter boats operate from Berwick. Fishing is similar to that from Eyemouth, drifting reefs with artificial lures and/or bait, expect to pick up cod, catfish, ling and coalfish. I understand launching is possible here at any state of the tide.

Amble
(Northumberland)

There are several charter boats operating out of this port with inshore fishing and wrecking available. Catches can include cod, catfish, ling, haddock, pollack and coalfish; in the summer a few turbot are taken.

Hartlepool
(Cleveland)

One of the largest charter fleets in the country operates out of Hartlepool. There is the chance to go offshore wrecking where 20lb (9kg)-plus cod and ling can be taken; and reef and open-ground fishing produces catfish, haddock, plaice and dabs.

Whitby
(North Yorkshire)

There is a huge fleet of charter vessels to choose from at Whitby, though early booking is advisable to be sure of getting one of the top boats. Offshore wrecking for ling and cod is the main attraction, though large catches of cod, the odd ling and catfish can also be taken on the inshore reefs. The open gullies between the reefs produce a few haddock at times. There is an excellent slipway within the harbour where launching is only difficult at extreme low water. The best of the fishing is during the summer.

Bridlington
(Humberside)

Another large fleet of charter craft run out of this harbour. Offshore wrecking and rough ground fishing for cod and ling is best in the summer, when pirks and muppets are favoured. There is inshore fishing for codling, plaice, whiting and dabs.

Grimsby
(Humberside)

A number of charter boats work from this old-established commercial fishing port, fishing the North Sea wrecks and gas rigs. Catches on the wrecks are made up mainly of cod with a few ling. Open-ground fishing can produce dabs, whiting and thornback rays.

Great Yarmouth
(Norfolk)

Several vessels are available for hire at this port. Codling normally feature in catches from late spring until the end of the year. Plenty of dabs can be caught and there is sometimes a chance for thornback ray and bass. Early winter whiting fishing can produce some big bags.

Lowestoft
(Suffolk)

The sport to be had from this established commercial fishing dock is similar to that from Great Yarmouth. Cod, thornback ray, dabs, bass, tope and whiting can all be expected.

● *30lb cod are not common off Felixstowe, Suffolk. This one, taken by local angler Jim Peacock, fell to a lugworm and squid cocktail presented on uptide gear*

Felixstowe
(Suffolk)

There are several vessels available for charter here, most of them based at Felixstowe Ferry at the mouth of the River Deben, which is to the north of the town. Cod and whiting feature in the autumn and winter; uptiding methods are favoured; good bags of dabs can be taken most of the year; and in the summer, thornback ray, bass, smooth-hound and tope may be taken. Small craft can launch at Felixstowe Ferry; however, be warned that there is a bank at the mouth of the river, that could easily catch out the unwary or inexperienced boatman.

Walton-on-the-Naze

(Essex)

A number of charter boats operate out of the marina; uptiding is the favoured method. Cod and whiting feature in the autumn and winter. Summer fishing includes smooth-hound, sting ray, tope, bass and thornback ray, and there are usually plenty of dabs around.

Brightlingsea

(Essex)

Several charter vessels are based in this little haven, and the fishing is very similar to Walton-on-the-Naze. There is a public hard that gets crowded at weekends. A launching fee is payable.

West Mersea

(Essex)

Cod and whiting in the winter; smooth-hound, bass, tope and sting ray in the summer and autumn. There are only a few charter boats available. There is a hard that can be used for launching at most states of the tide.

Bradwell

(Essex)

This is the home base for Bob Cox and John Rawle, charter boat skippers and of tackle designing fame. A number of other craft are available for charter at Bradwell Marina. Offshore summer and autumn uptiding for smooth-hound, tope, thornback rays, bass and sting ray; and whiting and cod in the autumn and winter. The fishing in the Blackwater estuary itself can be superb, whiting, cod, bass, sting ray and smooth-hound all being taken inside the river mouth. There is a steep ramp alongside the marina where small craft may be launched at most states of the tide.

Burnham-on-Crouch

(Essex)

Several good charter vessels are based at Burnham, and they enjoy the same fishing opportunities as the vessels working out of Bradwell. Burnham is slightly more convenient to get to.

Southend

(Essex)

Plenty of boats for hire at this location. Flounders, dabs, whiting, silver eels, thornback rays, smooth-hound and bass can all be expected in the catch. I understand there is a small boat slipway at the western end of the promenade.

Ramsgate

(Kent)

A major fleet of vessels ply for hire out of Ramsgate, the closest port to the infamous Goodwin Sands. In winter, cod, whiting and dab catches predominate inshore, and spring and summer usually bring runs of plaice and thornbacks. Offshore, wreck trips produce large cod, pollack and conger, while turbot may be taken off some of the farther banks. There are several slipways with access to both inner and outer basins of the harbour; for these, contact the harbourmaster.

Deal

(Kent)

Just a little south of Ramsgate, the fishing is very similar – though cod always seem a larger average size to me. There are several boats available for hire.

Dover

(Kent)

A substantial fleet of angling boats work out of Dover. Cod, whiting and dabs figure mainly in winter bags. Summer fish include plaice, turbot and bass with pollack, cod, conger and an occasional ling from the wrecks.

Folkestone
(Kent)

Folkestone experiences much the same fishing as Dover, being only a few miles along the coast. There are some top boats operating from the port, and trips to the Varne Bank as well as offshore wrecking can be arranged. There is a slipway in the harbour that can be used for a good deal of the tide. At the time of writing, launching charges have been imposed and the local anglers are counter-claiming right-of-way; the outcome remains to be seen.

Dungeness
(Kent)

Several charter boats work off the beach from here. Catches are high quality, much as is the famous shore mark, and include cod, whiting and dabs; summer species will include more dabs as well as turbot, brill, bass and conger.

Hastings
(East Sussex)

Boats have to be launched off the beach here; there are not many charter boats in the conventional sense, though a boat and boatman can sometimes be hired. There is, though, an excellent sea-angling club which has its own dinghies, winches and boat-storage compound on the beach. It should be possible to arrange something with them. There is inshore fishing for dabs and whiting throughout the year, and plaice from spring to autumn; cod are caught most often in autumn and winter. Offshore wrecks produce summer cod, pollack and conger. Lightweight boats can be launched and recovered across the beach; heavier vessels will need the assistance of the winch.

Pevensey Bay
(East Sussex)

This is another location where vessels have to launch across the shingle. The Pevensey Bay Aqua Club has a licensed clubhouse on the beach, and a compound with boat storage and winch facilities. Inshore fishing produces dabs and whiting most of the year, and cod in autumn and winter, while during the summer, bass, plaice, smooth-hounds and bream are taken; offshore catches include conger, spurdog, pollack and tope.

Eastbourne
(East Sussex)

This resort town has another active angling association, with a licensed club house on the beachfront. Once again, launching is off the beach. The club has a large boat-storage compound. There are a few boats that ply for hire, and it may be possible to arrange something with Eastbourne Angling Association; there is some excellent fishing to be had from here. Around Beachy Head, bass angling can be first class; dabs and whiting are present inshore most of the year, as are the cod in the autumn and winter period. Offshore, the reefs inside the Royal Sovereign produce conger, pollack, bull huss and black bream; while outside, tope and spurdog appear from time to time. Wrecking produces big cod hauls in the summer.

Newhaven
(East Sussex)

A number of charter vessels conduct operations out of this port, with mid-Channel wrecking for cod, conger and pollack a prospect. Some very large conger are taken out of here every year. Fish to be found on the open ground are spurdog, whiting, dabs and cod. In the summer a few smooth-hound are taken by anglers using crab.

Brighton
(East Sussex)

A substantial charter fleet operates out of Brighton Marina. There is some good offshore wreck fishing to be had, with large conger and cod, pollack and a few ling; spurdog also feature, though they are often undersize. Whiting and dabs are about nearly all year, though the best of the whiting fishing is late in the season. Fishing off the outfall at Rottingdean produces black bream, dabs, plaice and occasional bass in summer; a few cod run inshore in the autumn and winter.

Shoreham
(West Sussex)

Several boats now work for charter out of this port. The fishing is similar to that from Brighton. With offshore wrecking available for cod and conger;

inshore species include plaice, whiting, dabs and cod in the latter part of the year.

Littlehampton
(West Sussex)

There are plenty of angling boats for hire at Littlehampton. The Kingsmere rocks have long been famous for their black bream fishing in the spring, though it has had its ups and downs with catches in recent years; however, it still produces the fish. Conger are also a possibility on the same site. Whiting and dab figure strongly in autumn catches, when cod will also start to show. There are wreck boats operating from the harbour, with prospects for pollack, cod, conger and the odd ling.

Hayling Island
(Hampshire)

'Hayling Island' is the title under which the large fleet working from Langstone Harbour advertises. In fact in practice, the boats pick up at the ferry pontoon on either the Hayling or Southsea side as required.

There are some excellent opportunities for angling out of this large natural harbour. March sees a run of plaice in Hayling Bay, closely followed in April and May by smooth-hound, black bream and tope. There are genuine chances of a big thresher or porbeagle shark out to sea from off the Isle of Wight during the summer, though they are never easy to find: conditions have to be right, you have to have luck, and if you do find a fish you must have the skill to boat it. Thornback, blonde and small-eyed rays also feature in catches.

Offshore, wrecks produce ling, pollack and conger; in the autumn and winter, whiting and heavyweight cod show up; and I have not mentioned the grounds off St Catherine's Point. It is possible to launch across the beach at several places either side of Langstone Harbour mouth, though none is ideal. There is also a slipway at Portsmouth Harbour entrance, though this one gets very busy in season.

Anglers are reminded that Langstone and nearby Portsmouth, Chichester and Southampton harbours and or their approaches are involved in the bass nursery area scheme. They should find out exactly what the current regulations are, and observe them.

Lymington
(Hampshire)

With a dozen or so charter vessels, Lymington is well situated to serve anglers wishing to fish the Solent and west of Wight fishing grounds. This town has built its angling reputation on big winter cod, but it has plenty of other species to offer. In the spring the Dolphin Bank generally fishes well for rays, while at the same time in Highcliffe Bay a run of plaice occurs. In the late spring and early summer, Freshwater Reef takes over as the prime inshore fishing spot, producing small-eyed ray, dabs, bass and a few turbot and brill. Offshore wrecking can be very good in May and June, with some giant catches of cod and pollack. St Catherine's, on the southern tip of the Isle of Wight, offers conger and tope fishing when tides permit.

Offshore, blonde ray and spurdog are taken. In the Solent, smooth-hound and sting ray are regular summer visitors, while bass, thornback and spotted ray also show regularly. In the autumn and winter cod are taken in the Solent, as well as from the famous Needles mark. There is also fine inshore flounder fishing in December and January.

Lymington has two slipways, both giving access to Lymington River. Bath Road car park is of most interest to anglers, with a good ramp and ample parking. For an hour or so during mid-water it can be a bit awkward launching on the hard gravel, at the foot of the concrete ramp. Fees are chargeable.

Keyhaven
(Hampshire)

Keyhaven is a small village only a few miles west of Lymington, still within the sheltered waters of the Solent and close to Hurst Castle. It has a number of charter boats available. In fact it offers the same fishing opportunities as Lymington and is less distance to steam. There is a small concrete ramp but the slope is quite shallow, though a good set of rollers will see that craft to 18ft (5m) launch successfully.

Mudeford
(Dorset)

Only a few charter vessels operate from here. The grounds they fish are very similar to the offshore marks that the Lymington and Keyhaven boats will

● *Ron Cowling, skipper of the Keyhaven, Hants, boat* Our Mary, *does the honours with a small-eyed ray*

be occupying. They do have the advantage, though – if they think to use it – of Christchurch ledge right on their doorstep. Conger, cod, bass, pollack and bream can all be taken off the ledge; and there are some good plaice to be caught in the sandy patches along the reef's inner edge.

There is a shallow sloping ramp inside the haven entrance where small craft may be launched. Visitors should note the ebb tide can be very strong for an hour or so through Mudeford race, most notably on springs, and small displacement boats may not be able to make any headway against the tide.

Poole
(Dorset)

One of the largest natural harbours in the world, Poole can provide offshore fishing for huss, conger, rays and cod as well as long distance wrecking – it is some way to steam before the charter boats even get out of port. Outside the harbour, off Peveril Ledge and Durlstone, pollack, bass, some large wrasse and black bream can be expected during summer and autumn. Off the Durleys some really first-class plaice may be caught. Early winter brings some excellent flounder fishing inside the harbour; the new year usually sees a run of these fish over 3lb (1.3kg). There are several launch sites around the harbour suitable for small craft.

Swanage
(Dorset)

Swanage offers all the offshore fish you can catch from Poole, plus an hour's less steaming time. Charter boats seem to come and go a bit from here

and they are not always available; perhaps it is because there is no proper harbour. Locally, there is some superb small boat fishing to be had if the weather is kind. Plaice, small-eyed ray, pollack, black bream, huss, conger and bass can all be caught within a few hundred yards of the launching ramp which is just inside Peveril Point.

Weymouth
(Dorset)

A fine charter fleet sails out of this sheltered harbour. There is excellent and varied fishing to be enjoyed. Large blonde ray and turbot are hunted on the Shambles bank, conger, bull huss and black bream come from broken ground and from Portland Bill, while bass are found in the overfalls of Portland race (this should only be attempted with professional boatmen). Some superb wrecking can be enjoyed as well. There are a couple of slipways in town, giving access to the river mouth. There is also a very good angling club whose members will undoubtedly be prepared to offer advice and assistance.

West Bay
(Dorset)

This small harbour close to Bridport has several charter boats, though putting to sea can be difficult as any swell funnels into the narrow harbour entrance. There is some wrecking to be enjoyed, with pollack, bream, ling and conger. Inshore reefs produce pollack, conger, huss and bass, while off the sand, dabs and plaice are taken. There is a better-than-average chance of taking a trigger fish from here during the latter part of summer. A first-class slipway gives access to the harbour.

Exmouth
(Devon)

There is an expanding fleet of vessels chartering from this resort, and wreck, reef, inshore and estuary fishing can all be enjoyed. Pollack, ling, conger, bream, rays, turbot, huss, dab and plaice are all fish to be expected. There are several potential launch sites, though most are only suitable for light boats.

Torquay

(Devon)

A number of charter vessels operate from the harbour in Torquay, offering chances to fish wreck, reef and the Skerries. Fish to be expected inshore are plaice, rays and turbot; offshore there is pollack, ling, cod, conger and blonde ray. There are several launching sites in Torquay and nearby Paignton.

Brixham

(Devon)

A picturesque village, it was one of the first angling 'boom' ports; wreck angling was pioneered out of Brixham. It declined in prominence as an angling port for a while, as the financial attractions of commercial fishing lured boatmen away from the sport. However, the charter fleet has been growing again recently and top class catches are still being made. A top port for conger, ling and pollack, with chances for bream, coalfish and turbot. There are several ramps into the harbour, some of them a bit steep.

Dartmouth

(Devon)

Situated in a delightful setting at the mouth of the River Dart, the charter boats sail from Kingswear on the eastern side of the river mouth as well as Dartmouth to the west. From here it is only a short voyage to the famous Skerries bank, which produces specimen plaice, turbot, brill, dabs, rays and many other species. Offshore the wrecking potential is first class, with monster ling, conger, pollack and coalfish. There are excellent sheltered launching ramps, suitable for most small craft.

Salcombe

(Devon)

One of the most beautiful settings in the country to sail from, Salcombe offers some of the finest fishing to go with it. There are only a few charter vessels working from the estuary but they include the best. Inshore fishing can be superb, with the Skerries to the east and the banks and reefs around Start Point to choose from. Bass, brill, turbot and blonde ray can all be taken close in. For offshore fishing, start-ing from the most southerly point on the mainland cuts steaming time and increases catching time, and the angler can expect bumper hauls of pollack, conger and ling when conditions are right. There are several possible launching sites in and around Salcombe, giving access to the estuary.

The Channel Islands

The fishing must be good around these islands – why else would a large part of the south coast charter fleet spend so much time sailing to and from Guernsey?

Several craft are available for charter on both Guernsey and Jersey, and boat-fishing prospects are some of the best in Britain – year-round action from blonde, small-eyed and undulate ray, turbot, brill, pollack, coalfish, ling, conger and bass. That should whet your appetite!

There are several slipways on Jersey, mostly in St Helier; you may be required to register your craft if it is under 30ft (9.15m) and capable of more than 12 knots (21.9kph). Guernsey has a big ramp at St Peter Port; parking here may be difficult.

Isles of Scilly

Anglers wishing to try some boat fishing around these islands will either have to sail a boat there themselves, charter one from the mainland, or arrange something with a local boatman. Whatever the decision, there is likely to be plenty of action, as all reports indicate plenty of pollack, coalfish, ling, blue shark and rays, though the average size might not be as big as some people would hope. Unfortunately, the isolated and exposed position of these islands has meant that no in-depth angling study has been possible to establish which are the best local angling areas, tackles and techniques.

18 Boat fishing abroad

WITH THE RAPID INCREASE IN FOREIGN TRAVEL, more and more anglers find themselves looking for opportunities to enjoy their sport while on holiday overseas.

A spell as a merchant seaman, twenty years as an active member of the European Federation of Sea Anglers, coupled with angling forays to distant shores on my own, has given me the chance to sample various venues, types of fishing and ways of getting afloat abroad. Here are a few suggestions as to some possible destinations.

Ireland

Ireland's appeal must be due in part to the plentiful, familiar types of fish and the effectiveness of our own accustomed fishing techniques. This, coupled with the wide open roads and the friendly relaxed approach to life of the Irish people, can create a unique sea-angling experience. The Irish Tourist Board recognises that angling is a big revenue earner and encourages all aspects of the sport.

Belmullet and Westport in County Mayo, located on the western coast, are two of the leading boat-angling centres in Ireland, with plenty of charter vessels for hire. Catches from these ports will include pollack, monkfish, conger, cod and tope.

Further south in Galway, the harbour at Clifden has several boats available. There is the chance of blue shark, plentiful pollack and also cod, conger, ling and coalfish. Along the southern coast in County Cork are the harbours at Kinsale and Courtmacsherry. Here, a number of charter boats are available; blue shark are the traditional quarry, but pollack, ling, turbot, cod and coalfish are all species to be expected.

Further east, in County Waterford, is Dungarvan, with several angling boats available. Catches out of here include common skate, pollack, bass, cod, haddock and various rays and flatfish.

Ireland has a lot to offer the boat angler – but don't expect to be away sharp every morning!

Holland

Dutch boat angling follows similar lines to that in Britain. Sea-angling clubs are very popular, and a number specialise in various aspects of the sport including dinghy angling and offshore fishing.

There are charter boats to be found in most seaports, very often run from a café or tackle shop base on the quayside. Civic authorities in Holland seem actively to encourage sea angling, appreciating the revenue it generates for their towns. They even provide parking areas adjacent to the docks specifically for anglers.

Most charter craft in Holland are comparatively large, usually ex-trawlers that carry up to thirty anglers. Positions are generally pegged around the boat, and it is the accepted rule that anglers move along seven places every 100–120 minutes. There are reasonably priced bar and snack facilities aboard – it is a bit like fishing off a mobile pier. Boatcasting is the more productive way of fishing the relatively shallow waters. The Dutch generally favour the use of full-size beachcasters that can cast up to 12oz (345g), mounted with large fixed spool reels for boatcasting, though UK-style uptiders can be quite adequate. Paternosters are widely used. Common species caught are cod, flounder, plaice, whiting and sole, so the Dutch preference is to keep hook sizes quite small, 1s or 1/0s for most general boat angling. There are more specific opportunities for tope and bass, where different tactics may be called for.

France

Boat angling is very popular in France, with angling clubs popular and numerous. The vessels available for charter are often a good deal smaller than those we are used to in Britain – boats of 18ft (5.5m) to 24ft (7.3m) are quite common, taking just four to six anglers. Commercial fishing boats can also be hired

• A plump autumn cod safely netted

• This hefty amberjack took a bit of hauling up from 300ft (92m) below the surface. It was located on a deep, offshore Florida reef

for angling; a little judicious bartering on the quay can often arrange a trip for the following day.

Tackle, techniques, baits and species are similar to those in the UK, though to the south of the country on both the Atlantic and Mediterranean coasts, more exotic species are encountered such as the meagre, a beautiful copper-hued fish that grows to weights in excess of 143lb (65kg), and various tuna. Some fine fishing is to be had off Bayonne, in the southern Bay of Biscay. There is a reef here known as the Roche de la Barre which produces huge conger and pollack and the hard-fighting meagre.

Sweden

The Swedes are keen sea anglers, and have some excellent and varied fishing. Most Swedish sea anglers own their own boats, but it is possible to charter commercial fishing vessels for angling, and there are also some specialist angling craft for hire. Lure fishing with various muppets and pirks is widely practised in the clear waters of the Baltic, though bait such as mussel is used for the best catches of sea catfish and wolf-fish, tasty hard-fighting species common in some parts of the Baltic. Sea angling in the Baltic can be quite surprising, the brackish waters yielding freshwater species such as pike and perch alongside cod and catfish in some areas.

Norway

Boat hire can be arranged in most harbours, usually with small commercial fishing vessels. Stavanger is a major port where a number of big angling festivals have been held over the years. Catches here can include spurdog, cod, ling, catfish, torsk, redfish and coalfish. Pirks and rubber eels can be very productive.

Prices are high in Norway as compared to Britain, and for both boat hire and the cost of living, a deep pocket is essential if a prolonged stay is planned.

Denmark

There is some excellent fishing to be had in Denmark, especially in the north of the country. The fishing on the yellow reef, out of Hirtshals, can be superb – the Danes have a ban on commercial fishing on the reef, and this ensures sustained good catches of cod, pollack, coalfish and, from the clear patches amongst the rock, turbot and brill.

Some terrific cod hauls are made out of Helsingor: fish of 50lb (23kg) are regularly taken in the straits between Denmark and Sweden. Angling vessels are generally available for charter, and both bait and lure fishing can be successful. The Danes are great exponents of uptide pirking and frequently use two rods: one, an uptide rod, is used to

● *The author with part of the catch that won the 1985 TVS Championship for him in Iceland*

cast updrift and work a pirk back to the boat, when on the appropriate side of the vessel; and when the drift is the opposite way round, a standard rod is fished in conventional pirking style.

Though lures are quite reasonably priced, tackle in general is quite expensive in all the Scandinavian countries, so try and take anything you might expect to use with you.

Iceland

This is an exciting area to fish, where huge catches can be made, even close inshore. Iceland is the home of big cod, haddock, catfish, halibut and enormous coalfish. Only a few areas cater for angling, notably at Keflavik and again on the Westman Islands; therefore anglers contemplating a trip to Iceland should contact one of the specialist travel firms dealing in angling holidays in order to pre-arrange boats, as availability is limited. Alternatively Icelandair, the national airline, may be able to offer a deal of its own.

Bad weather can be a problem in Iceland, as severe conditions may last for weeks, preventing boats reaching the best fishing grounds; though some good catches can still be made in the sheltered fjords and inshore bays. To increase the chance of good sea-angling conditions, visits are best confined to the period May to September.

The Canary Islands

A lot of people take holidays in the Canaries, and while there are certainly boats on Tenerife and Lanzarote whose skippers will tell you they are available for angling, most are in fact just party boats, catering for swimming, snorkeling and booze cruises. It is sometimes possible to hire a diving boat specifically for a fishing trip – ideally you would need to take tackle with you, as these boats seldom have their own, though you might find the odd craft with equipment aboard.

There is an angling charter business operating out of Los Christianos on Tenerife, but it caters very much to the casual holidaymaker rather than the serious angler. Only one port in the Canaries is geared up for serious sea angling: Puerto Rico, on Gran Canaria. Here a fleet of charter boats offer perhaps the best value in game fishing this side of the Atlantic. Charter prices are reasonable, and boats have a full range of tackle available for use.

There is a variety of fish to be targeted, ranging from the gamefish, marlin and tuna; the bottom-dwellers, sting ray and skates; to reef-loving species such as bream and trigger fish.

● *This 288lb (130kg) hammerhead shark put up a good fight before it unfortunately rolled in the line and drowned, preventing it from being returned*

North America

Angling in all its aspects is widely catered for throughout the USA and Canada. Visitors from the UK will also find it is an excellent opportunity to stock up on tackle at bargain prices, especially if they can get to one of the large discount tackle stores that are to be found around the country.

There are several types of craft available to take boat anglers sea fishing. For game fishing, the vessels are large, high-speed cruisers equipped with fighting chairs, and all tackle is provided, though you can take your own if you wish. For general bottom fishing, some craft are similar to British charter boats, but the norm in the US is for large, high-speed party boats that can carry forty or fifty anglers, sometimes even a hundred. These boats are likely to have heated rails for winter fishing, air conditioning for the summer, and a galley providing hot food and drink. Your catch will be filleted or steaked, put in freezer bags and iced down ready for you to take home. On vessels operating offshore charters lasting several days, there will be sleeping accommodation and shower facilities. Full tackle requirements are catered for including, in some cases, electric reels.

Whatever size or type of boat you are on, you will find the mates fuss around, wanting to look after your tackle for you; this can be irritating, but it is best to learn to relax and enjoy it! You are expected to tip them – about 10 per cent of the cost for the whole day is about right.

Prices for *party boats* in the US work out to be approximately the same per head as a day's wrecking would be on a good boat in the UK. A *game-fishing craft* for the day will cost about the same as the total daily price of a wrecking trip in Britain, and will vary – as it would at home – with the quality of the boat and the standard of equipment aboard. It works out more expensive per head, because four anglers is a sensible number to carry and six generally the maximum.

New York State

Charter boats operate direct from Sheepshead Bay in the city of New York, but the place to make for is Montauk, on the tip of Long Island, about a two-hour drive from New York city. From here, a large charter fleet operates. In the summer bluefish, a toothy, hard-fighting gamester, dominates the party-boat catches. Game-fishing craft make the run to offshore canyons for tuna and billfish. In the winter there is no game-fishing activity, and the boats are either laid up, or head south. Winter party-boat fishing, weather permitting, concentrates on cod and some huge lunkers can be caught. On my last visit, one angler had two 50lb (23kg)-plus fish, on the same day. Check the availability of charter places and departure times before travelling to Montauk; US sportfishing magazines are a source of information, or inquire by phone.

North Carolina

Cape Hatteras is a Mecca for eastern seaboard sea anglers, and charter craft proliferate in the region. The gulf stream is about an hour and a half steam-

● *A typical Florida game-fishing charter boat. The price, about the same as the cost of a day's charter to go wrecking the UK, includes bait and the use of all tackle. Although you can get six anglers aboard, four is a better number*

ing in a fast boat and offers fishing opportunities for dorado, tuna, marlin and sailfish. Inshore catches can include red drum, snapper, grouper, black seabass and saltwater trout. The season runs from about April to November. The beach fishing is pretty spectacular as well.

Florida

Florida state is totally geared for tourism, and a large proportion of its effort is aimed at visiting anglers. Every dock and inlet has craft available for charter, and as well as game and party boats, in some areas you will find skiffs with guide available for full day, half-day and evening hire, with all tackle and bait supplied. A word of warning: use a high protection sun-tan lotion when going afloat in Florida, as the sun really is very strong.

The Florida Keys, a chain of islands linked by highway US 1, run some hundred miles south-west from mainland Florida. Fishing is a dominant part of the tourist trade in the Keys, with many motels having their own ramps and docks. Major fishing centres are located at Islamorada and Marathon. There is good fishing all year round, backwater, inshore and offshore, but a prime time is April to June. Then the climate is at its best, and tarpon over 100lb (45kg) are a real possibility from the backwater skiffs. Other species from skiffs

Boat fishing abroad

throughout the year include bonefish, permit, lady-fish, snappers, catfish, saltwater trout and redfish. Inshore fishing features yellowtail snapper, mangrove snapper, permit, barracuda, grouper and many more species. Offshore, sailfish, dorado, wahoo, kingfish, blackfin tuna and amberjack are all common.

Florida really is an angler's paradise!

Expect to see a rapid growth in overseas fishing holidays aimed at the boat angler. Sea-angling breaks are currently available in British Columbia and Alaska with halibut as a prime target. Other venues offering packages include Costa Rica, Venezuela, and, in Mexico, Baja California and the Yucatan peninsula.

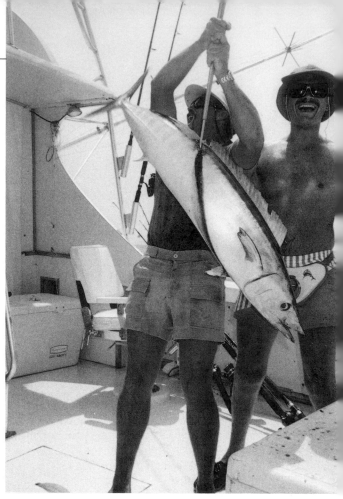

● (Above) *Yahoo! It's a wahoo! This 44lb (20kg) Florida gamester smoked 100yd (92m) of line off the reel on its first run when hooked by visiting UK angler Andrew Flintham*

● (Left) *Middlesex angler Tim Flintham with a 70lb (32kg) amberjack, taken off the Florida Keys*

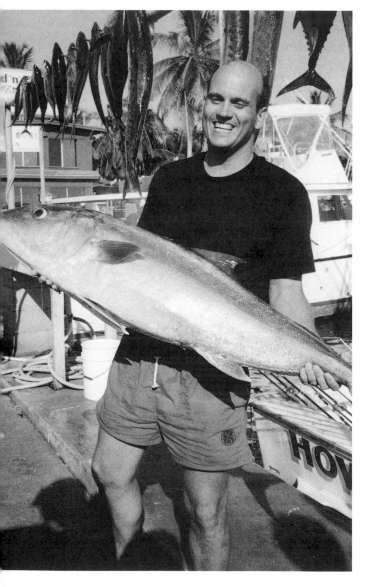

Appendix

Unusual catches

A NUMBER OF UNUSUAL FISH occasionally appear and are caught around our shores, that have not been mentioned in the foregoing pages. This is because they have either become so uncommon as to be not worth specifically targeting, or they are a species that does not respond very well to the baited hook. A number of these are listed here.

Angler fish
(*Lophius piscatorius*)

This ugly-looking customer gets its name from a lure that it dangles over its mouth to entice small fish, which are then gobbled up. Supposedly not uncommon in the seas surrounding Britain, though they seldom fall to the angler's bait or lures; and of those that do, many grab small fish that have already hooked themselves. So if we want to catch more angler fish, perhaps we should use more live bait. They grow quite large, and specimens over 90lb (41kg) have been recorded.

Catfish
(*Anarichus lupus*)

A member of the wolf-fish family. Actually this fish is sometimes caught in reasonable numbers in the far north of the country, though it is never as abundant as in Norway and Sweden, where it loves nothing better than to eat a mouthful of mussel, which the Swedes, who like eating catfish, are happy to offer. It has a most ferocious set of teeth, so if you should catch one, watch your fingers. These fish grow quite large; the British record stands at 26lb 4oz (11.9kg).

Dory
(*Zeus faber*)

If you saw how many of these are landed by commercial fishermen, you might wonder what anglers are doing wrong not to catch more themselves. Another strange-looking customer, the dory has a protrusible (ie telescopic) mouth. It is a predatory fish which stalks its prey and gulps it down. The British record for dory is 11lb 14oz (5.4kg).

Lumpsucker
(*Cyclopterus lumpus*)

Another ugly customer, and another fish that is not uncommon, but seldom caught – it is more likely to be washed up on the beach, than caught by an angler. The female actually lays her eggs in a nest, at the low-water springs' weed line. The male gets the dubious privilege of guarding the eggs, for which trouble he often gets attacked by seagulls on extreme low tides. They grow to weights exceeding 20lb (9kg). The eggs are sold as mock caviar.

Monkfish
(*Squatina squatina*)

A member of the angel shark family; it used to figure frequently in catches forty years ago, but apart from some areas off the west coast of Ireland where they are reputed to have bays full of them, these fish are no longer a common catch. They do grow to a large size: the British record caught in 1965 weighed 66lb (29.9kg).

Trigger fish
(*Balistes carolinensis*)

This fish is certainly not as rare a catch as it once was. During long warm summers they become a regular feature for shore anglers at Chesil Beach. A toothy fish, they are great fighters if you are lucky enough to hook one. They grow to weights in excess of 10lb (4.5kg) though the largest recorded British catch weighed only 4lb 9oz (2.07kg).

Wreck fish
(*Polyprion americanus*)

Years may pass without even one of these fish being caught, then a shoal wanders to our shores from the south and the British record is broken umpteen times in an afternoon aboard the same vessel. The name 'wreck fish' comes from their apparent habit of accompanying floating wreckage, though actually these are juvenile school fish – they stop chasing wreckage as they mature, and live deep on the bottom where they reach weights of 100lb (45kg). The British record stands at 10lb 10oz (5kg).

Index

Index